Land of Dreams

ALSO BY JAMES P. BLAYLOCK:

The Elfin Ship
The Disappearing Dwarf
The Digging Leviathan
Homunculus

Land of Dreams

JAMES P. BLAYLOCK

ARBOR HOUSE / New York

Manufactured in the United States of America

10 9 8 7 6 5 4 3 2 1

Library of Congress Cataloging-in-Publication Data

Blaylock, James P., 1950–
Land of dreams.

I. Title.
PS3552.L3966L3   1987   813'.54   87-11423
ISBN 0-87795-898-X

*To Viki
and to Lynn, Ron, Tim, and Katy,
who have the right inclinations*

Sainte-Beuve, as he grew older, came to regard all experience as a single great book, in which to study for a few years ere we go hence; and it seemed all one to him whether you should read in Chapter XX, which is the differential calculus, or in Chapter XXXIX, which is hearing the band play in the gardens.

—Robert Louis Stevenson
"An Apology for Idlers"

───── *Part One*

IN WHICH THE CARNIVAL ARRIVES

1

It had already been raining for six days when the enormous shoe washed up onto the beach. It was an impossible thing, as big as a rowboat, with frayed laces trailing a garden of pink hydra and blue-green algae.

It was almost evening, in mid-autumn. The sky was choked with clouds and with spindrift from waves breaking across exposed reefs—vast shadowy breakers that quartered round the headland and drove toward shore like skating hillsides, feeling for the shallows and throwing themselves over in a booming rush so that you could hear them break a quarter mile above the village, beyond Edgware farm and beyond the Tumbled Bridge. Along the horizon, like a wrinkled blue ribbon that stretched north from the headland toward the edge of the world, the hem of the sky shone beneath the clouds, looking like old porcelain, watery pale with a mist of rain falling across it.

The shoe lay on the beach and smelled of kelp and wet leather and salt spray. Its tongue had shoved up under the laces and was pointed cockeyed at the sky like the misshapen sail of a fairy-tale boat, and every now and again a wave greater than the last would wash up across the sand in a churning of sea foam and push the shoe a foot or two farther along, until, when Skeezix found it just at sunset, it sat high above the declining tide, as if some wandering giant had left it there and gone home.

It was full of seawater that leaked past the stitching in the soles, but the leather had swelled so much during its voyage that the water leaked out only very slowly, and it would still be mostly full even by morning. Under the threatening sky the water in the shoe was dark as well water. There was the shimmer of something in the depths, though, the silver-green shimmer of fish scales or silver coins; it was impossible to say which without rolling up your sleeve and reaching down into the cold and shadowed water.

Skeezix was what Bobby Wickham called himself and had called himself since he was five years old, ever since he'd seen a picture of an old man in an ostrich-plume hat on the wall of the library. He'd been told it was King Skeezix of Finland, who had, a century earlier, been so famous that now his picture could be found in any good illustrated dictionary. The name had sounded birdlike to him, and the ostrich feather, when he was five, had looked grand as anything. Now, at sixteen, it looked foolish, but the name had stuck and he probably couldn't get rid of it even if he wanted to.

He peered down into the depths of the water. The sides of the shoe rose almost to his neck. If it was silvery coins that lay within, they were too deep to reach anyway, and only looked like they hovered near the surface because of a trick of the slice of sunlight that glowed for the moment beneath the rim of the clouds above the sea. Skeezix hoisted his tattered umbrella when the breeze freshened and swept a patter of raindrops down the back of his coat collar. The glints of silver winked out, and he could see they had been nothing but the sunlit tails of a school of little fish.

There was no explaining the shoe. It had been on the ocean for a week or so—that was easy to see—but whether it had sailed across from some distant land or had drifted south in the longshore current Skeezix couldn't guess. Like the enormous spectacles found two weeks back in the tangled eelgrass of a tidal pool, the origins of the shoe were a mystery.

It occurred to Skeezix that he ought to hide it. He ought to drag it behind a heap of rock and driftwood so as to save it for Dr. Jensen. The doctor should be the first to see it, to study it. They'd taken the eyeglasses away from Dr. Jensen and hung them on the wall of the tavern beside the wonderful two-headed dog. The lenses were crusted with salt and sand and dried seaweed, and the brass of the frame was etched with turquoise verdigris as if it were turning into a jewel.

They'd scraped the muck from the lenses with a spatula and painted comic eyes on them, so that the glasses seemed to be peering at you from the tavern wall. Right next to them hung the two-headed dog, looking woeful, its fur sketchy and matted.

Skeezix didn't at all like the idea of it. They'd been making fun—of the sorry dog, of Dr. Jensen. There were some things that oughtn't to be made fun of. Heaven knows they'd made fun of *him* often enough, mainly because he was fat and because he walked on the beach every day, rain or sun. He'd almost given them up—his walks on the beach—when it had begun to seem like the rain wasn't going to quit.

On the first day of heavy rains he'd slipped out the orphanage window at dawn, after having lain awake most of the night listening to the rain drum on the tin roof and rush and gurgle through the gutters, and he'd spent the morning rummaging in tide pools under his umbrella. He collected a pail full of brittle stars, which Dr. Jensen could ship south to the city, and by ten or eleven it made little difference that he carried the umbrella, for he was soaked with rain and seawater despite it. He had built a fire of driftwood under the cavern in the hillside, and he sat watching the rain fall all afternoon through a veil of smoke, stringing seashells on line pulled from the ribs of the umbrella.

Dr. Jensen would want the shoe. Heaven knows what he'd do with it, but he'd want it, if only to study it. He'd wanted the spectacles very badly, but the tavern keeper, a man named MacWilt, who had a crooked nose and one eye screwed almost shut because of some wasting disease, wouldn't give them to him. He would hang the spectacles on the wall of the tavern, he'd said, and Dr. Jensen could hang himself. What would MacWilt do with the shoe? Make a planter box of it, probably, out in front of the tavern, then let it go up in weeds out of spite.

The sea swallowed the sun at a gulp just then, and the evening beach fell into shadow. Skeezix slipped his hands beneath the weathered shoe sole and lifted. It was like trying to lift a house. He'd have to bail the water out of the shoe before he could even think of moving it, and even then it might be futile unless he had help. His stomach was beginning to growl too, and he felt suddenly that if he didn't eat he was going to faint. The little bit of lunch he'd brought along hadn't lasted him past noon. He'd had nothing to eat since. He would eat at the orphanage—for what it was worth—then slide out and eat again at the doctor's. Somehow he wanted nothing more than hot potatoes with butter and salt on them, about ten, all steaming on a plate with the butter pooling around them. He'd get cabbage soup and bread again at the orphanage, but there were worse things to eat. He'd eaten raw mussels once when Dr. Jensen had gone south for three days; he could still remember the slimy liver texture of the things and the pier-piling flavor. He would have starved then, probably, if Elaine Potts, the baker's daughter, hadn't come through with doughnuts. Good old Elaine; she was gone now, though, on holiday down south, and wouldn't be back for a week. She'd miss the Solstice entirely.

Hunger overwhelmed him like a silent rushing wave, and he found himself clambering up the slope toward the Coast Road and the railroad tracks and the village beyond. Nightfall would hide the shoe. No one would find it in the dark, least of all MacWilt, who would be busy pouring ale into pitchers and scooping up coins until well past midnight anyway. The shoe was safe enough. From the hilltop along the road it looked like nothing more than an oddly shaped tide pool. He'd eat, then hunt up Jack Portland. Jack would help him with the shoe. They'd come back after it that night, and the two of them would haul it up to the doctor's house on a wagon, and old Jensen would answer the door in his nightshirt and cap, Mrs. Jensen at his elbow. It would be nearing dawn. He and Jack would be ragged and wet from having worked all night at saving the shoe, and while the doctor went out in lantern light in the pouring rain, wearing his slippers, Mrs. Jensen would hurry them in and give them cookies and coffee and cheese and pickles and slices of pie.

Skeezix loved to think about food, especially when he was hungry. Around four every afternoon he daydreamed about meals he'd sometime eat, and he had sworn, years earlier, that one day he'd travel from one end of the world to the other, eating in every café and inn along the way. He'd eat two desserts, too; if he was going to be a fat man, he'd be a good one. Halfway measures weren't worth dirt when it came to food.

When he got there, the village was dark beneath the clouds and the coastal trees. Living rooms and parlors were cheerful with fires burning in grates. Smoke tumbled up out of chimney pots. Skeezix trudged along through the wet, up a cobbled alley that wound along parallel to the High Street. Through lit windows he could see families already eating dinner around wooden tables—sisters and brothers and mothers and fathers all gobbling away at mashed potatoes and pot roast and slivered apples with cinnamon. He could remember his own mother's face if he tried, but he didn't very often try. He couldn't remember, though, ever having sat around a table like that and eaten with his family. He'd had no family, not really.

Now he had Jack and Helen—and, of course, Peebles and Lantz. Jack didn't live in the orphanage; he lived with Mr. Willoughby up the hill. Jack was in love with Helen, although he wouldn't let on that he was, even to his best friend, Skeezix. Helen did live at the orphanage and had lived there at least as long as had Skeezix. What she felt about Jack she kept a mystery, which no doubt confounded Jack.

Skeezix didn't like Peebles. Nobody did, really, except perhaps Miss Flees, who ran the orphanage, or at least came as close as anybody did to running it. Peebles "kept her informed." That was what she was always saying: "Peebles will keep me informed." And then she'd squint up her eyes like she had a sand grain in them and nod her head very slowly. Peebles had a nose like MacWilt's nose—like someone had yanked on it with a pliers—and he was always after Miss Flees to be after Skeezix not to eat so much.

She'd lecture Skeezix by the hour about diets. She'd eaten only whole-wheat muffins and well water, she said, when she was a girl. And it seemed to be true, since she was thin as a wind-beaten scarecrow and had dark hollows under her eyes. Skeezix couldn't see any profit in such a diet. And even if he could, he could hardly have eaten less of her cabbage soup and bread than he ate; there wasn't half enough to go around as it was. Helen very often gave him a piece of her bread, because she was small and didn't eat much, she said, and Skeezix would bring Helen dried starfish and the empty shells of chambered nautiluses and moon snails that would be tossed up onto the beach after a storm.

But you had to put up with Peebles. There he was, after all—what old Willoughby would call a "sad case," hated as he was by almost everyone except Miss Flees, and by himself most of all. That's how it seemed to Skeezix anyway, who climbed now over the little stile fence behind the orphanage, waded through the knee-high grass, slipped a copper ruler between a window rail and its jamb, and levered up the little slip lock that held the window shut. After a minute of groaning and hoisting and kicking, he tumbled in past the open casement and onto the floor. He stood up and dropped the ruler into the grass outside, along the clapboards of the wall. Then he shut the window and peered out into the hallway, where he could hear the sound of clinking plates and glasses.

The sour, heavy aroma of boiled cabbage hung on the air. Two cats wandered toward him down the hall, and he bent down and picked one of them up, a white and orange cat named Mouse, his particular favorite. He was half sure that the cat could speak, and more than once just lately he had awakened in the middle of the night to find it perched by his ear, whispering something to him, something he couldn't quite make out. It was the Solstice that did that, that turned everything onto its head.

Miss Flees blinked at him out of a pinched-up face. Her hair seemed to have lost its mind. Half of it was shoved up atop her head in a sort of geyser and clamped with a piece of twine. The other half had abandoned the twine and hung around her ears like the oars of a galley. The corners of her mouth drooped. "You're late," she squeaked, in a voice only half human.

"I fell asleep. I was awfully tired because of all the rain last night."

"You're lying again."

"That's right, he is," said Peebles happily. "He wasn't in his bed half an hour ago. I looked in, and he was still gone. He's been gone all day. Look at him, his clothes are wet, aren't they?"

"Yes, Mr. Peebles, I'm certain they are." Miss Flees gave Skeezix a shrewd look, seeming to mean that she saw right through him, that Skeezix would have to work a little harder if he wanted to fool someone like her.

"*You're* lying," said Helen to Peebles in a tired voice. "I saw him asleep myself an hour past, and then again just before supper."

Now it was Helen's turn to be squinted at. Miss Flees looked her up and down, as if she was just that second seeing her for the first time, or as if she'd just then *really* seen her for the traitor she was. "And the wet clothes?" she asked, smiling and nodding at Peebles.

"I was sleeping with the window open, actually," Skeezix put in, not wanting to make Helen lie for him. It was fairly clear by then that Miss Flees hadn't herself looked into his room. She rarely did. She sat and read dime novels in what she called the parlor, and she told fortunes for a penny.

She used to hold séances. Once Skeezix and Helen had watched through the window and were surprised to see a ghostly apparition appear from the direction of the kitchen in the middle of the spiritualizing. One woman had fainted and another had screamed, the fainting woman thinking it was the ghost of her dead son come back around at the bidding of Miss Flees. It hadn't been the dead son, though—although the woman had never found that out—it had been Peebles covered in baking flour and wearing a black robe. The fainting woman was the wife of the Mayor, the other was the Mayor's sister, and the Mayor himself had bitten the end off his cigar and nearly set his pants on fire with the ash. Peebles had fled through the kitchen door, and it took about a gallon of tea at five cents a cup to restore the party to the extent that they could walk home.

Helen and Skeezix had waited a day before they asked Miss Flees, very casually, why it was that Peebles had bathed in baking flour and what all the screaming had meant. Skeezix had gotten extra bread that night, and Helen was relieved of washing the dishes, and for two months afterward they had a better time of it than they had in years—coming and going as they liked, finding a scrap of salt pork in their cabbage soup, laughingly recalling now and again how surprised they were to see Peebles gotten up like that in the robe and all, and what a fine trick Miss Flees had played on the two ladies, who, heaven knew, were too stuffy for their own good in the first place. They could "throw the whole thing in their face," insisted Skeezix. It would serve them right. But Miss Flees seemed very anxious that such a thing be avoided, and although she shook with the effort of it, she'd even bought Skeezix a pie for dessert one night, and he'd eaten it—sharing a slice with Helen—right down to the last scrap of crust, while Miss Flees stood gaping and sputtering like a bomb about to explode and level the house. Miss Flees hated both of them. So did Peebles.

After supper Skeezix went out through the window again. He'd catch it from Miss Flees in the morning. She'd keep an eye on his room for sure that night. But so what? What would she do to him, put him on half rations? He could live with Dr. Jensen, couldn't he? Except that would mean abandoning Helen to Miss Flees and Peebles, and he couldn't do that. She was like his sister. He wasn't half a block up the hill to Willoughby's farm when Helen caught up with him.

"Where are we going?" she asked. But she knew the answer well enough; there was nothing beyond Willoughby's farm but redwood groves and meadows choked in berry vines and skunk cabbage.

"Only up to Jack's."

"Then where?"

Skeezix shrugged. He wasn't certain he wanted a girl along on such a night—not with the storm threatening to break loose again and the sky full of bats and clouds and wind. "Just hanging out."

"You lie as badly as Peebles. You and Jack are up to something. What is it? I'm going to help." She pulled her coat around her more tightly and turned the collar up against the wind, which was blowing almost straight onshore and was heavy with misty sea salt.

Actually, Skeezix was happy enough to have her along. He muttered something about girls out on a night like this, but Helen gave him a look and he shut up about it, grinning at her as if he'd said it just to provoke her, which, of course, was why he *had* said it. Higher up the hill, the wind blew along in gusts, kicking up newly fallen leaves as if it meant to sail them into the next county. But the leaves were heavy from days of rain, and they fell almost at once back onto the road and lay there dark and wet and glistening with moonlight. Creeks and rills flowed with muddy water. They'd continue to flow straight through until summer, all of them dropping finally into the Eel River, which, any day now if the rain kept up, would overflow its banks and flood the orchards and farmhouses in the lowlands along the coast. The Eel fanned out into little sandy islets and then disappeared into the ocean above Table Bluffs Beach, some miles up the Coast Road from the cove where Skeezix had found the shoe and where the enormous spectacles had washed up.

Wild fuchsia bloomed in the shadows of hemlocks and alders along the road, but the startling purple and pink of the blossoms was washed colorless in the shadow. The mossy forest floor was like a saturated sponge, so Skeezix and Helen kept to the road, counting on the leafy carpet that lay upon it to keep mud off their shoes. All was silent but for the occasional patter of rain flurries and the moaning of wind in the top of the forest, and once, when the wind fell off and there was nothing in the air but the *drip, drip, drip* of water falling from tree branches, they could hear, distant and muted, the crash of breakers collapsing along the shore of the cove behind and below them. There wouldn't be another high tide until almost morning. The shoe would be safe at least until then—plenty of time, it seemed to Skeezix, for the three of them to haul it away on a cart.

He didn't tell Helen about the shoe. She could hear about it when he told Jack. She tried to get it out of him, and that made him happy. Then she quit trying to get it out of him, and that made him happier yet, because he knew she was just pretending to be indifferent. So he shrugged and started talking about whether or not butterflies flew in the rain and, if they did, whether the dust that covered their wings would shed rainwater so they wouldn't get saturated like wet leaves and end up as a part of the carpet on the roadway. Dr. Jensen, he said, once owned a butterfly as big as an albatross that had beautiful aqua-blue wings with silver spots like raindrops in sunshine. Its body, though, was still the body of a bug—and a monstrous bug at that—and you couldn't stand to look at it, not if you wanted to sleep that night.

The story was a lie and Helen knew it. Dr. Jensen had *heard* of such a creature—almost everyone had. He'd traveled by rail up to Lilyfield where it had been netted by a butterfly collector, a man named Kettering, with whom Dr. Jensen had gone to school. Where it had come from neither of them could say, from some distant land, perhaps, on a wind out of the east. Mr. Kettering's cats got in through an open window one night and shredded the creatures wings until it resembled a tired kite that had hung through the autumn in the branches of a tree. It wasn't worth much to anyone after that. All that was left of it, really, was the bug part. Even a scientist like Kettering was repelled by such an enormity.

Helen told Skeezix that he was a fool; Dr. Jensen had never owned the butterfly and everyone knew it. In fact, most people wondered if the whole story weren't a lie. There was an awful lot about Dr. Jensen that people wondered about, and that was why almost no one, except people who hadn't any money, went to Dr. Jensen when they were sick or hurt. He could set a bone as well as the next doctor, of course, but he'd set it in an office that looked like a museum—an office full of bins of dried tide-pool animals and moths and beetles and the skins of snakes. And he had the jawbone of a skull on his mantel—a skull that he'd fairly clearly dummied up out of plaster of paris and dirt, for the thing was the size of a barrel hoop smashed in half and had teeth in it like ivory playing cards. There was a certain amount of suspicion in the village that Dr. Jensen's interest in the enormous spectacles was feigned, and some went so far as to suggest that he'd had the glasses built on one of his trips south and had tossed them into the tide pool himself and then arranged to have them found. Why he would have done such a thing they didn't know. He was a lunatic, some said, and that was reason enough.

Skeezix waved his hand at Helen, who had gotten to him by talking that way about Dr. Jensen. He'd been teasing her by avoiding the subject of the night's mystery, and now she'd gotten back at him. The doctor *had* to have the bins full of odd stuff, Skeezix said, in order to sell it down south to the biological supply houses in San Francisco and Monterey, because there wasn't enough money in doctoring to make it pay—not on the north coast, there wasn't. Helen said if he cleared the stuff out of his house maybe he'd get a little bit of business from people who didn't want to hobnob with salamanders and toads when they were getting their tonsils yanked out, and then Skeezix said she didn't understand anything at all, and after that he wouldn't talk. They were at Jack's by then anyway, so Helen gouged him in the side and slugged him on the arm in order to show him she was just kidding. Of course she understood everything. Peebles wouldn't have—that was certain. But Helen had the right in-stincts, as had Jack, and Skeezix knew that, and Helen knew that he knew. She'd proven, though, that she could irritate him as easily as he could irritate her, and so things had ended well.

Jack Portland lived on Willoughby's farm. No one else lived there except old Willoughby, who had been a friend of Jack's father—no one else unless you counted the cows and the cats. Skeezix and Helen threw rocks at the shutters high up in the barn loft, and Skeezix called Jack's name in a sort of shouted whisper. There wasn't any real reason to be sneaking about like that, since farmer Willoughby would be snoring beside his pint glass by then anyway and wouldn't care about them even if he weren't. But the night was dark and windy and full of portent, and Skeezix was anxious that everything be done right.

After a half dozen rocks the shutters opened and Jack looked out. They could see that a candle burned on the table beside him, and the dark cylinder of his telescope formed a long dancing shadow across his face and the open shutter op-posite. He had a book in his hand, and when he saw who it was on the meadow below, he waved the book at them and then disappeared back inside—gone after his sweater and jacket, perhaps.

In a moment he stood in the window again, hooking the iron hangers of his rope ladder over the windowsill. The tails of the ladder flopped to the ground, and Jack clambered down like a sailor down rigging. In a moment he was on the meadow. He hauled back on the end of the ladder, gave it a wavy sort of toss, and the hooks hopped off the windowsill. The entire ladder dropped onto the grass. Jack rolled it up and then ran around and tossed it in through the barn door, pad-locking the big hasp afterward. Skeezix liked the idea of Jack's coming out by the window even though there was a door at hand. And he liked the idea of reading by candlelight. Jack could as easily have used a lantern, of course, but it wouldn't have been the same. One did things right, thought Skeezix, or one might as well just go to bed. There wasn't much to be said for common sense—or for anything common, for that matter.

Skeezix had been right about old Willoughby, who, Jack insisted, wouldn't be likely to waken until morning and so wouldn't miss his wagon. In ten minutes they were rattling away down the road, the three of them wedged in together on the plank seat, bound for the cove through the dark and silent night. The sky by then was full of stars veiled by ragged clouds, like tattered curtains fluttering through the open window of a room inhabited by fireflies.

2

THERE WAS ENOUGH MOON to see by, but not to see well. Peebles could make out the dim shapes of cypress trees, bent and contorted like hunched creatures that might easily have crept out of the freshly opened grave before him—the grave he'd dug open by himself, blistering his hands until they bled. The trees bordered the cemetery where it crawled up into the hills, the farthest graves having disappeared long ago under a tangle of berry vines and lemon leaf, their tilted stones lost beneath moss and lichen. There was enough silver moonlight to throw shadows along the ground. The moon hung just above the horizon, and the shadows of more recently set gravestones stretched across the grass in stark black rectangles, making it seem to the boy, when he turned his head just so, that every grave was an open grave and every grave was empty.

He licked his hand, vaguely enjoying the coppery taste of blood but feeling as if he were part of a nightmare, the sort of nightmare in which you dare not move for fear you might jostle things, perhaps, and be noticed by something you'd rather not be noticed by. But the wind cutting down out of the mountains to the east, slicing across the back of his neck and freezing his fingers, hadn't at all a nightmare quality to it. You can't feel the wind in a nightmare, but you could feel this wind; and he wouldn't wake up in his bed and be able to turn over and see something else when he closed his eyes. There was a thrill in this, though—in the hovering death and darkness.

He looked uneasily at the cypress trees. He could imagine something menacing in twisted limbs or bent stumps and in the creak of tree branches on the night wind. He couldn't keep his eyes entirely away, either. They wandered, ever so little.

He'd see things out of the corners of his eyes—things that shouldn't be—and sometimes he had to glance at them straight on, just to know for sure. Here was a jumble of berry vines, almost luminous in the moonlight, that shifted in the wind like some loathsome thing from the deep woods put together out of leaves and sticks, creeping sideways inch by inch onto the open graveyard and sighing in the wind as if it mourned something dead.

What he feared most was what they'd find in the coffin. The body had been buried for nearly twelve years. He'd heard that the hair of a corpse continues to grow even after the bones are dry and brittle and old. Now and then, when the Eel River rose in flood, it washed open hillside graves, and the skeletons that tumbled out into the muddy current to go clacking away to sea had hair that wisped around the bones of their shoulders and in which was tangled the trinkets they were buried with.

There was a curse right then and the sound of a spade ringing against iron coffin handles and then scuffing off across pine boards. The man standing waist deep in the grave before him wore a black topcoat with cuffed sleeves. His hair fell dark and oily around his shoulders. Judging from the gray pallor of his bearded face, he might have been dead himself for a week and then dug up and animated.

The boy, who leaned on a shovel above and half hid his eyes and who was stricken with terror now that the coffin had at last been unearthed, was even more frightened of the man in the grave, whom he despised. Unlike the moon shadows round about them and the sighing of things on the wind, he was a flesh-and-blood horror. Though he was weak, as if he were starving and tired and ill, his eyes were dark and deadly. But he had offered Peebles something—hadn't he?—that would make it worth the terror and more.

The man cursed again and then hissed something through his teeth.

"What?"

"I said, give me the bar. Are you deaf?"

Peebles said nothing but picked up an iron crowbar that lay in the damp grass and handed it to the man, who looked back fiercely, as if he'd just as soon kill the boy right there and have done with him. The man bent back to his work, levering the crowbar under the coffin lid. There was the squeak of rusty nails pried loose and the scratch and scrape of the iron bar when the rotted wood of the lid snapped and broke away. The man cursed again and slammed the curved end of the crowbar into the lid, smashing and smashing it until the night rang with the blows and the man gasped for breath and there was nothing left of the coffin lid but splintered fragments still fixed by long casing nails to the edge grain of the coffin's side.

Peebles looked away as a cloud shaded the moon. The trees above him faded into blackness and the shadows of gravestones slowly disappeared. A drop of rain plinked down onto his hand, which grasped the shovel so hard that it shook. Another drop fell, and then another. In an hour the gravel road out of the cemetery would be a muddy rill that would bog the wheels of their cart in mire, and he'd find himself trudging the two miles home in a downpour. He pushed his glasses up onto his nose, shaded his forehead in an effort to keep the glasses dry, and looked back and the black-coated man, who stood beside the grave now, scowling and grinning in turn, as if he couldn't make up his mind whether to be insanely happy or insanely angry.

Peebles peered into the grave, imagining the gumless teeth, the empty sockets, the wisps of grayed hair, the dusty and worm-eaten clothing slumped across the xylophone curve of rib cage. It was a horrifying thought, to be sure, but it was fascinating, too. Something in him loved the idea of death and decay. He'd found a book once on a high shelf in the village bookshop, and in it were sketches of instruments of torture and of dead men hanging from gibbets. He'd torn the pictures out and kept them, fearful they'd be found and hating the people who might find them because it was their fault—

wasn't it?—that he had to live in fear of being discovered. Those were just pictures, though, and what lay in the grave, dead these long years, wouldn't be a picture.

He bent closer, relishing the anticipated shock of horror. What he saw was a disappointment. The skeleton lay buried beneath scattered debris. And it hadn't any webby, overgrown hair. The flesh had returned to dust, and even the bone seemed to be crumbling, so that the skeleton lay in moldering pieces, like an instructive illustration from an archaeology textbook.

What lay in the coffin was simply too thoroughly dead to be frightening. There was no rotted flesh, no grinning zombie, just the slowly vanishing remains of a man long dead and forgotten, lying beneath a heap of books and glassware as if beneath the earthquake-tumbled contents of a room set up for alchemical study. There were broken sheets of tinted isinglass and a half-dozen conical beakers. There were fragments of rolled copper and a length of glass tubing shoved in among the rest like a spear. There was a crockery jar big enough to hold a severed head, and in it was the cracked bust of a fierce-looking bearded man, whose jaw and left ear had been broken away. Scattered throughout were long-necked, unlabeled wine bottles.

The man in the topcoat crouched at the edge of the grave, silent now and stroking his chin. Peebles edged closer, gaping at the lumber in the cracked coffin and tugging his coat closer around his shoulders to keep out the rain. The moon appeared again like a lamp suddenly unveiled, and moonlight shone for a moment off the curved glass of a heavy, almost opaque bottle that was still half full of some dark liquid. The man leaned in and plucked out a book that seemed to have been bent by dampness. The pages were glued together, and the outside cover pulled away from the spine, as if worms, having reduced the corpse to a papery hulk, had gone to work on the leather binding. On the first page of the book, scrawled across the top in black ink, was the inscription *To Lars Port-*

land, from Jensen and then the month and day of a year twenty-five years past.

The book tumbled out of the pale hands and fell into the grave, sliding down the dirt incline and jolting to a stop against a half-filled bottle. "What are you gaping at!" cried the man, turning toward the face of the boy, who read over his shoulder. Peebles stumbled back, catching his heel on the spade that he still held, falling over backward onto the wet grass. The man laughed low in his throat and shook his head; then he reached again into the grave, hauled out the bottle, sniffed at it, and threw it end over end into the night.

He plucked out the skull next and peered at it intently, thumping his finger against the top of the thing's cranium. The brittle bone splintered under his nail, as if it were a termite-eaten husk of wood. He took it between his two hands and shredded it, letting the brittle teeth clatter down into the grave, and then he threw the fragments in after it. "Dead a thousand years," he muttered, and then he shook, as if from a chill.

The cemetery was lit just then by lightning through clouds, and with the boom of thunder that followed came a sudden downpour. The man arose without a word and slouched tiredly around the grass, tramping on graves with his boots and pulling his hat over his forehead. The boy watched for a moment, then sprang up and grappled with the shovels and crowbar and with a heavy pick, dragging the lot of them along in the man's wake until he caught up. The man struck him in the face with the back of his hand, tore the muddy tools out of his hands, and flung them away. Then, looking at the cowering boy, he said, "What do we want with stolen tools?" as if his explanation would justify his hard treatment, and he helped the boy roughly into the cart before climbing in himself and taking up the reins.

They clattered away toward the Coast Road, a peal of wild laughter howling away behind them on the wind; then the sound of a racking cough followed the laughter, with a string of curses to bind it all together. The graveyard, in moments, lay empty and dark beneath the cloud-veiled moon, and the rain beat down onto the moss and grasses and pooled up until it ran in little rivulets down the hill toward the sea, some of it edging into the mouth of the freshly opened grave and pouring over onto the strange litter of glass and books and bones and alchemical debris like a rising tide of seawater submerging the curious inhabitants of a long-evaporated tide pool.

The shoe still sat on the night-dark sand like a beached whale. They drove the wagon down onto the slick, packed dirt of the beach road, blocked the wheels, and put a feedbag on the horse. There wasn't much time; it was past midnight, and they'd want to be at the doctor's by two if they were going to wangle a meal out of Mrs. Jensen. Helen didn't much care about eating in the middle of the night, but it appealed a little bit to Jack and especially to Skeezix, whose stomach felt at the moment like a collapsed balloon. He wished he'd brought a lunch, but he hadn't, so there was nothing to do but hurry.

Jack set a hooded lantern on a driftwood burl, so that the light was shining down onto the shoe, and then all three of them started bailing water out of it with milk buckets. Big as the shoe was, though, more than anything else they got into each other's way, and when Helen splashed a bucketful of seawater down the back of Skeezix's pant leg, he quit and went away mad to hunt up driftwood to use as sleds.

The heel end of the shoe angled away uphill, so they emptied it first, and then tried heaving the toe end up into the air in order to dump the rest of the water onto the sand. But Helen and Jack couldn't budge it. When Skeezix appeared out of the darkness dragging long, waterworn timbers in each hand, he tried tilting the shoe with them, but it still wouldn't move. They shoved one of the timbers—an immense broken oar, it seemed, from a monumental wrecked rowboat—in under the toe and then wedged the other timber under it, levering away at the first until the heel edged around and down the hill. They inched it along, burying their fulcrum timber in the soft beach sand and pulling it out and resetting it and burying it again, until water rushed from the toe to the heel. Then they bailed it clean, shoved it farther, bailed once more, and then pushed the shoe entirely over onto its side, ocean water cascading out past the tongue and the laces and the heel edge along with a school of silvery fish that flopped and wriggled on the wet sand.

Helen plucked up the fish and dropped them into her bucket. Then, realizing that the bucket was dry, she ran down to where the waves foamed up along the beach and waded out ankle deep, scooping up water and then running back up to where Skeezix and Jack were busy yanking the shoe over onto the two timbers.

"Leave off there, can't you?" shouted Skeezix, who was still mad about his pants.

"I've got to save these fish."

Skeezix gave her an exasperated look, a look which said that there was no time to save fish, but she acted like she hadn't seen it and went right along with her task. Groaning aloud, as if he'd never understand girls like Helen, Skeezix quit messing with the shoe and started picking up fish himself, dropping them into Helen's bucket with exaggerated care so as to let her know that, although he had more important work to do, he'd humor her for the sake of her fish. Helen said thank you very politely each time he dumped in a fish, and then she started to pretend that the fish were saying thank you, and she made the fish talk to Skeezix in high, burbling voices, like bubbles through water. Skeezix made a threatening gesture, as if he were going to eat one of the fish—bite its head right off and swallow it raw.

Helen ignored him, turned, and walked down once again to the water, emptying the several dozen fish into a receding wave. Skeezix ran along after and pitched his in too. Then, with a clever look on his face, he said something to Helen about her not taking the bait, but a forked bolt of lightning and a simultaneous crack of thunder buried her equally clever reply, and both of them ran back toward the shoe, hunkering down now under a fresh torrent of rain, which washed in on the driven wind, beating on the surface of the sea and soaking them through in moments.

They debated taking shelter in the cavern in the cliff, but that seemed pointless—they were already as wet as they were likely to be that night—and the longer the shoe sat in the rain, the more water it would catch and the heavier it would be. So they slid it heel first over the timbers, all the way across and down onto the beach, where it pushed up a sort of bow wave of sand and lodged there, its sad, seaweedy laces trailing along on either side.

"We need two more boards," Helen announced, and immediately all three of them went off searching, Jack carrying the lantern in such a way as to keep rain out of the shade, playing the feeble light over the dark beach. There were any number of snags of driftwood, none of which would do them any good at all, tangled as they were, with any useful boards trapped beneath stumps and branches and half buried in sand. Then, just when searching any farther began to seem pointless, Skeezix found a sort of graveyard of old railroad ties, tumbled from the ridge above. They dragged two free. With the rain beating into their faces and the surf roaring against the rocky edge of the cove, they hauled them back toward where the shoe lay beyond a veil of falling water.

None of them questioned the foolishness of their mission. Here was a beaten and water-soaked shoe, after all, useless to anyone but a giant. But there were no giants living on the coast, or anywhere else, as far as any of them knew for sure. It was a shoe which, come morning, would still be sitting on the beach—had they left it alone—and so didn't, perhaps, require their slogging through wet sand and cold rain at past midnight.

There was something wonderful, though, in doing useless work. You could turn it into a sort of art. They'd spent the better part of a day and night once building a fortified sand castle on that very beach. Dr. Jensen had promised an eight-foot tide the following morning, and they'd calculated how high to build the castle so as to assure its doom. There was no grandeur in a sand castle that was safe from the tide. They'd built a wall around it of stones carried in buckets from the rocky shingle to the south, and inside they'd dug a waist-deep moat, and then, between the moat and the castle, they'd set a line of stakes driven two feet into the sand and they'd woven kelp strands through the stakes, along with whatever sorts of flotsam looked likely to stop an ounce or two of encroaching seawater.

They'd worked at it until late in the night and then slept above the beach in the cavern. All three had awakened past midnight to work again on the sand castle in the light of the moon, and they were still working—building a city of minarets and domes and troweled avenues beyond the castle—when the eastern sky had paled with the dawn and the moon had disappeared beyond the watery horizon after lying for a moment like a smoky island on the sea. They had watched from the cavern as the tide swirled up the beach, but they were too tired by then to be anything but silently happy when the rocks and the moat and the wall held up against the first onslaught of waves. More waves had followed, marching up in long straight lines out of the dark ocean, nibbling away at the sand beneath the rocky wall, collapsing the woven sticks in a heap, filling the moat and cascading across the towers and spires and domes and flooding subterranean tunnels. In something under a minute there had been nothing on the beach but a vague mound of wet sand like the back of a turtle, and a little fan-shaped tumble of smooth stones and sticks.

They were twenty yards from the shoe when the shriek of a train whistle erupted from the hill above. Skeezix shouted in surprise and dropped the end of the timber he'd been dragging along the sand with both hands. Jack threw his down, too, and with Helen at his heels set out at a hunched run for the cavern. They climbed the sandstone slope, slipping and clutching and hauling themselves into the mouth of the cavern and out of the rain. From there they could just see, misty and pale through the curtain of falling drops, the train trestle where it crossed above the stream eighty feet farther down the beach.

The train tracks were a ruin, and had been for as long as any of them could remember. They were rust-pitted and twisted, and a good many of the ties had long ago fallen prey to termites and to sliding hillsides. But there was something in the night, in the rain and the wind and the tide, in the dark bulk of the giant shoe that sat like a behemoth on the sand, that made the impossible appearance of the train seem half expected.

Years ago there had been a northbound coastal train, the Flying Wizard, from San Francisco to the south and all the way up from subtropical border towns before that. The population of the north coast had dwindled, though, over time. And in the rainy season, water off the coastal mountains crumbled cliff sides and swept train trestles and tracks into the heaving ocean below. The tracks fell into disrepair. The train—strangely—had run anyway during the Solstice twelve years earlier, but it had never been settled whether the tracks had been hastily repaired for that last journey or whether it had been a miracle that brought the train and the Solstice carnival to Rio Dell and Moonvale.

There was another whistle blast and the screech of brakes, and from where Jack crouched in the cavern he could see steam roiling from beneath the cars. The train was slowing. It wound around a curve of track, appearing for the moment that it took to clatter across the trestle, then almost at once disappearing beyond the rain and the redwoods that climbed down the hill toward the sea. One by one the hazy cars lurched past, dark and low and open and freighted with strange, angular machinery.

"What is it?" Skeezix whispered, referring not to the train but to the junk heaped in the cars.

Jack shook his head, realizing suddenly that he was shaking with cold too. Wind off the ocean sailed straight into the cavern, swirled round in back of it, then sailed out again. It was drier than it had been on the open beach, but at least there they'd had their minds on something other than the cold and wet. The chill seemed to have come with the train, carried, perhaps, on the steam that whirled away into the misty might. They could hear that the train had stopped, although they could no longer see it, and Jack supposed he could hear the soft chuffing of the waiting engine, even though the wind was blowing in the opposite direction.

"Carnival stuff," Helen whispered.

Skeezix jumped, as if Helen had poked him in the ribs. "What?"

"On the train. That arched framework was a Ferris wheel, and there was one car piled with little cars of some sort. Didn't you see that?"

"Yes," Jack said, because he *had* seen it, although he hadn't had any idea what he was looking at. Helen came from down south, from San Francisco, and she would have seen carnivals. But there hadn't been any such thing on the north coast since the last Solstice, and Jack had been too young to remember it much. What had happened there, though, at the carnival, was something he couldn't entirely forget, ever— even though there were times when he might have wished to. He'd seen pictures of carnivals in library books, and he knew well enough what a Ferris wheel was. Seeing one in a book, all put together and lit up and with the rest of the carnival laid out below, was a different thing from seeing the dim pieces of one dismantled and howling past in a distant, darkened train.

"Why're they stopping at the bottom of the grade, do you suppose?" asked Skeezix, whispering just loud enough to be heard above the rain. Neither Jack nor Helen answered, since they didn't know, so Skeezix replied to his own question. "Some sort of mechanical trouble, I bet. We could ride down the Coast Road and have a look."

"I'm freezing," said Helen. "If I'm riding anywhere, it's home to bed. None of us knows anything about that train, and that's fine with me. It's got no business stopping here. It's got no business *being* here. If we're lucky, it will be gone before we've reached the Coast Road, let alone driven around to the bluffs, which is where it is now, from the sound of it."

After that, both she and Jack stepped out into the rain and skidded down the wet scree to the beach, where they picked up the railroad ties and lugged them along to the shoe. Jack watched Helen carry the timber across her shoulder, balancing it there like it was nothing. He admired that. She was beautiful with her dark, wet hair and musty wool sweater. She saw him watching her, and he looked away in embarrassment, dropping his timber onto the beach and then grappling it back onto his shoulder, thankful that the rainy night would mask the color in his face.

Skeezix and Jack pulled and pushed and slid the shoe across the top of one pair of parallel timbers and onto the next, then stopped while Helen dragged the two abandoned timbers around and flopped them onto the sand, and so on until, cold and weary, they found themselves at the beach road, where the cart stood in the rain, the horse asleep.

Jack shoved a railroad tie in front of the rear wheels just in case. Then the three of them lifted the toe of the shoe onto the back of the wagon. Helen and Skeezix held it firm while Jack ran around to the heel and put his shoulder against it to make sure it didn't slide back off onto the road. His two friends joined him then, and together they lifted the shoe and pushed it entirely up onto the rain-slick cart until it bumped against the slats in front. The horse awoke with a whinny, shaking her head to clear her eyes. They tied the shoe to the side rails with the heavy, water-soaked laces, letting half the heel overhang the rear of the wagon.

By quarter past two they were rattling Dr. Jensen's door knocker, and ten minutes later they stood shivering by his fire, watching Mrs. Jensen light the oven and haul a pie out of the pantry. The fire hadn't, thank goodness, burned down yet, since the doctor had gone to bed late, and the coals were so hot that it had taken no time at all to get the fire banked and roaring in the grate.

They had hauled the shoe into the doctor's carriage house, where there sat a number of other treasures with which it shared a strange affinity: a round, convex sheet of cracked glass, like the crystal of an impossible watch; a brass belt buckle the size of a casement window; and a cuff link that might as easily have been a silver platter. The shoe was the best of the lot, though, for while the crystal and the belt buckle and the cuff link might have been tricked up by an enterprising craftsman intent on playing a prank on someone, the shoe hadn't been. It had clearly been worn. It was down-at-heel to the point at which the sole tacks showed through, and it was scuffed and ragged about the toe, and there was a bulge in the side, as if it had been too small for the giant who had worn it and the side of his foot had pressed against it and stretched the leather out of shape.

Dr. Jensen was speechless with joy. It seemed to prove something to him, as did the unlikely appearance of the train, which troubled him too. But what it proved and how it troubled him he couldn't entirely put into words. That didn't matter to Skeezix, who didn't much care for words right then anyway, and who had one eye on the lamplit kitchen window the entire time. But it bothered Jack.

Something was happening, and it involved him. He was sure of it. Something had come with the rain. The air had shifted, it seemed, like a season turning. He could almost smell it on the breeze through the loft window in the morning. The ocean was restless. The wind blew day and night. The cattle were moody and suspicious, and they looked around when they grazed as if they heard someone approaching across the open fields, even though nothing could be seen but the long grass rippling in the wind or the shadow of a passing cloud.

Two days earlier Jack had awakened in the middle of the night to the sound of a cow lowing in the barn below, and he'd thrown open the window thinking that someone was prowling around out in the darkness. He'd seen nothing but night shadows and the moonlit meadow with the forest and hills rising beyond. Low on the horizon, though, out beyond Moonvale, the sky had been alive with a flickering of lights like an electric storm—except that the lights were faintly colored, blue and azure and green, and there was no thunder, not even distant thunder, only a silence hanging in the air like a storm about to break. Rain began to fall then. It seemed to wash the sky clean as if it were a watercolor painting.

Later that night he'd heard the sound of a voice. He'd awakened to find no one at all nearby, only a mouse scuttling away across roof joists. But it stopped some distance out onto the span to look back at him, standing oddly on its hind legs, regarding him curiously. Then the following morning he'd made an odd discovery: his bathwater, when he pulled the plug, dumped straightaway down the drain, over the edge and gone, like in an old drawing of ocean water falling off the edge of the flat earth. It ought to have swirled around, creating a little vortex, but it didn't. The Solstice had that sort of effect; it altered things, sometimes for a couple of weeks, sometimes forever. He'd forgotten about it, though. There were cows to milk and hay to be forked, and he was off that afternoon with Helen and Skeezix to take food and clothes to Lantz, a scatterbrained friend of theirs who lived alone in a shack on the meadow above the sea.

Lantz might have lived at Miss Flees's, had he wanted to. The village would pay for it. But he liked solitude better. He kept a menagerie of stuffed animals, too, bug-eaten and falling to ruin, which he talked to in low voices and which he'd gotten when Riley's taxidermy shut down for want of business. Lantz looked just a little bit like one of his animals—tall and stooped and ragged, like the stuffing was coming out of him—and he walked in a loose, disjointed sort of way that would have made Miss Flees shout to see it. As far as conversation went, he accomplished more with his stuffed creatures, probably, than he did with anyone who spoke out loud.

Although he might have stayed at Miss Flees's, he wasn't exactly an orphan, or at least no one was certain that he was an orphan. Some said that he was the son of MacWilt, the taverner, and a hunchbacked gypsy woman who had kept birds in the attic rooms above the tavern. Years earlier you could hear her singing to the canaries on warm summer evenings, high trilling songs that sounded eastern, somehow, and ancient, like they were being sung in the tongues of the birds themselves. It had been discovered one day that a boy lived there among the birds, a mute, it was thought, although later it turned out that Lantz had simply never been taught to speak any language other than the language of the canaries. MacWilt insisted that the child was a foundling whom he'd given to the gypsy woman, along with a certain monthly sum, just out of the kindness of his heart. This last had become a sort of joke for days, people insisting that the story must be a lie, since MacWilt was widely known to lack such an article of anatomy.

Beneath the joke was a certain amount of scandal. It was true—MacWilt would no more house a foundling or feed a gypsy than he'd give a gold piece to a beggar, which is to say never. The woman died, some said in childbirth, when Lantz was eight, and there was a brief, wicked rumor that the unlikely offspring had been a monster and that MacWilt himself had borrowed a skiff, rowed three miles out to sea in a calm, and cast it into the deep ocean. Some went so far as to whisper that he'd murdered the woman himself, out of sheer horror, but it had never been proved.

Lantz, though, fled into the woods and stayed there, and village children brought him what he needed to stay alive. He avoided the village, although he sometimes helped Skeezix fish for tide-pool animals, and now and then Mrs. Jensen hiked out to his shack above the bluffs with a basket of food. Helen one time had brought him a caged canary, but Lantz had fled in horror at the sight of it and they hadn't seen him after that for months.

It was all very strange, and the later at night Jack thought about it, the stranger it seemed. There was no profit in thinking after midnight. Some little bit of the darkness slipped in and cast shadows across what ought to be commonplace details and events. The late hour changed their countenance in subtle ways until you began to see patterns in the stones in the tumbled countryside of your mind, patterns that were the vague outlines of almost recognizable shapes.

Jack shook the sleep out of his head. Mrs. Jensen was laying the remains of an apple pie on the table, and beside it a pitcher of cream and a cold joint of beef and a great wedge of cheese. Skeezix nodded to Helen by way of politeness and then sat down and helped himself to the beef and cheese. The sight of Skeezix eating swept the doubts and suspicions and vagaries out of Jack's mind. There was something about an apple pie, he thought as he sat down at the table, that made a mockery of late-night fears. But as he at it, sleepy and drying out in front of the fire, he couldn't quite rid his thoughts of the sound of the moving wind and the pattering rain.

3

JACK PORTLAND AWOKE LATE in the morning, feeling as if he'd just eaten. It took him a moment to realize that he had, that he'd spent two hours in the middle of the night at Dr. Jensen's, following Skeezix's lead and shoving down food.

The sky had partly cleared. What clouds were left blew across the heavens on a rushing wind, throwing a scattering of raindrops now and then, just to keep their hand in, but clearly put to flight at last.

From his loft window Jack could see halfway to Moonvale on a clear day. Only the rise of the Moonvale Hills and the low, drifting fog that shrouded them stood in the way. It would have been nice, perhaps, to have been able to see on a spring dawn the distant pinnacle of a shingled church steeple or plumes of sleepy smoke hovering above distant chimneys like the misty promise of enchantment just beyond the hills. But Moonvale was too far away and its church spires hidden. Any smoke from chimneys might as easily be cloud drift, and the only evidence of a city at all was that at night there was the faint glow of lights along the horizon, stretching down almost to the sea.

He hadn't even been to Moonvale, although Helen had. If his father were alive the two of them would have been there and beyond. Someday . . . Jack thought. But the idea of it, of leaving Rio Dell and wandering off alone, was better left a dream. It was safer that way; like most dreams, it might lose just a little bit of its charm coming true.

A rush of wind blew through the open window, fluttering the pages of his book. Jack reached out and yanked closed one of the two shutters, fixing it tight with a wooden peg just as the wind threw the second shut with a bang. Though feeble light shone through knotholes and between the oak slats of the barn, it was not enough to read by, so Jack lit three candles on the table beside his bed, then watched the flames dance and flicker in the little gusts that found their way through the slats. He wanted the sort of book that didn't seem to need a beginning and end, that could be opened at any page without suffering for it—slow, candlelight reading.

He could have slept in the house, of course. Mr. Willoughby might easily have preferred it. At times Mr. Willoughby wanted more company than his cats. Jack rarely wanted any company beyond his friends. A year or so after his father's death Mr. Willoughby had asked Jack to call him "Pop," of all things. Jack had made a painful effort, and they had stumbled along with it for about a month, but it was never natural for either of them, so Jack gave up on it. He'd stuck to "Mr. Willoughby" for a time thereafter, then settled finally on "Willoughby" in the years since.

Jack had known his mother for a few short years and could recall almost nothing about her, depending upon the sad, usually drunken, reminiscences of old Willoughby. Jack owned a picture of her too, a faded photograph in which she wore a velvet dress—the dress she died in. Willoughby was her uncle and was the only family Jack had left. He did his best at it, too, but wasn't cut out entirely for the raising of small orphaned boys. Willoughby wasn't cut out for much of anything, but he had the right instincts.

"I'm not much of a farmer," Willoughby would admit, shaking his head as if remembering something that he hadn't the power to speak of. It was what Jack called a three-glass revelation—maudlin and sad, but without the edge of despair that set in after the fifth glass. And Willoughby was right, as far as it went. His farm was a ruin of weedy pastureland and broken fences and a half dozen or so independent-minded cattle who, Jack was certain, understood *themselves* to be the owners of the farm. Jack had found one of the cows clopping through the village not half a block from the town hall one sunny afternoon, on his way, Jack was certain, to have a go at altering the deed to Willoughby's land, in payment, perhaps, for sixty thousand quarts of milk given on loan.

But Willoughby's "I'm not much of a farmer" sentiment seemed to hint that there was work he was more suited to. Things might have been different, it seemed to imply. He'd think of Jack's mother and shake his head. Then Jack would change the subject—happy though he would have been to glimpse bits and pieces of the past. Dr. Jensen had told Jack that someday he'd see through it all clearly, and Jack supposed he was right. He often was, in his way.

When Jack had moved from the house to the barn at the age of twelve, Willoughby had said that Jack was exactly like his father and would one day be moving along into realms much farther removed than a hayloft.

But Jack's father was dead, shot to death on the meadow. That was Willoughby's way of being philosophic about death, Jack supposed—calling it a "realm," as if it were something more than nothing. That was two-glass optimism on Willoughby's part and was accompanied by squinting and nodding and an immediate third glass, which, at a blow, would level any such mystical talk and set Willoughby's head from nodding to shaking. Seven glasses would set it to nodding again, in time to deep, sonorous snoring. That would continue until morning and was half the reason that Jack had moved to the loft.

The other half had to do with an evening on which the seven glasses had failed to put Willoughby to sleep, and he had muttered halfway through an eighth glass something about Lars Portland orphaning his own son. Nonsense had followed, giving way to sleep, and although poor Willoughby wouldn't have remembered the slip the following morning anyway, Jack waited two weeks before announcing that the loft had taken his fancy. He wanted a view, he'd said, and that was the truth.

The ruined farm couldn't pay. By the time Jack was six he knew that Willoughby had some little bit of money put away somewhere. Where it had come from was none of Jack's business. Jack had never wanted for anything beyond a view—that and the unveiling of a few shrouded mysteries. Now he had a strange feeling, what with the change in the weather and the sky lit up at night and the tub water behaving like it did, that someone's hand was on the curtain and at any moment would snatch it aside.

He realized, of a sudden, that his mind wasn't at all on his book. Two of the candles had blown out and one of the shutters rattled against the window casing. Wind whistled softly through chinks. Rusted hinges squeaked downstairs and the barn door slammed. Yellow lantern light leaped up the walls, and Willoughby, come to work on his cheese, hummed softly and tunelessly after barring the door against the wind. There'd be coffee in the house.

Jack pulled on his pants, shirt, and sweater and stepped across to the stile railing that fronted the loft. The rear half of the barn floor, separated from the cattle by a tight, low, paneled wall, was swept clean every afternoon. Tables and benches lined the walls, cluttered with tubs and buckets and shrouds of cheesecloth. Cheeses hung in nets from the ceiling and sat in molds along the walls, heaped together, one atop and beside another like buildings along a street.

Jack and Willoughby couldn't begin to eat that many cheeses, and Willoughby never sold any. The cheeses were an excuse to keep six cows. *One* cow would have been enough to keep them in milk and butter. Years ago Jack had assumed that the cheeses would one day come to something, that there would be some end to them. "Some things are never finished," Willoughby had said cryptically. "They can't be. Finishing doesn't enter in."

Many of the cheeses had long since become dust, and the rest had become a sort of mouse township, complete, Jack assumed, with aldermen and a mouse mayor. "Let the mice have them," Willoughby had said patiently. There was a lot in Willoughby to admire.

Jack could see the mice working the cheese. They appeared from little gnawed avenues and then disappeared again, toting chunks from deep in the interior toward secret destinations. Why they bothered was more than Jack could say. Why haul cheese from house to house in a city *built* of cheese? It had to do with aging it, perhaps; the mice were connoisseurs.

Willoughby meddled with a cheese mold for a moment, cursed under his breath, and went out again through the door, shutting it after him. Lantern light flickered across the cheese, guttering in the cool, moving air of the barn. There was a noise in the shadows—the meowing of a cat and the scraping of claws against the boards of the barn wall. The cat pounced, suddenly, out into the circle of yellow light, landing on all fours but with its front paws together, trying to pin something to the floor. It was a mouse, running higgledy-piggledy, scurrying toward a crack in the floorboards.

"Hey!" Jack shouted at the cat, thinking to take the side of the mouse. He bent over to pluck up his shoe in order to pitch it over the railing. But then he saw that the shout had been enough. The cat had stopped where it landed in the lantern light. It stood there gaping, as if it had seen something it hadn't half expected to see. Jack gaped too and straightened up slowly. There wasn't a mouse on the floor of the barn at all; there was a tiny thumb-sized man. He clutched in his hands the head of a mouse, a mask, actually. All Jack's gaping and goggling lasted only a fraction of a second; before Jack could speak, before he could shout at the man, compel him to stay, the cat leaped at him and he dashed through a chink in the barn wall and was gone.

Jack fairly flew down the ladder. The little man had disappeared, lost in the high grass. Jack started after him but gave it up almost at once, fearful he'd step on him by mistake. He walked back into the barn and yanked the lantern off its hook and then held it near the chink in the barn siding, trying to illuminate it in such a way that he could see what lay beyond—outside. There was nothing but morning gloom and grass blades, just as he'd known there'd be.

The door opened and Willoughby strode back in, looking grizzled and tired. He chased the cat out and then asked Jack what it was he was looking for, down on his knees on the barn floor like that. Jack shrugged. It was an impossible question to answer.

"See something, did you?" asked Willoughby, looking at him sideways.

"Yes. I think so. Might just have been a mouse, I suppose."

"You don't *know* if it was a mouse?"

"It was too dark. I couldn't see clear. It looked like, like—"

"Something that wasn't a mouse?"

"Exactly," said Jack. It seemed to him suddenly that Willoughby wouldn't at all be surprised to hear that little men in costume came and went in the darkness. "What was it?"

Willoughby shrugged suddenly, as if he were weary of the whole subject. "Nothing you should meddle with," he said, taking the lantern and hanging it again on its hook. "It probably *was* a mouse, now that I think of it. What else *could* it be? You leave it alone. It'll only waste your time. There's trouble that comes from peering through cracks like that; you can mark my words. Your father found it—you already know that. So you leave it alone. There's better things to do. Weather's broke, if you ask me, and when I come up from town this morning I found this on the cottonwood at the fork."

He handed Jack a sheet of grainy paper, gaudy with color even in the shadowy barn. CARNIVAL! it said across the top, and below that were the words *Dr. Brown of World Renown* in smoky, languorous lettering that might have looked mystical and exotic if it weren't for the cheap and tawdry effect of the color-washed sketch below: a bird's-eye glimpse of a carnival spread out in an open field: vast coasters and whirlabouts, a Ferris wheel with a rainbow of colored cars leaning off it at jaunty angles, wild-eyed, broad-faced people staggering out of a funhouse through the window of which peered a tilt-headed skeleton with jewels in its eyes, wearing a slouch hat.

Jack studied it for a moment, then climbed back up into the loft to pull on his shoes. He unpegged the shutters and pushed them open, surprising a crow that had evidently been sitting on the sill. The bird was immense; it flapped there outside the open window, seeming to look in at him. Grasped in one claw was a gnarled little stick. The idea of it appealed to Jack—a crow with a walking stick. It circled round in a big loop out over the meadow before making away toward the coast. It flew astonishingly fast; it seemed to Jack that he could hear the creature's wings beat the air even when it was nothing but a black dot silhouetted against the blue-green of the sea beyond Table Bluffs.

On the bluffs themselves stood the half-erected scaffolding of the Ferris wheel, and across the meadows was strewn a litter of mechanical debris—the angular, disjointed skeletons of the curious carnival rides depicted in the poster that Jack still clutched in his hand. He grabbed his hat and set out. Coffee could wait.

There was a vast migration of hermit crabs that morning, all of them scuttling south down the beach, up the rocks, around the headland, then out into the shallows again and up onto the long strand that stretched nearly to the town of Scotia. By late afternoon there was a more or less continual line of the creatures, all of them wearing seashell hats and bound for unguessable destinations. Skeezix spent the morning on the beach, chasing the things down and dropping them into gunnysacks for Dr. Jensen. The doctor himself called a halt to the collecting at noon, when it became clear that the creatures intended simply to *walk* to the city and that his sending down a cartload would be pointless. The coals, apparently, were walking to Newcastle. There was a limit, it seemed to Dr. Jensen, to the hermit crab market.

Besides, as the day wore on, the crabs seemed to be growing in size. The first trickle of crabs on the beach had involved periwinkle-housed creatures no bigger than a thumbnail. By ten the crabs sported conch shells of varying sizes, some as big as rabbits, running wonderfully fast along the sand. At about noon a crab the size of a grown pig crept out of the green ocean, festooned with seaweed and making clacking sounds, as if someone were knocking together two lengths of dried bamboo.

It went on that way for hours. The crabs chased both Skeezix and Dr. Jensen from the beach and ripped one of the burlap bags to shreds, releasing the hundreds of smaller crabs within and herding them back into line and away south. Dr. Jensen had gone home to get his brass spyglass and then come back to watch, hidden in the bushes beside the ruined railroad tracks on the cliff above. It seemed to him, when he put his ear to the hot, rusty steel of the tracks, that he could hear the distant roar of the old Flying Wizard as it plunged along into the north coast. But what he heard, obviously, was something more akin to the sound of the ocean in a seashell. Against that roar he could barely make out the faint *clack*, *clack*, *clack* of the migrating crabs, sounding weirdly metallic when telegraphed like that through the railroad tracks.

The sky that same morning was deep blue, like evening, and Jack could see stars faintly luminous beyond the thin sunlight, so that the whole circle of the sky looked like the mouth of an upended bucket brimming with water and reflected stars. Jack walked along toward the bluffs, his hands in his pockets, hoping that he'd see Helen, who hadn't been at Miss Flees's when he'd stopped by. He heard in the village about the migration of crabs, so he knew where to find Skeezix. He heard too that a man had been murdered just after sunup, and that his body had been bled white and pitched off the cliffs into a tide pool. Dr. Jensen himself had found it.

Jack walked across the meadow toward the carnival, kicking his way through high autumn grass and listening to the silence of the ocean and the occasional ringing of hammers. The air barely moved. He wished he'd taken the time to go after Skeezix or made a greater effort to find Helen. Even Lantz would be good company. He felt suddenly lonely, on the meadow by himself, nothing around him but grass and wildflowers and the carnival, shrunk by distance.

He had no idea on earth where he was going. There was really no carnival yet, nothing but half-built skeletons. But they drew him curiously, as if the jumble of debris was somehow magical, the product of enchantment, perhaps, and held him in thrall. He could have turned around and walked back the way he'd come, or he could have angled over toward the Coast Road and strolled south to where Skeezix almost certainly was messing around on the beach. It seemed to him, though, that the appearance of the carnival hadn't been just a random happenstance; it had drifted in on the weather and the strange tides and on the colors that had stained the horizon and now tinted the sky.

Only a handful of men worked to assemble the carnival rides, gaunt, pale, wretched-looking men in rumpled, ragged clothes, none of them talking. Two of them knocked together the framework of a wooden arch that spanned the dirt road from the beach, curving down into the weeds and ending there, as if it were a disattached gateway.

Jack saw MacWilt suddenly, talking to a man he didn't recognize. The stranger's back was toward him. He had long, black hair that hung round his shoulders, and the skin of his hands was peculiarly sallow, the white of a fish too long out of water. He wore cuffed boots caked with mud, and he wore a black top coat, which, along with his black hair, gave him the appearance of a great black bird.

The man turned to scowl at Jack, as if he'd expected him but didn't half like it that he'd come. The scowl was replaced for a fragment of a second by a look half of recognition and half of surprise, as if he'd been caught out. Then once again there was a scowl, and a malicious scowl at that. Jack nodded and walked past, noting the long bullet scar on the man's cheek. He kept his hands in his pockets and looked at the ground, as if he were just strolling toward Table Bluffs Beach and had passed the carnival out of necessity, because it was in the way. But he could feel the man's eyes against his back as he made his way toward the beach trail. Somehow Jack knew that the man was Dr. Brown, of the poster. And he knew that he didn't at all like him.

Jack stepped around wooden sheds painted with grinning clowns and gaudy whirling acrobats and impossible, shadowy freaks. The paintings had been wonderful, in their time. But their time had passed many years since, and now they were so faded by rainwater and sunlight that they were just the tired ghosts of paintings. There was an enclosed wagon with a canvas flap for a door. Above the flap were the words *Alligator Child*, painted long enough ago so that whatever sort of freak lived within couldn't very likely be a child any more. And beyond the wagon, lying in a heap on the meadow grass, were a half dozen skeletons, dirty ivory in the shadowy daylight, their bones wired together with silver thread.

The crossbraces and gears and rails stacked round about were rusted and ancient. They'd been painted in the distant past too, but the paint had flaked off, so that what had once been the depiction of a bicycle-riding clown in a pointed hat and ruff collar was now nothing more than a severed head drifting above a nearly spokeless wheel, half the head peeling away in a sheet of dirty blue and pink. Partly built amid the heaps of machinery sat a contrivance that seemed half beehive oven and half steam engine. A calliope lay on its side a few yards off, and between the oven and the calliope, cordwood was stacked shoulder high beside a heap of coal.

All talk had stopped as he passed, as if they'd been uttering things that weren't for the ears of an outsider. He found himself scrambling down the beach trail and out onto the sand, with no earthly reason for being there but mightily relieved that he was. The tide was low. He could pick his way around the cliffs by skirting tide pools and clambering over normally submerged reefs until he got to the cove. The only alternative was to hike back up the trail and stroll once again through the midst of the carnival—something he wasn't inclined to do. He'd wait until it was more of a piece, and he'd take his friends with him.

Jack didn't find Skeezix on the beach. He found Dr. Jensen on the bluffs with his spyglass and a little leatherbound notebook in which he was keeping count of the crabs. He explained that his counting wasn't worth as much as it ought to be; numberless crabs had no doubt crept past in the night, and earlier that morning Skeezix had been counting but had boggled it a half dozen times, had started over and then over again, and finally had estimated by multiplying numbers that Dr. Jensen hadn't yet fathomed.

What did it matter, after all? Jack asked. Dr. Jensen shrugged. Maybe it didn't. When you thought about it, *nothing* much mattered—did it?—beyond a sandwich and a plate to eat it on. And even the plate wasn't worth much. Clerks spent their days chasing down numbers and writing them into columns and adding them up and, as often as not, growing agitated at what they found. Well, Dr. Jensen chased down numbers too, and his numbers were as good as theirs, better maybe. There hadn't been a migration of hermit crabs in twelve years. Another opportunity wouldn't come for twelve more. Dr. Jensen was going to make the most of this one, just in case he could make it pay. He'd missed part of the last one, and he'd regretted it since.

Jack sat on the bluffs for a time, watching the sky out over the ocean. The stars had faded, but the sky was still a deep evening blue, and the sea, calmer now than it had been last night, was bottle green and rolling beneath an oily ground swell. It looked for a moment as if the sky were flat, like the surface of the sea, and was a thing of substance, hovering in the air miles overhead. Then, although nothing identifiable had changed, the sky seemed prodigiously deep, as if he were peering into the clearest sort of ocean water and it was only distance that obscured his vision. He had the uncanny feeling that something was hidden from him in the depths of the sea and sky—something pending, something waiting.

Dr. Jensen said he felt that way too, especially at the time of the Twelve-year Solstice. Why they called it a "solstice," he couldn't say, since it seemed to have little to do with the sun. He'd seen two of them since he'd moved to the north coast to open his practice. Each time there'd been the arrival of a carnival—the same carnival, for all he knew. There'd been ceremonies and a festival and a few people had floated baskets of bread and autumnal fruit out onto the ocean and into the longshore current. Fishermen took a holiday, either because they deserved a holiday or because they caught things in their nets during the solstice that they'd rather not catch.

The few boats out on the water this morning were new-comers. It was doubtful that villagers would buy their fish even if the fishermen caught something they had the stomach to keep. It was more likely that they'd catch other sorts of oceanic flotsam—things that had been swept out of the east by deepwater tides and had been under the sea so long they'd become hoary with seaweed and worms.

Twelve years ago the taxidermist's son had gone mad after eating Solstice fish, and for days had spoken in the voices of long-dead townspeople. In the moonlight it had seemed as if the boy *looked* like the corpses of the people whose voices he mimicked, and the taxidermist, whose business never amounted to much in the first place, had put away his glass eyes and stuffing and had set up as a spiritualist in one of the carnival tents.

But he failed as a spiritualist too, although for the first few hours it seemed as if he'd finally made his fortune. Dead men clamored to be heard, but it turned out they hadn't anything more interesting to say when they were dead than when they'd been alive. The entranced son gibbered out a steady monologue of tiresome complaints until he was possessed finally by old man Pinkerd, who'd been struck and killed six years earlier by a wagon driven by a drunken stranger from Moonvale. He wanted the stranger brought to justice, he said. He couldn't abide any more delay.

Through the mouth of the boy the old dead man had mumbled about lawsuits but had obviously gotten the idea confused with the sort of suit you wore, which made it seem to everyone that death turned a man into an idiot. To make the complaint even more foolish, the wagon driver from Moonvale had himself been killed by lightning a week after he'd run over Mr. Pinkerd, and so all talk of lawsuits was foolishness. There was speculation about why old man Pinkerd, being dead himself, hadn't heard about the lightning strike, hadn't had a chance to confront the stranger from Moonvale himself, beyond the pale, as it were. It was generally agreed upon, by the villagers who were listening to the taxidermist's son, that it was simply more evidence that dead men didn't know half as much as they were generally given credit for and were the same sorts of pains in the neck dead that they were alive. There was the same sort of general relief among the audience, in fact, when old man Pinkerd finally ended his ghostly harangue and the taxidermist's son fell asleep in his chair, as when the old man died six years earlier.

The taxidermist's son had awakened a half hour later to a diminished audience, but by then there were so many ghosts trying to talk at once, and none of them in the mood for answering questions, that the boy had seemed suddenly to go insane and burbled his way up into a rising shriek that ended when the chair he sat in collapsed over backward and he had to be helped to bed.

Dr. Jensen said he'd never seen anything like it before. It was entirely possible that the whole thing had been a hoax. It seemed possible, if you thought about it, that *all* the strange business of the Solstice was a fake—a matter of suggestion. People expected the dead to speak, and so they heard cryptic messages uttered in the chirping of crickets and the croaking of toads. They accepted without question the arrival of the two-headed dog, which was found dead in the street outside the tavern. Had it appeared six months earlier, heads would have nodded and eyes would have squinted, and it would have been murmured that it wasn't a two-headed dog at all but a clever fake, got up by the taxidermist in league with MacWilt. During the Solstice, said Dr. Jensen, people were ready to believe anything.

The more Jack thought about it, the more he was willing to admit to this last part. *He*, at least, was in a mood to believe anything. And maybe being in such a mood made commonplace things seem extraordinary. Maybe. The train last night, though: that had been anything but commonplace. The tracks were half wrecked yesterday afternoon. Ties had slid down onto the beach. The iron was etched with rust and twisted by moving earth. They were half wrecked again this morning. You could see them lying crooked in the sun from where the two sat on the bluffs. And yet at midnight a train, pouring steam, had flown atop them, out of the rainy night.

"Did you hear a train whistle last night?" Jack asked idly, peering through Jensen's spyglass at a hulking crab that was just then tramping up out of the sea.

Dr. Jensen was silent for a moment. Then he admitted that he had. That was another of the Solstice phenomena—the arrival of the train, but always so late at night that no one actually saw it. Some said that the carnival *was* the train, for there was no evidence that the train ever got beyond Moonvale, and there was nowhere between Rio Dell and Moonvale for the train to turn around. It couldn't, then, come and go in the night.

Once, years ago, when Dr. Jensen and Kettering were students in the university, they'd paid a visit to an old man whom Kettering had met in a Chinatown bar. He was a curious and indefinably malignant old man named Wo Ling, and he claimed to be prodigiously old. It hadn't sounded like a lie. Kettering had agreed to supply him with laboratory animals, mostly lambs and chickens, although what he wanted the beasts for he wouldn't say. Jensen hadn't liked the idea much, but then the idea wasn't his anyway; it was Kettering's, and Kettering didn't ask questions.

The old man had been an engineer in his day—had piloted trains, as he put it, unimaginable trains. But he was tired of it. He lived on the waterfront in a half-abandoned warehouse that he shared with bats and owls and crows. The front rooms were scattered with rusted machinery, the decayed remains of a dismantled carnival that had been stored there years past and left to rust in the ocean air.

A section of roof had caved in and windows were broken and hanging. Blackberry vines and creepers supported tilting walls that were little more than papery termite-eaten husks, and when the wind blew it whistled up through the termite tracks and sounded like the hollow music of a bamboo flute. The man was an alchemist, and he was dying. From the look of him he might already have been dead a dozen times over and brought back to life by some revivifying drug.

They'd wandered through the interior of the ruined warehouse, out into a broad empty room that fronted the harbor and was built on pilings. A train trestle ran along beside it, the cold tide swirling below and rocky islands floating on the bay, visible through dusty window glass. Fog seemed to have blown in through broken panes and through the ruined roof, for the room was misty with ocean air and the smell of tar and salt spray and drying kelp. There was the sound on the breeze of distant train whistles, although neither Jensen nor Kettering could swear that it wasn't just wind through the termite caves.

The fog swirling in the room had drifted toward the veiled ceiling to dissipate like steam, and the entire time they stood there, listening and waiting, the ground swell in the bay sighed through the pilings, clattering stones and seashells along the rocky shingle. The combination of steamy fog and ghostly whistling and the perpetual rush and clatter of the ocean filled the air with the uncanny atmosphere of a train depot. Then, although it might have been his imagination, it seemed as if the warehouse were nothing but an enormous museum of steam machines, of locomotives and calliopes and engines, and that the entire structure shook and clattered where it stood, as if through some sort of enchanted metamorphosis it was turning into the very curiosities it housed.

Then the wind had fallen off and the sea calmed and the fog cleared, and once again they stood in an abandoned, decayed warehouse. It was imagination after all. And yet later that week, curiously, when the two had passed along the waterfront in a coach, they couldn't see the warehouse at all, although the train trestle still stood there, its pilings sunk into the mud of the bay and covered below the tide line with mussels and barnacles and starfish.

Kettering was foolish enough to think that the warehouse had *been* the train, in some curious way, and the carnival too— that it was all one. But then Kettering always had been a sort of mystic. The old man didn't return to the city while they were there, although Jensen saw him again twelve years later, during the Solstice in Rio Dell, the year old man Pinkerd came back from the dead. He operated the carnival that year—Wo Ling did—but he said he was giving it up. He was tired of it, he said; there were certain conditions that went along with it that he hadn't the stomach for any more.

Dr. Jensen's story didn't clarify things much, and when Jack told the doctor about the train last night, the doctor shrugged. "There you are," he said, as if that explained things well enough, and he went back to watching his crabs—the occasional stragglers that were left. He seemed disinclined to talk. Skeezix appeared then, eating a doughnut and wild with excitement. Something had been caught by one of the fishermen, had entangled itself in his net in shallow water. Skeezix wouldn't say what it was. He shook his head and grinned and puffed up the beach trail behind Jack, both of them hurrying toward the village to see it. Dr. Jensen stayed behind, studying the sea through his glass.

4

THE VILLAGE SHOPS CLUSTERED along the High Street where
it wound up the hill and eventually up to Willoughby's. There
was a grocery and two inns, a barber and a hardware store,
MacWilt's tavern, the open market, a store that sold cast-off
furniture and crockery, Potts's bakery, and the taxidermist's
shop. This last, of course, had been locked up for years and
the windows dusted with grime. Streets and alleys ran off at
angles, some dead-ending a half block down, some winding
up and away into the hills past outlying farms, then turning
into logging roads or just petering out into trails that disappeared into orchards and woods.

The ocean itself pushed in behind the High Street when the
tide rose. When it fell again it left mud flats and eelgrass behind, dotted with oyster beds and with mussels clumped
along pier pilings and rocks. The ribs of decayed rowboats
thrust up out of the mud. Beside them sat tethered boats,
gone aground when the tide fell, waiting for it to rise again.
The open market, which was nothing, really, but a dozen
pineboard shacks with tin and copper roofs, sat on the broken remains of an old pier that ran out into the mud of the
bay. The pier had been longer once, and at the end of it had
been what passed for a fashionable restaurant. But that was
forty years ago, when Rio Dell had been more prosperous and
when the old Flying Wizard still ran the coast route to
Moonvale and Sunnybrae and Crescent City. Two thirds of
the pier had finally canted over into the soft silt of the bay and
twisted itself apart. The restaurant—condemned a year and a
half earlier—had smashed to kindling wood. Over the years,
it had been piece by piece carried out with the tide. Fishing
boats still docked along what was left of the ruined pier, and

the fishermen themselves lived either on their boats or in the shacks of the market.

It seemed now as if half the town milled about the market. Jack caught sight of Miss Flees skulking along with a net bag full of cabbages, and Skeezix insisted they were severed heads and not cabbages at all. Almost no one was intent on buying anything. It was late in the morning for that sort of thing; most of the greengrocers had hauled their carts home an hour since. People were intent on something else. Jack saw MacWilt's hat wagging along beside one of the fish shacks, and then he saw the hat sail off, like someone had shoved a firecracker under it. The crowd roundabout the foot of the pier broke into raucous laughter, and people farther back on the edge pushed in to see what the row was about. Skeezix slipped in among them, disappearing from Jack's view.

In a moment he heard Skeezix whistle but couldn't see him. Skeezix whistled again. There he was, on top of the balcony that ran along the side of the Harbor Inn. There was a door leading onto the balcony from the interior of the inn, though it had been nailed shut years earlier when a sleepwalking traveler had strolled out at dawn and pitched over the railing onto the street. You could climb up the copper drainpipe, though, and pull yourself over. In the summer Jack and Skeezix slept up there sometimes, climbing up silently in the darkness and watching the village, waiting for the moon to rise out of the midnight sea, listening to the trill of canaries from the room above the tavern across the street. They'd be chased off if anyone saw them up there during the day, but everyone was too busy making fun of MacWilt. The laughter sounded forced, though; it had an icy, hollow edge to it—as if maybe what they were laughing at hadn't ought to be laughed at, but, like idle hands occupied with twiddling fingers or twirling hair, laughing gave them something to do with their voices.

The laughter died and was replace by MacWilt's cursing. Jack could easily see why. In a wooden tub, sloshing with seawater in front of a fisherman's shack, swam a finny sort of creature with great popping-out eyes. It looked as if it had been netted deep in an oceanic trench, and that the lessening pressure of its ascent had started to explode it, to pop its eyes out like corks out of a toy gun.

If flopped there, sucking in great gulps of water through its undulating gills as if there wasn't enough ocean in the little tub to satisfy it. Along its sides shone scales the size of half dollars, glinting like overlapping rainbows in the sunlight. It had something very much like a neck, odd as it seemed to Jack, and fins that might as easily have been hands. Its tail, though, was the tail of a fish, and it whumped against the bottom of the tub in a steady rhythmic motion, as if it were trying to pound out a coded message. It struggled suddenly, thrashing sideways and flopping up on edge, and then hooked its ventral fins over the side of the tub as if laboring to throw itself into the murky waters of the bay.

The fisherman who had caught it flipped it back into the tub and told it to stay there. He called it a sport and wondered past a drunken grin whether such a thing had ever before been filleted in the village of Rio Dell. There wasn't as much laughter, apparently, as he would have liked. A little knot of fishermen standing nearby and smoking pipes shook their heads—not in answer to his question but with the air of washing their hands of the whole dark business. They were old-timers. They hadn't even taken their boats out that morning. It was better to wait a week or so, until the ocean got back onto an even keel and the strange flotsam stirred up by Solstice storms settled back into the shadows of submarine grottoes and stayed there.

Jack gouged Skeezix in the side with his elbow and pointed at the crowd. There in the shadows stood Miss Flees, her hair swept back out of her face and clutched with a strip of ribbon. She smiled blankly, as if it were expected of her, and she cocked her head and fluttered her eyelids in rapid little blinks in a sort of parody of flirtatiousness, all the time staring at the thing in the tub. No one spoke to her, although every now and then she turned her head and widened her eyes as if she'd just seen an old friend coming along toward her through the crowd. Once she cast a little trifling wave in the direction of the street, but both Jack and Skeezix could see that there was no one there. She couldn't keep her eyes off the fish for long, though.

"Did it sing?" shouted someone from the edge of the crowd.

"Did it sing! You should have heard it!" The fisherman tipped the creature back into the tub again but jerked his hand back quick, as if he'd been bitten. He grinned weakly and shrugged, sucking on his finger. "'*Course* it sung. I caught him on the junk line, but he warn't after the bait. I snagged him, is what I did, when I was reeling it in. He was drifting in toward the harbor on the tide. Thought it was a damned jellyfish at first."

"It don't look like a jellyfish to me," said Potts, the baker, wiping flour onto his apron.

"That's because you ain't a fisherman," shouted the man who'd asked about the singing. "It would have looked like a jelly *roll* to you." With that he laughed like he was going to collapse, but no one else laughed much at all, which made him mad. He coughed once, then turned to the woman standing next to him and said in a stage whisper, "Spitting image of Wilt, ain't it?" then burst into laughter again.

MacWilt, who had been eyeing the creature as intently as Miss Flees had, spun round and took a step toward the man, who straightened up with a jerk and squinted at the tavern keeper. "You shut up," said MacWilt, giving him a dark look.

The man snickered, cast a wink at the woman beside him, and reached out to flip MacWilt's hat off his head again. The hat somersaulted into the air, landing neatly in the tub, to the vast amusement of most of the crowd. The fish thing thrashed beneath the hat, cascading water out onto the pier. "Can you beat that!" cried MacWilt's tormentor. "It's wearing its daddy's hat!"

The air seemed suddenly to have a serrated edge to it. No one cared that MacWilt was being insulted, and most of the crowd hoped it would come to blows. It felt to Jack as if storm clouds were blowing in and the pressure were dropping. He heard something on the freshening wind, but he couldn't identify the sound—a sort of tooting, faraway music, rising and falling in the breeze, muddled up with a distant booming, like waves, perhaps, breaking in the cove. Skeezix started to say something about Miss Flees, but Jack shushed him and told him to listen. He tilted his head. Skeezix seemed to hear it too. A calliope, that's what it was. Jack clumped along the boards of the balcony toward the street, until he could see round the corner. It was coming from out on the bluffs, from the carnival. He could see a distant slice of meadow between the tavern roof and the chimney of the bakery—the curve of a little grass-covered hill that ran down toward the bluffs and the sea. Edging up above it, turning round and round in cadence with the slow whistling of the steam-driven calliope, was the top arc of the Ferris wheel, its cars empty but moving.

MacWilt had retrieved his wet hat by the time Jack rejoined Skeezix, who was grinning with delight and pointing at the two glowering men. MacWilt shook a fist in the other man's face. "Don't you meddle with me! I'm warning you!"

"I won't meddle with you, I'll put you in that there tub!"

"You'll live to regret it, if you try! And you won't do no more than try."

The other man reared back and cast MacWilt a look that was intended to topple him over. "I come from down south. If you ever been down there you'd of heard of me. You'd lick my boots if you knew who I was."

"Who *are* you?" shouted a voice from the crowd, and everyone laughed.

The man turned around and looked, as if he was sorry he couldn't discover who'd said it and take care of him too.

MacWilt spit into his hands and rubbed them together. Then he took his wet hat off and punched his fist into the crown, straightening it out. He put the hat back on and said, "My advice to you is to go *back* down south, before you run into a world of trouble. I ain't a man to be meddled with."

Then he dusted his hands together, as if he'd taken care of his end of the conversation.

The other man swelled up and stepped forward a pace, balling up his fist. "I've chewed up bigger men than you and used them as bait," he said. "I'll tear your lungs out, is what I'll do. Just as quick as that!" And he snapped his fingers in MacWilt's face.

"There ain't nothing I'd like better—" MacWilt began, but he was interrupted when someone in the crowd reached out and pushed MacWilt's opponent in the small of the back, catapulting him forward into the tavern keeper.

"Too much talk!" somebody shouted, and the core of an apple flew out of the shadows and struck the man in the side of the face. MacWilt, seeing his chance when the man turned to curse at whoever had thrown the apple core, hit his opponent in the back of the head. But he overreached himself and toppled forward, clutching at his hat, and the man spun round and swung wildly at the air, a good foot over Mac-Wilt's head.

The force of the swing threw him against the fisherman's shack, knocking the tub sideways and dumping the now quiet creature onto the pier in a cascade of seawater. The fisherman shouted and went groping along after the slippery creature, wary of getting bitten again but fearful he'd lose it into the bay. MacWilt rushed in at the man from down south, who calmly knocked his hat off again with a single blow that he brought down onto MacWilt's head. Jack could hear the rattle of MacWilt's teeth as his mouth slammed shut and his chin jammed against his neck.

In moments both men rolled and struggled on the pier, clutching each other, gouging and hitting. The crowd pressed back to give them room. They rolled back and forth, accomplishing nothing until they heaved up against the fisherman's shack. The fisherman himself, abandoning the flopping creature from the tub when it slid, finally, off the edge of the pier and was gone, sailed in to pummel both of them with his fists. "Damn it!" he shouted. "You—" But before he'd gotten the words half out, the shack canted over and collapsed in a ruin of rotted boards. "By God!" he cried, infuriated now, and he grabbed MacWilt by the seat of his pants and the collar of his shirt and pitched him into the bay. The other man leaped up cursing, waving his fists in a sort of windmill frenzy and inviting everyone there to step up and take his turn. So the fisherman very calmly and deliberately knocked him down, then dragged him off the edge of the pier too.

The crowd cheered the fisherman. Then they cheered MacWilt, who hauled himself out of the water, dripping mud and weeds and still, miraculously, holding onto his hat. The fisherman, on his hands and knees, looked over the edge of the pier into the mud below, trying to find his escaped fish— if a fish is what it was. His creature was gone, back into the bay. The other fishermen, looking as if nothing they'd seen was worth remarking on, peered into their pipe bowls and shook their heads.

Skeezix grinned at Jack. This was just the sort of thing Skeezix liked—bullies beating each other up. The two boys leaned on the railing, both of them animated by excitement and by the unspoken determination to stay on the balcony until they were chased away. The crowd was breaking up. The second man slogged out of the bay and strode away in disgrace when he found that his lady friend had abandoned him. After ten steps or so he turned and stared back at the dispersing crowd as if there was one last thing he intended to say to them, but that it was powerful language and might confound them. Then he made as if to shake his fist, but a roar of laughter at his expense made him think better of it. In ten minutes there was no one on the pier but fishermen, mending nets and coiling junk lines and drinking beer out of tin cups. The fisherman who'd lost his catch had put back out in his dory. Jack could see him hauling on the oars with a passion, disappearing around the little swerve of shore that angled out to form the mouth of the harbor.

Just then, as the street fell into an early afternoon quiet, Miss Flees hurried out from under the pier, cutting across the mud toward the stand of overgrown pepper trees that had consumed the back yard of the abandoned taxidermist's shop. Both boys watched, knowing she'd been lurking under the pier this last half hour. She carried a wet burlap sack clutched against her frog-colored dress, as if whatever was in the sack might make a noise and give her away. And it seemed to Jack for a slice of a moment as if he could hear the twitter of small birds on the air, mingling with the whispered exhalations of the calliope and the screams of wheeling gulls.

Jack and Skeezix grew tired of sitting on the balcony. They'd watched the street below for a while, but nothing much was going on. The villagers had already had a day's worth of excitement and had gone back to work. Old Mrs. White hung sheets out to dry in the back yard of her house beyond the taxidermist's, and Skeezix insisted that they were corpse shrouds and would inflate with the night wind, haunting the countryside until morning. They weren't, though. Maybe they'd be more when the moon rose above the mountains at midnight, but at the moment they were only sheets, not worth anything at all in the way of entertainment—even imaginary entertainment. Then Mrs. Barlow's dog ran through one of the sheets and yanked it out of its clothespins, and that was pretty good, though it only lasted a minute. After that there was nothing for a long time. A half hour passed, and they heard MacWilt yell a couple of times. Then he smashed out of the tavern and hung the CLOSED sign on the door. For a moment it seemed that something would come of MacWilt's raging that would serve to enliven the afternoon, but actually MacWilt rarely did anything *but* rage, and so his antics were simply tiresome.

They decided, finally, to stroll up to the orphanage and find Helen, who was sure to be up in the attic painting "views," as she called them. She wouldn't tolerate interruptions in the morning, but now it was well after noon. Maybe they'd bring her something to eat in order to make the interruption seem worthwhile. They'd make fun of her paintings, of course, although they had admitted to each other any of a number of times that the paintings really were very good. Jack couldn't get over that Helen could make a brush or a pencil or a piece of charcoal do whatever she wanted it to do. She could make the cheekbones of a face look like cheekbones, with shadows and glints exactly where they ought to be; or, even better, where you wouldn't have expected them to be, so they'd lend the face a surprising expression, and you couldn't quite define what it meant or exactly where it came from.

Jack had tried his hand at it. Helen owned a tablet of enormous sheets of paper, and a wooden box too. It was very intricately built, this box, and full of slivers of charcoal and pastel chalk and tubes of oil paints half squeezed out. There were fifty brushes in it: fat, squat brushes made of sand-colored hairs; long, tapered brushes, only a couple of strands thick at the ends and suitable, maybe, for painting eyelashes; and any number of conical, fluffy-looking brushes for daubing on skies. The paint box seemed magical to Jack, and the big grainy sheets of paper were full of promise. It seemed it must be true that, like magical amulets, the box and the paper would enchant his hand into cooperating, into painting what it was he saw in his mind.

So once, with Helen's encouragement and advice, he painted a tree that looked almost like a tree, especially if you stood across the room and squinted or, better yet, crossed your eyes so that there were two trees run together; then it had what Helen had called an "intriguing sense of dimension." Skeezix suggested that it would be even better if you were blind, so it could have an intriguing sense of anything you wanted. Jack gave up on trees and painted a face, but with the eyes tilted, like a stiff wind had blown them haywire. The nose, to his great despair, turned out to be on sideways, even though it had seemed to him as if he were painting it on straight. Also, there wasn't enough forehead on the face, which gave it an inexplicably idiotic look, and its ears stood away on either side like Christmas ornaments. Skeezix had been wonderfully happy with it, pointing out tirelessly what it was that made Jack "unique" among artists. There hadn't been any magic in the box or in the paper. The magic was in Helen.

Jack and Skeezix wandered along now, kicking stones, taking the long way around. As they drew abreast of the mouth of a skinny little alley—Quartz Lane, it was called—they heard the wild clucking and squawking of a chicken. "Dogs," Skeezix said, and turned up the alley, meaning, Jack supposed, that dogs were worrying the chicken—something Skeezix wouldn't stand for. Jack picked up a rock in either hand, and Skeezix picked up a stick, and the two of them trotted around the first bend, past a wooden fence covered with blooming passionflower vines. The alley was full of trash pitched over back fences: old straw ticks, cracked wagon wheels, garden tools that had broken and gone to rust. There was a stuffed chair that housed a nation of bugs and, beside it, a half dozen paint cans tilted on edge and spilling dirty paint that had dried months since.

It didn't sound like a dog to Jack. There was no growling, only the frantic clucking of the chicken, cut off, just then, in a screech that made both boys leap down the last few yards of alley and tear aside the tangle of vines from before a sort of little alcove between two tilting fences. There, kneeling amid brown leaves and crumpled newspaper, Peebles hacked away at the now dead chicken with a keyhole saw, pinning the bird to the dirt with his left hand. He jerked around and gaped at Jack and Skeezix, sweat standing out on his forehead, his eyes wide. He'd managed to haggle the chicken apart along its breastbone and seemed to be trying to empty its organs into a little cloth sack rolled open next to his knee.

Neither Jack nor Skeezix spoke. Neither could believe what he saw. Peebles rocked back onto his feet and shuffled farther into the recesses of the alcove, stuttering out a jabber of syllables that were nonsense in the stillness of the alley. He goggled in fear at Skeezix, who couldn't find any appropriate words but, instead, cocked his arm and swung his stick at a point an inch above Peebles's head, smashing it into a wooden fence rail. Then he threw the stick down as if it were a serpent. "What—" he said, then stopped, staring as Peebles, who, cowering away from him, jammed the chicken parts into the bloody sack and shoved the sack beneath his jacket. Jack stepped backward into the alley and Skeezix followed, treading on Jack's feet.

Peebles crept out, with such loathing and mortification on his face that it looked as if he'd just as soon have been cutting up his two friends and dropping *their* entrails into a sack. Skeezix's desire to hit him—to do something to punish him— was replaced by a wondering terror at the act. What did it mean, Peebles killing the chicken? Was he going to eat it? Had he stolen and killed the chicken for Miss Flees? Was this lunch? Why the business with the keyhole saw? Why commit the deed in the shadows of a dusty alley? There was a perverse quality to the thing that made both Jack and Skeezix quail, perhaps because they didn't entirely understand it. Neither was surprised, though. In fact, as they watched him jog away toward the High Street carrying his bag, it seemed to both of them that they'd always half expected that sort of thing from Peebles.

They walked in silence to the orphanage. There seemed to be nothing to say about the incident. Making jokes about it didn't work. It was another one of Peebles's secret activities to add to the list, along with his burning himself on the palms of the hands with candle flames and his collecting snippets of human hair. They slid in through Skeezix's window, stepped into a narrow closet off the hallway, and climbed a set of steeply angled stairs up into the cobwebby darkness. Counting the steps, Jack held one hand out in front of him, feeling for the door in the ceiling. There it was. He stopped and Skeezix banged into him, grabbed his elbow, and nearly hauled both of them down backward. Jack shushed him and tapped three times on the wooden panel, waited for an instant, and tapped again, twice. There was an answering tap and the scrape of a wooden swivel latch being slid back. Light shone suddenly around the perimeter of the panel as it swung open, Helen's face framed beyond it. Jack and Skeezix climbed up into the middle of the attic, where the gable raised the roof high enough to stand without cricking your neck.

The attic of Miss Flees's orphanage was lit largely through a half dozen gable windows. On a sunny day the sprawling room was a confusion of shadow and light, and on a dark day it was mostly shadow. Helen had found a pair of candelabra in among the lumber of stored furniture that heaped the walls and floor, so even on the most overcast of days she could paint by candlelight. At night she didn't go into the attic. Neither did Skeezix.

There were a few clues that Peebles inhabited the attic at night, or at least crept up there on occasion. Miss Flees certainly didn't. There was a ghost in the attic. Miss Flees, in years past, had played at spiritualism in order to swindle people, but she never much believed in her own antics. She never much believed in anything. Very recently, with the coming of the Solstice, she'd begun to develop a sort of unhealthy curiosity in the occult, looking to use magic to accomplish some vague and nebulous goal. The ghost in the attic terrified her, though, and she resented it for that. She could hear it muttering, sometimes, through the ceiling vents. Helen heard it too. She called the ghost Mrs. Langley, which was the name of the woman who had owned the house before she'd died and it had been given by the village to Miss Flees for use as an orphanage. The furniture in the attic had belonged to Mrs. Langley too, but it hadn't been used in nearly twenty years and was covered with dust and cobwebs. Miss Flees could have used it, but she didn't care about it. She preferred an empty house and was easily confused by clutter. Also, she half supposed the furniture was haunted. It had sat so long in the attic, after all.

Helen didn't get along at all badly with Mrs. Langley. Jack had heard her talk to the ghost on more than one occasion, although he hadn't heard the ghost say anything back. The ghost played occasional pranks on Helen—like locking the trapdoor from the inside so Helen couldn't get in. That had happened twice. Skeezix had had to climb a pruning ladder and shove himself in through the only casement window in the attic gables that would open, and he wouldn't do it at all until Helen promised to buy him pies and ice cream and root beer. Even then he hesitated. Helen told him to hold the ladder and let *her* climb in at the window, if he was afraid to do it, but Skeezix wouldn't hear of that. This wasn't the sort of thing, he'd insisted, that a girl should undertake. When he was inside, he'd turned to wave back down at Helen, to show her, perhaps, how successful he'd been, and Helen had seen a face hovering above and behind him, wavering ghostly pale against the darkness of the attic. Skeezix hadn't seen it, thank heaven, or he'd have gone head first back down the pruning ladder. He'd heard something, though—faint tittering laughter from the hundred corners of the room like the scurrying of mice. He hadn't visited the attic again for months.

Helen had found the crusts of a sandwich on a windowsill once, and shortly thereafter an origami paper ball, painted over with symbols and containing a lock of human hair tied with a tiny bit of copper wire. It gave Helen "mites," or so she said to Jack and Skeezix. She had knocked both the crusts and the paper ball out the window onto the weedy lawn below, and later that afternoon she watched Peebles find the ball there on the lawn. He'd been furious, and he'd scowled up at the window, surprised to see her looking back down at him. She'd waved and grinned, just to infuriate him, but she hadn't been half so complacent about the business as she forced herself to appear.

Not having grown up in the orphanage, Jack wasn't as familiar with the attic or with the stories attached to it as were Helen and Skeezix. It seemed to him to be a cosy enough room, despite its size. Perhaps it was the quantity of wood that did it: the rough-hewn roof rafters, the rain-stained shingles showing through the sheathing, the stud walls clothed with unpainted backs of clapboard paneling. There were a hundred rich tones in the wood, heightened by Helen's candles. Gables jutted off here and there with their respective windows, so that light shone in and was almost immediately interrupted by a bit of wall or the dip of a roof valley, and the floor was crosshatched with shadow and light.

There were books, too, shoved into bookcases back in the piled furniture. They couldn't pull the furniture aside to get at the books, because Miss Flees would hear them and cause trouble. Once she'd threatened to lock Helen and Skeezix in, had accused them of intending to steal Mrs. Langley's goods, which were now, of course, Miss Flees's goods. She threatened less, now that Helen and Skeezix had witnessed the business involving the Mayor's wife, and was likely to do nothing at all about their being in the attic unless they made an issue of it by banging around and making a lot of noise. Miss Flees, in fact, was a sort of pudding, who wanted nothing more than to be left alone to read cheap novels and talk complainingly to herself. She demanded only that she not be crossed. Her pronouncements, then, were worth very little, as Helen and Skeezix had realized long ago. They could sneak around and do what they pleased, as long as they didn't confront Miss Flees with their shenanigans.

Then there was Mrs. Langley to think about. The books, after all, were hers. She hadn't given them up altogether yet. Helen wouldn't risk upsetting her. She liked her attic studio too much and did what she could to humor the old dead woman. But Jack couldn't get the idea of the books out of his head. Now, with rain clouds swirling in from the east and darkening the sky, and the attic lit by the glow of dozens of candles, it seemed to him a perfect time to have a look at them. They might, of course, be nothing: old textbooks or impossible-to-read romances or technical books. On the other hand they might be something more.

By lying on his stomach and peering beneath the apron of a low table and between a forest of chair legs, he could see a row of dark book spines stacked on the bottom shelf of an otherwise hidden case. Helen and Skeezix held candles, and Jack pulled himself under the table upside down. He slithered around half sideways so that he could get his feet in after him. The beaded frill of a dusty tablecloth dragged across the side of his face and into his eyes. He hauled himself past it, peering up at the distant vaulted ceiling, past towering furniture draped in yellowed bed sheets, most of which had sagged and slid and pulled themselves off over the years.

"Give me a candle," he whispered.

"You'll set the place on fire," said Helen, grimacing at him past the table legs.

"I won't. I want to be able to read these book titles. Just give me a little piece."

Helen shoved herself partly in under the table and reached a lit candle along the floor to him. Jack took it, then crept forward as far as he could, climbing in among the chairs. He held the candle on its side and dripped wax onto the pine floor, then settled the candle into the hardening pool. He pushed himself past a tall carved sideboard and in among a maze of chair legs stacked against a wardrobe that still smelled of aromatic cedar.

He could see Skeezix and Helen's faces, dark outlines against the candle glow behind him, and he was clutched with the idea that he'd at any moment see Mrs. Langley's face there too, hovering pale in the air. Suddenly he wasn't at all happy to be crawling around amid that odd furniture. The smell of dust, of decaying bed sheets and musty wood, and the strange odor of camphor and cedar swirled around in the attic air and made it seem as if he were creeping through a deep woods at night.

He plucked his candle up and set it again six feet farther on, where it cast a glow on the books. Wafering himself against the back of a massive wardrobe, he shoved his head and arm in between the legs of a stuffed chair, the coiled springs combing his hair, cotton fluff raining down around him. He stretched out his arm and reached for the bookcase. He could just brush it with his fingers. He jammed himself farther in, got a finger on the top of a tall book and pulled it out, then dragged it back into the candlelight.

Corridors through the stacked and heaped furniture seemed

to run away in every direction, like tunnels through a goblin cave, all of them disappearing into shadow. Rain began to patter on the roof above him, then to pound down, and in moments the gutters were gurgling and rattling with running water. He jerked out from beneath the chair, snuffing his candle with his elbow, and found himself plunged into darkness. The lights of Helen's candelabra shone away off behind him like firelight through a forest, and he heard, as if from somewhere deep inside his ears, a curious commingling of sounds: the singing of birds and the tooting of the calliope and the soft whispering of voices trying to tell him something, though he couldn't at all make out what it was.

He jerked around, his candle spinning away across the floor and out of sight. The other books, suddenly, didn't interest him. Nothing interested him but getting out. He pushed the book along in front of him, sliding and pulling, very nearly toppling chairs. He grabbed the dangling corner of a draped sheet, tugged to see if it was anchored, then, pulling on it, towed himself past the outthrust legs of a smoking table. The sheet jerked loose with a sudden pull and slid off the table it had covered, dropping like a dusty shroud onto his face.

Jack shouted, tearing at the sheet, imagining for a moment that it was the ghost of Mrs. Langley, come for him at last. He felt hands on his shoes, and he kicked at them, barking his shins against a chair leg. Then he felt himself being dragged, and he rolled onto his back, clutching the book, his head bumping out from under the sheet and along the floor. He raised his face, cracked his forehead on something, and flattened himself out once again, finding himself abruptly in the candlelight and Skeezix holding his ankles.

"*Will* you shut up?" Helen said to him, pulling the book out of his hands. "Is this all? *One* book? What was all that banging and snuffling about? Where's my candle?"

"I lost it," Jack said, ignoring the rest of her questions.

"I need that candle. Candles aren't cheap. Go back in and get it. And pull out a couple more books as long as you're there; this one looks pretty good." She stared at the cover, then stepped across toward the window and set the book on a table.

Jack stood up and brushed himself off, ignoring Helen's suggestion. Skeezix strolled away toward a shadowy gable and peered down a floor vent through which there glowed the light of a gas lamp from a room below: Miss Flees's kitchen. Jack's curiosity about the books had diminished more than a bit. He smoothed down his hair and tucked his shirt in, rumpled as he was from creeping around beneath the furniture. His hand shook mutinously, so he shoved it into his pocket, then turned to have a look out the window toward the street and to catch his breath.

Rain beat through the trees along the curb. The sky, in the last half hour, had darkened from end to end, and only on the very horizon, out over the ocean, was there any sunlight. It was almost evening, the sun setting over the gray Pacific. In the thickening rain the west was nothing but a haze of raindrops laced with dying orange. He could see beyond the rooftops of the houses across the street, all of them running with rainwater, which was already pooling up on saturated lawns. There was the taxidermist's shop, way down toward the harbor, and beyond it, mostly hidden, was the pier, empty now even of fishermen.

MacWilt's tavern was still closed up; Jack could see the tiny sign dangling from a nail in the door. It was possible that MacWilt was out on the bluffs meddling with the carnival, which had picked a peculiarly bad week to set up—if it had *picked* the week at all. The carnival, partly because of MacWilt's being connected with it, had become strangely ominous. And Dr. Jensen's talk of waterfront warehouses hadn't done anything to lessen the feeling. It attracted Jack a little, adding weight to his suspicions that something was happening, that the Solstice was more than simply harvest ceremonies and holidays.

MacWilt wasn't on the bluffs. He was atop the roof of the tavern. As Jack watched, he climbed out through a door in the flat roof, hunching into the rain and dragging an empty whiskey keg. There as an open-walled lean-to shed on the roof, under which was a heap of stuff covered with a tarpaulin. He hauled the keg under that roof, in out of the rain, then went down the open hatch and emerged again moments later, this time carrying the giant glasses with their painted-out lenses. He hurried them through the falling drops as if anxious to keep them dry and set them alongside the keg. He paused under the roof to light his pipe. After wiping rainwater out of his face with his shirt sleeve, he yanked the tarpaulin from off the jumble of debris. Beneath it was a sort of trestle of scabbed-together boards with tilted two-by-four legs. The two in back were shorter than the two in front, so that the whole construction pointed away at the sky like the mount for an enormous telescope.

Jack gestured Skeezix over to the window and nodded at MacWilt's antics. The tavern keeper had hoisted his keg into another keg, slightly larger, and was banging away at the end of the smaller inside keg with a hammer, breaking it to flinders. He yanked off the end hoop, and the staves fell outward like the petals of a flower but were caught by the larger keg. He worked one of the lenses out of the giant glasses and fitted it into the now-empty groove in the loosened staves, shoved the hoop back down over them while holding the lens awkwardly with one hand, and knocked the hoop tight. Then he turned the keg upside down and repeated the procedure on the other end.

MacWilt knew something of the putting together of kegs; Jack could see that. He found himself vaguely surprised that a man as thoroughly rotten as MacWilt could do anything at all beyond lie and cheat, but that vague surprise turned into a more solid sort of surprise when the tavern keeper hoisted the whiskey keg out of the larger barrel and onto the wooden contrivance and then blocked up the rear legs so as to lower the angle at which it pointed at the sky. He tied the keg to the boards with a length of rope, blocked the legs some more, and shoved his nose against the end. What he saw, Jack guessed, was Moonvale, or rather the line of misty hills that hid it, and which were already dim with evening.

Those hills were blue-black against the sky, and stars shone right above the horizon as they had earlier that morning. It didn't seem to be a night sky, though; it seemed a morning sky above the hills—gray and pink with dawn light, even though it was five o'clock in the evening and even though when the sun *did* rise it came up 90 degrees around the compass to the east, above the coastal mountains.

"Will you look at that," mused Skeezix, pointing at the tavern, and although he whispered it, his tone was such that Helen stood up from her book and muscled in between her two friends to have a look.

"A telescope," said Jack, half to himself and half to Helen. MacWilt had built a telescope out of a whiskey keg and a giant's pair of glasses. With a rain-soaked rag he began swabbing the paint off the lenses. He went about the business methodically, stopping twice to consult his pocket watch and once to refill his pipe. Then he picked up the brass frames of the glasses and shoved them into the empty barrel, which he rolled away to the edge of the lean-to as if he were clearing the decks and getting down to some really serious work. By the time he was finished the sun hung just above the sea and beneath roiling clouds, threatening to be swallowed on the instant by one or the other. At the same time, impossibly, there seemed to be a sun rising above the Moonvale Hills.

Jack was struck with the notion of sprinting for home. He suddenly wanted his own telescope. MacWilt was setting up to look at something, and Jack wanted to know what it was. But even if he ran all the way, it would take him fifteen minutes in the mud and rain. The sun would set without him. He'd be cheated of discovering MacWilt's secret and would accomplish nothing. And besides, it was moderately possible that the lenses of a commonplace telescope like his own wouldn't have been ground for work like this. Even if he beat the sun home, he'd probably see nothing from his loft window but a commonplace evening sky, and Helen and Skeezix would have had all the fun of watching MacWilt.

The tavern keeper threw down his rag and set his pipe on the hood of a vent protruding through the roof. Shading his eyes from the waning light, he peered into the end of his keg telescope. He kicked out two of the shims under the rear legs and peered again, hauling the whole contrivance a half inch to the right as if to get exactly the right angle. He pulled out his pocket watch, squinted at it for a long moment, looked about him at the rain as if wondering whether it was lightening, then squinted at the watch again. His head nodded with the ticking seconds.

Toward Moonvale, beyond the clouds that veiled the heavens, stretched a streak of deep blue, a pastel slash of sky that lay upon the hills like a pool of sunlit water. The glowing orange arc of the sun, just a slice of it, shone in the blue, as if it had gone down in the ocean minutes earlier, then run off behind the hills to rise once again, forgoing its journey around the earth.

Above the hills the sky was all mist and sunlight, and stars showing weirdly above the sunlight like fireflies, all of it shivering through the rain, wavering like air above hot pavement. It seemed as if it were an image projected against the sky and would at any moment dissolve into particles and fall with the rain onto the grassy hillsides. Shadows deepened against the blue, lit golden around the edges in the light of the peculiar sun. The shadows formed the vague outlines of buildings, of a city, perhaps, as if somehow the church spires and bell towers of Moonvale were reflected against the sky. Jack had the curious feeling that it wasn't Moonvale, though; it was the shadow of Rio Dell itself reflected there, rendered enormous by the oblique angle of strange sunlight. The rain slackened. Above it, distant and muted, sounded what might have been the chuffing of a great steam engine, a train, perhaps, rolling in over the hills toward the distant smoky city, the puffs of cloud on the horizon having been blown from its enormous stack.

A wind rose off the ocean and blew leaves out of the trees across the street, swirling them away toward the forest. MacWilt's tarpaulin blew into the air like a hovering spook and enveloped his knees. Jack could hear the echoes of his curses even above the wind, but he paid them no mind at all. The shadows in the sky thickened, swirling, growing angular and sharp—buildings now, with windows and turrets and gables and pitched roofs towering so high above the hills that giants might live in them.

MacWilt stared through his odd glass, seeming to be oblivious to the piece of canvas sailing off the roof, to the debris that followed—broken stools, mops and buckets, a pair of huge framed oil paintings—all of it leaping on the rain-laden wind, whirling away through the air, and clattering on the cobbles of the street.

There sounded the crack of breaking glass, as loud and sharp as if a crystal chandelier had fallen against the floor-boards of the attic. Jack saw great shards of the outer lens of MacWilt's telescope fly out, as if exploded from pressure within the keg. The tavern keeper shouted and reeled back, clutching his face, even though the lens he had been peering through hadn't been the one to shatter. His screams tore through the wind and rain, and he alternately snatched his hands away from his eyes, peering wildly around him, then jammed them against his face again, crying out, stumbling, dropping to his knees finally in a puddle and huddling there in the descending darkness.

In moments the night had grown black enough so that Jack, Skeezix, and Helen could see only MacWilt's hunched shade. Toward Moonvale the false sun blinked out as if it were a candle flame, and the city of shadows with it. Thunder pealed, lightning forked across the hills, and the sky was nothing but darkness and rain and wind-lashed trees.

5

SKEEZIX STOOD with his mouth open. He shut his eyes and then opened them slowly, as if expecting something to have changed. Helen passed her hands in front of Skeezix's eyes and snapped her fingers. Then she opened her mouth and mimicked his gape, goggling her eyes. "Soup's on," she said, poking Skeezix in the stomach. Her friend blinked and looked around, first at Jack and then at Helen. The smell of cabbage broth drifted up through the vent.

"Soup," said Skeezix in a disgusted voice. "I won't eat it."

Helen laughed, as if she thought it unlikely.

"What do you suppose . . ." Skeezix began, but his voice trailed off into nothing.

Helen sat at the table again and began to leaf through the book. "I suppose you two had better look at this." She pulled the candelabra across the tabletop in order to illuminate the frontispiece. Jack bent over her, unbelieving. There was a drawing of a city in a china-blue sky: narrow towers built of hewn stone, arched bridges stretching over what might be rivers or what might be cloud drift, red clay roofs rising out of thickets of trunkless trees, high windows looking out on meadows that stretched into nothing, into the deep blue mirror of the heavens. It wasn't the city they'd seen, but it floated in the same enchanted sky, tinted with twilight colors.

"Forget the soup," said Jack, pulling up a chair. "We can eat at my place later."

Uncharacteristically, Skeezix nodded, fetching a chair for himself. "Then we can eat again at Dr. Jensen's, after we show him this book and tell him about MacWilt and the glasses."

"Shut up about food," said Helen, "and listen to this: 'Ours is one of many worlds,' " she read, starting at the top of the first page, " 'of millions of worlds, unending numbers of worlds, all the same and all different, all of them spinning past each other like the shadows of stars. We fancy ourselves alone in time and space, conceited as we are, and it is during the Solstice that we are reminded of just how inconsiderable we are in the vast eyes of eternity—an insight that should cause us to laugh at ourselves, but doesn't. The mind, instead, freezes at the thought, and we go clambering after some means of fleeing from the little tract of countryside on which we have mapped our existence. Some of us are successful. Some of us are destroyed.' "

"Some of us are mystified," said Skeezix, stepping back across the floor to have another look down the vent.

"You're mystified about everything," said Helen, "unless it's on a plate. This is simple as pie."

Skeezix grimaced. "I wished it *was* pie. We all *knew* that something happens during the Solstice. It's like during a hot wind; everyone's on edge. People skulking in alleys and on rooftops. Voices in the night. Villagers babbling in funny languages. And the carnival train on the ruined tracks—where did it come from? What happened to it? What did MacWilt think he'd see? That's what I want to know. What *did* he see?"

"I bet he saw his own face," said Helen, "reflected in the spectacles. Imagine what that would have done to him. Imagine what it would do to *you*. Look at this and shut up. This is all about legends concerning these 'many worlds,' as she calls them—"

"Who?" asked Skeezix.

"Pardon me?"

"Who is *she*?"

Helen looked up and grinned. "Guess."

Skeezix shook his head tiredly, as if he couldn't be bothered with it. Helen knew that he was bursting to know. So was Jack, but Jack wasn't as much fun to bait as was Skeezix. Helen acted as if she were satisfied with Skeezix's pretended indifference. She grinned at him, turned a page, and began to read silently. Jack peered over her shoulder, not half so mystified, in truth, as Skeezix had claimed to be.

Jack was used to mysteries. He'd known for years that there had been odd circumstances surrounding his father's death—or disappearance, whatever it was—that had been kept from him, perhaps because Willoughby didn't entirely understand them himself; perhaps because Dr. Jensen thought it safer. And it wasn't just the bare facts of the business. He'd kept his ears open wide enough to have gleaned a fragment of the story here, a shard of it there. There was no shame in it—at least not in his eyes. That his mother had been loved or sought after by a trio of men, including his father, was nothing to keep hidden. Dr. Jensen had been one of those men. So what? Jack had known for years that she'd died four years after childbirth, and that his father had insisted the death was the deliberate doing of a doctor—one Algernon Harbin—who had, along with Dr. Jensen, been an abandoned lover.

The details of the murder on the bluffs at the Solstice carnival were scandalous enough to satisfy an entire village full of gossips, even when they were busy elsewhere—with MacWilt's monster and the canary gypsy and the taxidermist's son. Lars Portland had called the murderer out, had shot the villain Harbin in the head, at close range, and had himself been shot through the heart. It was cold-blooded murder in the eyes of the law. But not half so cold-blooded, in Jack's eyes, as the murder of his mother for the sake of—what?—revenge against her husband? Against *her* for having rebuffed the dark and clever Algernon Harbin?

The corpse of the murdered Dr. Harbin had disappeared. It was thought that he'd pitched over backward off the bluffs, into the moonlit Pacific. His body had quite likely been borne south on the longshore current, food for fishes and crabs and, finally, for sea birds on the sands of some deserted cove north of San Francisco. The operator of the carnival disappeared with it, and the carnival with him. He was sought for weeks afterward by the county sheriff, although the search could hardly have been carried out with much enthusiasm. Both parties were dead, after all. There was no one left to prosecute. Dr. Jensen had been coroner at the time, and he'd buried Lars Portland in the cemetery beside his wife, after coming to conclusions that would have seemed pointless to question.

Dr. Jensen had always seemed to Jack to be the real victim: denied the woman he loved; burying his best friend, who had not been denied that woman. And Jack had suspected for years that Dr. Jensen knew more than he let on, that there were remnants of the mystery that had not been buried beneath the last spadeful of dirt in the Rio Dell cemetery. Dr. Jensen, he had always supposed, would reveal them in good time, but now it was beginning to seem as if certain of those revelations were blowing in on the wind, or along the ruined tracks of a years-decayed railroad.

"I give up," said Skeezix, grimacing at Helen. "You win. You've got the book and I haven't. I won't wrestle you for it, because you're a girl and might cry."

"Because I'd twist your nose, you mean. Forget it. Ask me nice or eat cabbage soup."

Skeezix strolled across and plucked up Helen's braids, one in either hand, dancing them above her head so that their shadows leaped on the wall. "This is Perry and Winkle, the battling braid boys, reenacting the battle of the pier," he said, making the braids bow to each other and then launch themselves forward, pummeling each other while he made realistic battle noises with his tongue. Helen twisted around in her chair and slugged him twice in the stomach, at which he jerked back, hooking his foot around her chair leg, causing the chair with Helen in it to topple over backward onto the floor in a clatter of knocking and laughing. Helen shoved her hand against her mouth and managed to punch Skeezix one last time before rolling clear of the fallen chair and standing up.

During the melee Jack had picked up the book, and so Helen slugged him too and took it back. Skeezix hooted with laughter, *mumph*ing through this fingers. A voice sounded from below. "Who is that?" it shrilled—the voice of Miss Flees. "Is that you, Bobby? Are you in the attic? Who's in the attic? I'll find out! Come down out of there! Is it you, Helen?" There was a pause as Miss Flees listened. Skeezix, Jack, and Helen stood still, barely breathing, but grinning at each other. Jack crept across and looked down through the vent. There was Miss Flees below, holding a wooden spoon in her hand, with her head cocked sideways. Peebles was there, sitting atop a stool.

Jack motioned to Helen and winked, and Helen—very softly, almost birdlike—began to mimic the high, windy voice of Mrs. Langley the attic ghost, reciting, as the ghost often did, snatches of romantic poetry about dead lovers and ruined lives. Her voice rose and fell in the still attic. There wasn't a sound from below. Miss Flees stood as before with her head tilted and listening. Helen abruptly shut up and gave Skeezix a fierce look, as if to advertise what she'd do to him if he didn't contain his laughter.

Miss Flees stood just so for a moment longer, then, apparently satisfied, bent back to what it was she'd been doing before the ruckus started in the attic. Jack wondered what that was. She hunched over a big galvanized tub, looking intently at something within it. Peebles stared along with her, sticking the end of a spoon into the tub and jerking it back out, his shoulders shaking with what must have been suppressed giggles. Miss Flees stood up and stepped across to lock the door. In the tub, swimming in lazy circles, was the thing from the ocean, the existence of which had kindled such a ruckus earlier that afternoon.

Jack squinted down at the creature. It looked oddly unlike a fish in the gaslight of the kitchen—fleshy and pink and with fins that might as easily be arms—as if it had been built by someone intending to make a human being, then forgetting halfway through and trying to make a fish instead and winding up with heaven knew what. It seemed vaguely possible, now that Jack looked at the creature, that MacWilt's anger on the dock had been born out of fear, that it hadn't merely been a reaction to an insult. Jack waved his arm at his two friends, shushing them past a finger in order to keep them quiet. Helen joined him and Skeezix followed, stepping along in slow, enormous steps, his arms held out to his sides, fingers waggling, as if he were mugging the part of a secretive conspirator in a particularly gaudy stage production. He seemed about to burst over his own antics, so Helen gave him a look to shut him up. She had more at stake, after all, than Jack and Skeezix had.

Miss Flees folded open the top of a little bloodstained cloth bag, reached in, and pulled out the chicken parts that Peebles had fetched back from the alley. She seemed half repulsed by them, as if she did not entirely want to do what she was doing. Peebles watched in fascination. He offered the creature in the tub a spoon again. The spoon was jerked out of his hand, and Miss Flees hissed at him. Then the two of them tried to snatch it back out of the bucket, reaching in furtively and pulling their hands back as if they were trying to pick something up off a hot griddle.

Miss Flees finally came up with the spoon; glaring at Peebles, she set it out of reach on the sink. She dimmed the gaslight and lit a half dozen candles that were little more than heaps of black wax. A moaning began—an incantation of some sort. Jack listened. It sounded at first like the wind blowing under the eaves, drifting on the darkness. It was Miss Flees. She stood with her eyes closed, intoning what must have been a song. Then she picked up the sugar bowl, pinched out a heap of sugar, and emptied a trail of it on the kitchen floor in the shape of a circle. She laid the chicken entrails in the center of the circle and the five black candles at even intervals around the perimeter, chanting all the time. Peebles watched from his stool.

It seemed fearfully dark to Jack all of a sudden. He could hear the wind lashing at the trees out in the night and the rain pattering on the shingles. For a moment he felt as if he were floating above the vent, hovering there with darkness all around him. He forced himself to look at Skeezix, who stood transfixed beside him, his face bent into a curious mixture of fear and curiosity and disgust.

Miss Flees gathered up a scraping of the wax that ran off one of the soft candles, rolled it in sugar, then dragged it across the entrails, which were sticky with half-dried blood. She dropped the marble-sized pellet in the tub. There was a splashing and the noise of the creature slurping against the surface of the water—then silence. Her chanting continued without pause as she prepared another glob of wax. This time, though, she laid the sugary ball on the slats of the table and handed something to Peebles, who didn't seem to want it, whatever it was. Peebles shook his head. Miss Flees shook hers back at him, but continued to chant, louder now, as if she were yelling at Peebles in the only way open to her. Peebles shook his head again. Miss Flees snatched up his hand, pinioned his arm beneath her elbow, and jabbed at his palm. It was a needle that she'd offered him, but he'd been unable or unwilling to draw his own blood. He winced when the needle struck him, but he didn't cry out. There was a brief look of hatred in his eyes, and then fascination as he watched droplets of blood fall onto the sugared wax, tinting it deep red in the dim light. Miss Flees dropped the wax ball into the tub, and again the creature consumed it.

Jack could see the thing's mouth this time as it lashed up out of the shallow water and took the ball at the surface. It swam round and round its tub then, searching frantically, it seemed, for another of the morsels. The chanting diminished, low and whispery now. Joining it, high-timbred and burbling, like the piping of tiny underwater birds, was a second voice—obviously the voice of the thing in the tub. Miss Flees modulated her own chanting, heightening the rhythm so that it seemed to fit within the spaces of the creature's song.

A third voice joined in. It rose in the darkness of the attic.

The rain on the roof seemed suddenly to be beating in time, and this new voice sang what sounded to Jack to be a hymn, the words utterly distinct and yet utter nonsense.

"Shut up!" whispered Skeezix.

The singing continued. Miss Flees began to rock back and forth on her heels below. Peebles sat on his stool, eyes shut, holding his thumb against the palm of his hand.

"*Will* you shut up!" hissed Skeezix at Helen.

Jack wished Helen would shut up too. He didn't half like what was going on in the kitchen. The smell of the cabbage broth mingled with the perfume of the candles and the thin, coppery smell of blood, all of it swirling up into his face and sickening him. This wasn't at all like Miss Flees, or like earlier episodes with Peebles. This was something else, something that was causing the dense, wet atmosphere of the attic, of the entire house, to shimmer and shift.

"It's not me," whispered Helen.

Jack and Skeezix both looked at her. They'd assumed that she'd been impersonating Mrs. Langley, still playing a joke on Miss Flees. But she wasn't. She was silent and staring. Before them, back in the dusty recesses of a low shadow-hidden gable, there seemed to be a gray veil dangling in empty air. It was visible despite the darkness, hovering there like the city of shadows they'd seen above the Moonvale Hills. It swirled and congealed and formed itself into a face—the face of an old woman, turned sideways and staring against the dark wall. Long gray hair stood away from her head, and her eyes focused unblinking on nothing at all. Her mouth opened and shut like the mouth of a wooden puppet as she sang along with Miss Flees and the thing in the bucket. What it was she was singing, Jack couldn't make out. Part of him made an effort to listen to it; part of him wanted very badly to be anywhere else on earth.

Miss Flees herself appeared to be horrified. Her enchantment, whatever its purpose, was working to some inconceivable end or another, but the thought of a voice from the attic made her uneasy. Peebles listened intently to it, though. His eyes were half shut, as if he were studying the results of Miss Flees's conjuring. He'd gotten hold of the spoon again, and he tapped it idly against his knee, in time to the weird rhythms. He bent over the tub, glanced at Miss Flees, whose eyes were shut with concentration, and tentatively poked the end of the spoon at the fish creature. It ceased its canary singing, lashed up out of the tub, and buried its teeth into Peebles's finger, thrashing and banging its tail until, amid Peebles's shrieking, it dropped back into the tub and lay there.

Peebles slid from his stool, waving his hand and groaning. His little finger was bitten off. Miss Flees, coming up out of her trance, stared fixedly for a fraction of a second and then slapped Peebles with the back of her hand. Peebles stopped his capering and stood still, his finger dripping onto the floorboards. Then, very deliberately, he wrapped a tea towel around it, turned mechanically, and walked from the room, his face ghastly white in the candle glow.

The attic seemed to Jack to have gone mad. The air, suddenly, was filled with a sort of swirling mist, like ice crystals in the wind, and in it and around it were the sounds of cats and birds, all cheeping and peeping and meowing as if they were being stirred together in a pan. The hymn singing grew louder, in competition with the cacophony that circled roundabout it. Back in the corners of the attic the shadows lightened to a sort of twilight purple, and in among them there glowed what might have been little stars or hovering fireflies or sparks born spontaneously out of the charged, whirling atmosphere.

Miss Flees was thrown into abrupt confusion. She waved her wooden spoon and shouted for Peebles. Then she bent in to have a look at the fish and cracked her bony hip against the edge of the table, lurching backward and cursing with the pain of it. The activity in the attic diminished, the air growing suddenly more quiet. It seemed to Jack as if something had slumped, as if the atmosphere had tired itself out and sat down for a rest. The starry recesses of the room faded again into shadow; the cats meowed into silence; the canary trilling fell off with one last tired tweet.

Miss Flees resumed her crooning, but it was no good. The fish wouldn't sing. Mrs. Langley had fallen mute. Nothing was left but silence, doubly empty in contrast to the jungle of noises that had preceded it. Miss Flees cleared her throat, warbled just a bit, and gave it one last go, but the result was the same—nothing. Two of the candles had flickered out, and Peebles, when he'd been dancing around waving his finger, had kicked through the sugar circle and stepped on the entrails, smashing them flat on the floor.

In the attic, the ghostly face under the gable was gone. The only sounds when Miss Flees fell silent at last were the wind and the rain and the bubbling of boiling soup. Jack and Skeezix and Helen tiptoed back over to the table, all of them silent. Helen picked up the book and flipped it open, but she paid no real attention to it. Skeezix said, "Huh?" in a half befuddled, half bemused tone, then said to Helen, "Who *did* write the book?"

Helen shut the book and then turned to stare out the window. "Viola Langley," she said, and gestured at the book as if inviting them to take a look for themselves.

The streets were dark and wet and silent. Clouds scudded across the deep sky. The moon, two days away from full, peeked past the clouds now and again like an eye carved out of fossil ivory. Moon shadows danced and leaped in the wind like goblins, stretching up the sides of houses and waving their arms over their heads, then melting away to nothing when clouds hid the moon and the streets fell once more into darkness.

Lantz stepped along through the night, wary of the shadows and wary of the light. There were faces in the whorls of wood grain in the slats of a cedar fence, and there were faces grinning and evaporating in the whirling, moonlit clouds. The hooting of an owl, lost somewhere among the limbs of a leaf-less oak, chased him from the open sidewalk of the High Street up a narrow twisting alley. There was something lurking in the rain-dark emptiness of the oak, something pending. It was waiting in the alley too. He couldn't see it, but he was certain it could see him.

At the same moment that a cloud shadow cast the alley into darkness, he saw the tilted shape of a black scarecrow silhouetted against the whitewashed wall of a lean-to shed, the wind blowing the straw-stuffed arms of the thing back and forth as if they were hinged. He could hear it rustling. He stopped and stood still, waiting, thinking that he heard the sound of wings flapping, of things flying in the night. Suddenly he felt surrounded by pressing shadows, by sprites and hobgoblins and the sliding, sentient wind. The alley bent so sharply ahead that he couldn't see beyond ten or fifteen feet, but he felt something crouching there in the mud and the cast-out furniture. He turned and ran, the wind at his back.

Out of the corner of his eye he saw the scarecrow dance in the sudden wind, jiggling and flailing and tugging at the broomstick that pinned it to the dirt of a weedy garden. Its hat blew off, sailing like a saucer onto the roof of the shed, then tumbling across the shingles and clicking across the pickets of the low stile fence. Lantz ran back out toward the High Street, the xylophone clacking of the hat, the rustling of the straw, the hooting of the owl, and the creaking of the wind all playing through the avenues of his mind like the music of a goblin orchestra.

His house in the woods had slid down the hillside. Seven days of rain had turned the ground to mud, and the shack had set out toward the sea in a rush. His stuffed beasts had gone with it, squawking and mewling and screeching, their eyes dark with fear and wonder. Lantz had fought to save them, but in the slick mud and the pounding rain and the darkness he could do nothing at all.

Perhaps there'd be something left of them when the sun

rose. They might easily have pulled up short along the bluffs and be waiting for him there, near the carnival. But probably not. In two or three days they would wash up along the mudflat beaches of San Francisco Bay like a drowned zoo. People with their pant legs rolled, poking after razor clams at low tide, would find them there in a litter of glass eyes and cotton stuffing, kelp snails and periwinkles.

Lantz could see it. He could close his eyes and see it as if it were painted on a canvas the size of a barn wall. But he couldn't think about it; he couldn't, step by step, trace their strange odyssey: washing down the hill, teetering on the edge of the crumbling bluffs, roiling in the sea foam of a breaking wave, and drifting out into the current, entangled in kelp and flotsam. He could picture only bits and pieces of it that flickered across the evening hallways of his imagination like fragments of a landscape glimpsed through a telescope held wrong end to.

He shut his eyes and there they were, all of them moving swiftly in the darkness of an oceanic trench, sweeping south on a deepwater current. There was the ostrich and the elk head, the stray dog and the fish with its mouth gaping and rows of neat teeth like clipped-off bits of piano wire; there was the ape with patchy fur, and there was the bit of plywood with sixteen shrews pinned to it, all of them lined up in ranks and swirling now past a surge of seashells and tube worms and coral fans that waved and bowed in the shifting tides.

He found he was outside MacWilt's tavern. He'd just drifted there, awash himself. The night seemed to draw him along, as if it had in mind for him a destination he couldn't quite fathom. He looked up at the attic window, imagining that he could see himself looking back out, and for a moment he could. He heard the high trilling of two score of tiny birds, and he could smell the musty odor of their uncleaned cages and of spilled birdseed and gunnysacks and the mess of shredded potatoes and onions and bacon that cooked on the stove top.

He was thin, and his clothes hung on him like the clothes of the scarecrow that had chased him from the alley. He had years ago ceased to care about food. There were pine nuts and blackberries and mushrooms to eat. There was Mrs. Jensen now and again. He could trust Mrs. Jensen. He heard music on the wind that blew off the ocean and across the bluffs. It was carnival music, and there in the west where the clouds were breaking he could see what might be winking stars or what might be the lights of the carnival, like a thousand lit candles glowing above the sea.

There was a light on in the tavern. Lantz crept to the window and peered past the edge of muslin curtains at the interior. There was MacWilt cracking his knee against a wooden chair. He cursed, then stepped back and tried to kick the chair, but he was wide of the mark, and he nearly fell over backward with the effort. His eyes were bandaged with a rag, and he felt his way around his own tavern like a blind man, pushing over stools, pounding his fist against the bar top, shrieking horribly.

Lantz couldn't fathom it. Why had MacWilt wrapped a rag around his head? Lantz put his face to a cracked pane of glass and started to say something, then stopped when he couldn't think of anything to say. He blew through the broken pane, making a sound like wind under a door, watching MacWilt's head swivel round, his mouth springing open in sudden surprise. Lantz chattered like a squirrel and then made a noise like water burbling down a drainpipe. MacWilt shouted hoarsely and swept a half dozen glasses off the countertop with his forearm. He shrank toward the wall, feeling with both hands, his head swiveling from side to side as Lantz whistled through the crack, like a canary now, high and thin and distant.

"Look there!" Jack cried, standing up from the book and pointing out the window. Someone was peering into the window of the tavern. In the darkness Jack couldn't at all make out who it was, but as the person moved away, around the building and onto the side street, Jack saw that it was Lantz, lanky and dressed in rags and walking with his odd, shuffling sort of sideways gait.

Skeezix was already lifting the trapdoor. Jack and Helen followed him down, slipped into one of the bedrooms and out the window. Peebles had gone out a half hour earlier, still holding the rag to his finger and skulking away toward the bluffs, looking roundabout himself as if suspicious that he was being watched, which, of course, he was.

They didn't want to surprise Lantz. If they slid up behind him without warning he'd be gone. So they stood in the shadows across the street and watched. Lantz bent over something that lay beneath a curb tree. He reached down and picked it up with both hands. It was a piece of MacWilt's telescope, of the giant lenses. The shard was almost as big as Lantz's head.

The moon came out just then, lighting the street. Lantz held the glass up to his face and peered through it, looking straight across at his three friends. Jack waved, feeling foolish, startled at the way Lantz's face was suddenly magnified through the glass. His eye seemed to swell to the size of a plate. There was a rustling above them in the trees and the flapping of heavy wings. An enormous crow soared out of the branches, circled once above the top of the tavern, and then landed on the cobbles of the road, not six feet from where Lantz stood. Jack stared at it. It was the same crow; it still carried its stick.

Lantz regarded the crow through the glass, jumped just a bit as if startled, and then peered over the top of it as if to make sure of something. The crow hopped toward him, then flapped awkwardly up and onto his shoulder, scrabbling precariously there and seeming to whisper into Lantz's ear. The boy stood still, listening, then pitched the piece of glass into the weeds as if it were a piece of rubbish, turned on his heel, and set off up the High Road, leaving his uncertain friends behind. The crow soared away, winging toward the bluffs, which were lit now by the lights of the carnival.

Jack hurried across and found the glass in the weeds, but when he looked through it he could see nothing magical at all, nothing but the faces of Helen and Skeezix, who looked to be tiny and distant, about a mile away on a hilltop. It must have been the peculiar convex surface of the lens that accounted for it, and for Jack's face seeming to them to be the enormous moon face of a leering giant.

Part Two

THROUGH THE LOFT WINDOW

6

THEY FOUND DR. JENSEN at work on the shoe. It was coming on to nine o'clock, and he was in the carriage house caulking seams. He'd rigged a mast through the laces and fitted a tiller across the heel. He planned to sail it, he said. There seemed to Jack a dozen easier ways to obtain a boat: there were half a dozen small sailboats in the harbor that might be rented by the day, and there were skippers aplenty, especially during the Solstice, who had nothing very much better to do than hire themselves out.

Dr. Jensen wasn't interested merely in sailing in a "boat." He couldn't much stand sailing, in fact, although he'd done a good bit of it on San Francisco Bay as a boy. When he'd gotten older he'd gotten colder too, and he would enjoy the ocean now from the shore; he didn't have to go out on it. It was going sailing in the enormous shoe, he said, that particularly appealed to him. There was no telling where a man might end up. He would set sail tomorrow. The tide fell at nine in the morning, and he intended to be on it, so to speak. He didn't know when he was coming home, but he undertook to believe that with the strange weather and seas, and with the coming of the Solstice, it wouldn't be a long voyage. Mrs. Jensen wasn't going along, but she understood his going and wouldn't stand in the way. Jack and Skeezix and Helen nodded, although Jack, for one, wasn't entirely satisfied with the doctor's logic. It seemed to imply something more than it actually said.

Helen showed the doctor Mrs. Langley's book. He wasn't particularly surprised. He warned them about taking too great an interest in it, though, and said it might be best if they considered it the stuff of fairy tales, and nothing more.

Jack scratched his head at that, but he didn't say what he

might have said in regard to the sailboat shoe. He regarded Dr. Jensen, with his caulk and his overalls and his unlikely boat, and said, "It seems like everybody's going somewhere all of a sudden, doesn't it?"

"Oh?" said the doctor.

"Well, maybe they're not *going* somewhere, absolutely, but they're *up* to something. There's a sort of something in the air, isn't there? Like right before an electrical storm, only it's been going on all week, and it's getting—what? Not worse, more so—or something like that."

"Very mysterious," muttered Dr. Jensen, smearing away at the shoe sole, seeming to pay little attention to what Jack had to say. Either that or he simply didn't think much of it as a subject.

Jack told him about Miss Flees and the monster from the sea. Dr. Jensen shook his head, half in disgust. The news of Mrs. Langley's appearance, though, and her joining in with the conjuring seemed to interest him, but only for a moment. Then he shrugged and bent back to his work.

"Mrs. Langley been unusually active lately?" he asked casually, wiping his hand on his overalls and looking up at Helen.

Helen nodded. "In fact, yes. You can't shut her up sometimes. Usually if I talk back to her she'll be happy and quiet down. She'll be carrying on, say, about a pink dress or a Thanksgiving turkey, and I'll say that the dress is very beautiful or the turkey was the best I've eaten. Then there'll be nothing, like she'd been worrying about the dress or the turkey, but she's satisfied now, heaven knows why. This past week, though, she's been moaning and talking in a rush. And there's the sound of cats, too, meowing around the attic. I think there's more than one—maybe three or four."

"Do tell," said Dr. Jensen, lighting his pipe. "Cats, is it? Ghost cats?"

Helen shrugged. "I haven't seen any live ones up there."

"There's graves ripped open along up toward Moonvale," said Dr. Jensen, and he gave them all a look, as if he was

suddenly willing to talk about the mysteries they'd been referring to, but it was a very serious business and required a
careful choosing of words. "You've heard that?"

All three of them shook their heads.

"And one out at Rio Dell Cemetery. You ought to know
about that one, Jack, if you don't already."

Jack widened his eyes. There was only one reason that Dr.
Jensen would say such a thing. "My father's grave?"

The doctor nodded, puffing on his pipe and squinting at
Jack. He gave up on his boat entirely for the moment. The
conversation had come round to a point at which it required
all his attention. "I had a look, early this morning. I would
have told you out on the bluffs, but I wanted to look at the
graves up near Moonvale first. This isn't the first time such
a thing has happened. If you read far enough in Mrs. Langley she'll tell you about it—glorifying it just a little bit, like
she does. She didn't see anything wrong with meddling with
the truth if it made for a better yarn. But it's the truth we
want here, and as I said, I'd have given it to you earlier if I'd
figured it out. I went up to the farm this evening on purpose
to find you, but Willoughby said you'd been gone all day.

"Those graves up toward Moonvale weren't robbed. They
were half washed out by the Eel, and if the rain keeps up
there'll be dead men out to sea by morning. A few weren't
opened by the river, though. At least I don't think they were.
I think the corpses stood up and walked away."

Skeezix laughed hollowly, as if he were half embarrassed
to laugh but found the idea silly enough to demand it. Jack
didn't laugh at all. The grisly notion of his father's corpse
having walked away from Rio Dell Cemetery wasn't any
laughing matter. Dr. Jensen must have read the look on his
face, though, for he held his hand up and shook his head.
"Your father's grave was dug up. That's the difference. The
bones are still in it."

The idea of bones didn't appeal to Jack at all, but he was
relieved anyway. "Why?" he asked, certain, somehow, that
Dr. Jensen knew the answer.

The doctor shrugged, puffed a half dozen times on his pipe, paused to tamp and relight it, then said, "They aren't your father's bones."

Jack stood silent.

"I filled that coffin, Jack, and the bones I put in it belonged to a man who should have been dead years earlier. His bones were turning to dust when I was laying him out, and I had to toss in a heap of your father's junk to weight it right."

"You're telling me my father's not dead?"

"Nope. I'm not telling you anything of the sort. Only that he's not buried in that coffin. He might be dead, or he might not. This might be his shoe that I'm caulking here."

"He wasn't shot?"

"Oh, he was shot, all right, but not bad. Harbin shot him in the arm. Your father shot Harbin in the face. I wish I could say it was self-defense. No, that's a lie. I don't care at all about self-defense. Harbin deserved to die, if any man does. Worse than that. I'm not sure that he didn't *get* worse in the end. They didn't find his body. You heard that. He went off the bluffs into a high sea. It was the Solstice, of course, and it wasn't any different from this one: rain and wind for a week; tides running too high one day, too low the next; storm surf out of the north falling off flat in an hour and then an hour later kicking back up again. There was that little bunch of houses out near Ferndale washed away in the night. No end of people drowned. They found those bodies—every one of them. But they never found Harbin, even though they looked up and down the coast for a week."

"Whose bones were in the coffin?" Jack asked, fascinated enough by the disappearance of Dr. Harbin, but unable to get his mind off the opened grave that wasn't his father's grave after all. The news that his father might still be alive left him feeling curiously deflated. It seemed somehow depressing. If it were true, if his father had shot Harbin and fled, then Jack had been abandoned to Willoughby all these years when his father might as easily have come back after him. No one in the village thought him guilty of any real crime. There was no one to prosecute, or at least no one who would particularly care to file charges.

"They were the bones of the man I was telling you about this morning. The old Chinese man from San Francisco, who lived in the warehouse on the bay. There were three others of us on the bluffs: Willoughby and I and Kettering. I wanted Harbin dead as much as Lars Portland did, but I didn't have the courage to do it myself. There was nothing vile that he hadn't done. Killing your mother—which he did, there isn't any doubt at all—was only one of his crimes, but it was enough. Your father said he'd kill him, and he did, or he tried, anyway, and went away thinking that he had. I made an effort to stop him, but not much of a one, and I watched with Willoughby while the two of them called each other out. If Harbin had killed your father, I'd have shot him dead myself, there and then, and taken the consequences. But as I say, your father shot him full in the face—knocked him over backward—and he rolled over the cliff. We saw him go into the ocean like a rag doll. We could see the white of his coat washing against the rocks with the surge, and then a big swell pulled him out into deep water and he was gone. Food for the fishes, we though. Now I'm not so sure."

"Who's dead then besides the man from San Francisco, the engineer?"

"No one's dead."

"Where's my father?"

"Ask Mrs. Langley. She knows."

"Where's Dr. Harbin?" When Jack asked he realized that he really didn't want to know—that if he knew for sure he'd want to kill the man himself. That wasn't true either. He *ought* to want to kill the man, maybe, for what he'd done to his mother and father. But then Jack hadn't much known his mother and father, had he? He had only vague childhood memories. And the idea of killing anything was foreign to him. It was the sort of thing that would appeal to Peebles or

MacWilt or to Harbin himself. "I don't get it," said Jack, feeling foolish for stating the utterly obvious. "I mean about the old bones in my father's grave."

"We didn't need any corpses, to tell you the truth. What happened out on the bluffs was going to take some explaining anyway. The old man wasn't anything but a mummy when we found him. He was lying in the rain. Looked like an old leather bag sewed up into a sort of doll. There were sounds coming out of his mouth, but they didn't mean anything, or they were in a language we couldn't understand. Inside of five minutes he'd dwindled to nothing but a heap of bones and dust. His dust is part of the mud of the meadow still; his bones we put in a gunnysack and hauled home. I put them into the coffin along with ballast, like I said, and I told everyone that asked that it was Lars Portland in the coffin. I was the coroner then, and there was no reason for me to lie, not really. No one suspected me of having a hand in the business. And I didn't, up to a point. I just wanted to keep things neat. They've been neat, too—as a pin—up until a couple of days back."

Skeezix had sat in silence atop a nail keg, listening to Jack and Dr. Jensen. It was their affair, really, and he had enough sense to stay out of it. When it seemed that Jack was played out, though, he asked, "What about the carnival? You said this old man who—what, decayed on the bluffs there?—*ran* the carnival. What happened after he was gone? Carnival close down? Where did it go?"

"A mystery, I suppose," said the doctor, squinting at the floor. "It sat in the rain for two days, looking like it was going to rust to pieces. I'd have bet that by the end of the week there wouldn't be anything more of it left than there was of Kettering's friend—nothing but dust and carnival bones. But then it left in the night. Pulled up stakes and was gone. I heard the calliope whistle. Woke me up around midnight, but by the time I got the wagon out and drove down to the Coast Road it had vanished. Nothing but moonlit steam rising in a line down toward Scotia. I put an ear to the tracks, and I could hear it, traveling south. I followed it, is what I did—next day. I drove all the way into San Francisco and stayed for a fortnight, looking in on the warehouse, even though I knew I wouldn't find it there, and even though last time we'd been there the warehouse itself had been gone. It was a fool's errand, and I knew it, and yet there was something in the atmosphere of the whole thing that compelled me. Well, it was back, after a fashion—the warehouse, that is. It wasn't what it had been years earlier, and you'll recall that it was falling into ruin then.

"Now it was the skeleton of a building. Termite dust was ankle deep in the sheltered corners. Wind had scoured the floor where it blew off the bay. There was a litter of iron debris, and of brass and bronze and copper, but most of it was massed together with rust and verdigris so that I couldn't say for certain what any of it had been. There were old posters glued across the few walls left teetering there, circus posters, mostly, or carnival posters, and all of them peeling off in the weather to expose more of the same underneath, layer after layer. It was as if the walls themselves hadn't ever been plastered, but were nothing but papier-mâché, glued together with the ooze from mussels and barnacles. It certainly smelled so. The whole place, even in the wind, had the smell of a tide pool too long out of the water, boiled by the sun.

"The berry vines had grown luxuriantly, though they seemed to be dying back now. There was scarcely a place in the tumbled warehouse, though, from which you could see either of the buildings that flanked it beyond weedy yards. The only view was out onto the bay, across the railroad trestle. On the street in front, off the Embarcadero, there was an iron fence, tilted and broken, that ended on either side merely by burying itself into the vines. I had gotten there at low tide and had had to climb down onto the mud flats and pick my way up from the bay. It was that or cut my way through the blackberries.

"Anyway, that's what I found. I convinced myself that we'd been mistaken on the last trip. We hadn't made much of a search of it then, and it was coming on dusk. We had peered past the fence and through the vines and had *thought* there was nothing left of the place, but clearly we'd been fooled by the dying sunlight. Maybe we'd mistaken the broken framework of the place for part of the railroad trestle." Dr. Jensen ran out of steam suddenly. He stood up and surveyed his boat, which didn't look at all seaworthy to Jack. But it had floated ashore from somewhere without capsizing or sinking. Perhaps it could stand another voyage.

"So you haven't been back since?" asked Jack, not entirely satisfied that the doctor had come to the end of his tale.

"Oh, I went back, all right. Three years later. I'd gone into the city again after certain amphibians and stopped in Chinatown for supper. I drove around the Embarcadero in a coach—not to visit the warehouse, mind you, but to collect salamanders at the wharf—and en route we passed the gates. I hadn't been thinking about the place, so it took me by surprise, and I'd passed them in an instant and was rattling away toward the wharf before I could collect myself.

"The gates, you see, had been repaired and either painted or brushed clean of rust. The vines were clipped and green and covered with ripe berries. The warehouse itself had been repaired and shingled and the windows glazed. The paint had been enlivened, and through a lit window I could just see someone tinkering with a bit of machinery, bending over it and working at it with a wrench. Then we were gone. There were problems with the salamanders—half of them were dead and the rest weren't worth bothering with. I spent hours chasing down money I'd paid for nothing and then raced into the station and caught the evening coach for Inverness with moments to spare. I never got back around to Embarcadero, to discover who it was that had rejuvenated the warehouse. All I know for certain is that it wasn't Kettering's old friend. His bones were in the coffin in Rio Dell Cemetery, and they're there now, covered up with dirt again and likely to stay that way."

"So who was it?" asked Skeezix, looking at Jack and then

at Dr. Jensen, as if he knew something was being discussed that was beyond his understanding but mightn't be beyond Jack's.

He was wrong; Jack didn't know. Dr. Jensen shrugged and said he couldn't be sure, but he was beginning to suspect. He wouldn't invent any tales, though. He'd wait until he was sure; then he would tell them. Anything else might cause trouble, and it seemed to Dr. Jensen that the three of them got into an adequate amount of trouble as it was. They didn't need help.

Jack asked him what they ought to *do*. They couldn't just stand idle, could they, while the rest of the north coast was caught up in mysteries? What if they missed out? What if everyone got there and they were left home?

Where? Dr. Jensen wanted to know. Jack couldn't say but went him one better by asking again exactly where it was he was sailing to in his shoe. Dr. Jensen shrugged and said there was no way of knowing where a man might end up. And so they were back around to where they'd started.

Later, after Skeezix had been satisfied with the remains of yesterday's turkey and cranberry sauce, Helen asked Dr. Jensen about what Mrs. Langley referred to as the "land of dreams." Helen had, quite clearly, been trying to piece together something coherent out of all the fragments, while Skeezix's time had been spent half smirking and Jack's thoughts had been torn by curiosity, regret, and anticipation and so had come to nothing in the course of the evening.

Helen could see patterns in all this strange behavior—it involved Mrs. Langley's magical land, didn't it? That's where everyone thought they were going. Heaven knew how many villagers were making preparations to set sail, just like Dr. Jensen: this one, perhaps, by fashioning a stupendous kite; that one by conjuring a monster from the ocean; the next one by building—what?—an enormous telescope out of a whiskey keg and the spectacles of a giant. And where *had* the spectacles come from? Mrs. Langley's land of dreams, obviously. It had begun with the Solstice. Any of a number of things began to arrive with the Solstice. Lars Portland had disappeared with the Solstice. He'd gone to the land of dreams, hadn't he?

Dr. Jensen shrugged. Maybe he had. He'd wanted to. He certainly hadn't been seen again in the twelve years since, nor had Kettering, who'd been on the bluffs with them. The road he'd pursued had been opened to him through alchemy. He'd talked of an elixir, a wine that smelled of tar and dandelions and ocean water, all at once. But it hadn't been the elixir alone that had done it. The carnival, somehow, was an ingredient, as were easterly winds and a swell out of the north and a change in the weather. It was all very unlikely, is what it was, although Algernon Harbin hadn't thought so.

Harbin had sought some such avenue until the search had made him wretched. Whatever parts of him hadn't been tainted with ruin and greed had languished and died, and when it seemed to him that Lars Portland had succeeded where he himself had failed, well . . .

Dr. Jensen shook his head. They'd covered this ground before, and there was no need, he said, to drag themselves across it again. Helen was right, of course. None of them knew where they were going or what they'd find there. Dreams were often not very pretty items, and there were precious few of them that we'd want to come true, as the saying went. There was the mystery in it, though, that attracted us, said Dr. Jensen, and there was the sad notion that there must, in our lives, be something more than the continual decay of the world we fooled ourselves into thinking was solid. We totter along the brink of a crumbling precipice, it seemed to him, balancing on the dubious edge, and all around us we watch our friends toppling off and smashing to the stones below, and no way on earth for us to anticipate when that little bit of dirt on which we've thrown our weight will disintegrate below us and we'll plunge headlong in the wake of all the rest. There must be some way, he insisted, to map things out, to grasp the tiller and steer for a shore less fogbound and precipice-ridden than the shores we've known.

Dr. Jensen looked at his pocket watch and sighed. It was late, and he was starting to talk maudlin. With the morning sun things would look brighter. He was off on a pleasure cruise, he said, and nothing more. He had enough faith in his dreams to suppose he wouldn't go blind when he caught a glimpse of them. He offered everyone a second helping of pie, but only Skeezix had an appetite for it.

Skeezix, forking out a chunk of pie, said that if he found himself suddenly in the land of his dreams he'd set out to cross it on foot and would eat at every inn along the way, good or bad. He'd let the bad ones remind him of just how good the good ones were. It was a sad business, he said, all this about strolling along the edge of a cliff, and true enough in its way. But for him it seemed that the precariousness of the business lent a sort of flavor to it; it would be a dreary place all in all if his existence were mapped out too thoroughly. Dr. Jensen smiled at that and said Skeezix was young, and some day he might easily see things through a different pair of spectacles.

Jack slept fitfully that night. The wind gusted outside and rain beat against the walls of the barn now and then while Jack drifted off and awoke with a start, thinking he'd heard something, and then drifted off again. Once he woke up, climbed out of bed, and shoved his hand under his mattress, feeling around until he found the little bottle of amber-green liquid that he'd had hidden there for a week. The bottle wasn't quite three inches high. It had no label but had a screw top, which was good, since if it were corked he'd probably never have gotten the cork out. It had been left—he was almost certain of it now—by the little man in the mouse suit. He'd opened it after he'd found it, left beside his book and his candle on the bedside table, and the barn in an instant had been filled with the aroma of tar and dandelions and ocean water, all of them at once and yet each of them distinct, as if a bottle of each had been opened simultaneously and their aromas hovered roundabout each other in the air.

He'd told Skeezix and Helen about it; there had been no reason not to. Peebles had overheard. He'd been skulking outside the door to Skeezix's room but had sneezed and given himself away. Jack hadn't cared much one way or another; Peebles, after all, had seemed to him little more than a sad, irritating blotch. But now, after the last couple of days, Jack wasn't sure. Peebles had begun to seem like something more. Still, Peebles would hardly be interested in the elixir—if that's what it was—and even if he wanted it passionately, he was too much the coward to sneak round and steal it.

Jack shoved the bottle back in under the mattress. It seemed to him that he could hear the calliope in the distance, that he had been listening to it in his dreams. He wrapped a blanket around him and opened a shutter. The sound of music seemed to leap just a little, as if it had been lurking without, waiting for a chance to push its way into the barn. The rain had fallen off for the moment, and it was clear and dark. Jack could see the black line of the ocean away off beyond the bluffs, and it seemed to him as if he could see the glow of lights from Moonvale too, although heaven knew why Moonvale would be lit up in the middle of the night. Perhaps it was the aurora that glowed there, low in the sky above the Moonvale Hills.

The carnival was lit like a Christmas tree. Jack could almost see the green of meadow grasses roundabout it. He swiveled his telescope toward it, focused, and made out the shadow of someone moving about amid the machinery of the rides, all of which, weirdly, were spinning and whirling and lurching on the firelit meadow. The shadow—Dr. Brown, no doubt—strolled here and there, throwing levers, turning great iron wheels, stepping back and shading his face from the issuance of whirlwinds of steam. Two figures beyond him pitched split logs into the beehive oven. It was too dark at first to make them out.

The door of the funhouse opened in a sudden spray of glinting light, and someone wearing an enormous pointed clown hat stood in the doorway for a moment before the door slammed shut in his face. The fire in the oven leaped, the calliope played louder and wilder, the two stood in the fire-light, holding an armload of wood each, and seemed to leap and dance in the flickering light. They were both skeletons, animated somehow, in the employ of Dr. Brown.

Jack sat back and blinked, then looked again. The oven door had been shut. What he'd taken for skeletons were mere shades now, chopping away at driftwood with axes. He could hear the distant blows ring out above the sound of the calliope. Had they *been* skeletons? It hardly seemed likely. It might very easily have been a trick of moonlight through broken clouds—that and the suddenly leaping fire and the strings of lamps overhead had all mingled to fool him. That had to be the case.

He noticed abruptly that the rides weren't all empty, not entirely anyway. Someone rode the Ferris wheel. It spun very slowly skyward, counterclockwise, an enormous hoop of lights and a dozen rocking chairs set round it like numbers on a clock. The spokes of the thing and the struts that spaced the spokes were silver-dark against the glow like the web of a spider in moonlight. A shadow sat slumped in one of the chairs, rising from two o'clock to one, one to twelve, dropping to eleven and ten and down and swinging round to rise skyward again. Jack searched for him through the telescope, a strange hollow certainty developing in his stomach. He couldn't swear it was Lantz, but the stooped figure might easily have been, huddled there at the edge of the little rocking seat. He'd been wandering through the streets, after all, in the darkness. He'd been searching for something. He'd listened to the crow that had landed on his shoulder, and set out toward the bluffs with enough resolve to make him ignore the shouted greetings of his friends.

Jack watched for ten more minutes, until the north wind began to ignore the blanket and the dark rain began to fall again, blowing in through the shutters and against the lens of his telescope. It was getting on toward dawn, time to sleep. The carnival was open and doing business, in a limited way; Jack and Skeezix would have a look at it in the morning, if they could slide out without Helen. She'd probably be in the attic painting and reading Mrs. Langley's book anyway, perhaps shooting the breeze with the old dead woman herself. Jack felt once again for the tiny bottle, then, satisfied, drifted away into sleep, dreaming of Helen and Skeezix and Dr. Jensen, but mostly of Helen, all of them adrift in a giant's shoe on a sea so deeply blue that they might as easily have been sailing through the night sky toward shoals of stars.

7

"IT MIGHT BE HIM."

"Changed, though. I caught a glimpse myself, and I wouldn't have thought it; not just from looking at him."

"All of us have. It's been a few years."

The voices murmured out of the parlor, carrying into the kitchen but not much farther. They were low and secretive. One belonged to Dr. Jensen and the other to Willoughby. Neither could disguise his voice if he tried—not enough to fool anyone—and they weren't trying here anyway. Jack stood just inside the service porch door, listening. He'd gotten up early. He couldn't sleep, not with the mysteries tangling up his thoughts all night. And he'd come inside after a cup of coffee and a hunk of bread and jam. He stood in his shirt sleeves, head cocked, shivering in the morning chill that seeped through the screen door. He'd have shut the kitchen door, but it creaked, and he didn't, right then, want either of the two in the parlor to know he was there.

"Twelve years." Willoughby paused after saying it, as if studying. "Can we know for sure?"

"No, I don't suppose we can. We can't stroll up and *ask* him, after all, can we? It doesn't really matter much, I suppose. Too many years gone, if you ask me, for any of us to start stirring up the dust. Let it lie; that's my advice, but keep it from Jack and the others. Jack especially. It wouldn't do him a bit of good to know."

"And *we* don't *know*," said Willoughby almost at once, as if he were anxious to agree with the doctor. There was a silence then. Jack wondered who it was they were talking about. He supposed it was his father. Some one had "come back," that much was certain.

"Anyway," continued the doctor after a moment, "I saw it

down on the bluffs, near where I found the body in the tide pool. There was something awfully strange about that whole business. And then the kids were telling me last night that they'd seen it in town, near MacWilt's."

"It's been here too. I took a shot at it yesterday afternoon, but it was too far off. But I've got my gun by the door there, loaded. I'm ready for it. I don't think I could shoot a man, not unless I had to. But I could easy enough shoot—"

There was a shuffle of feet and the scrape of chairs being pushed back. Jack turned and shoved out through the screen door, onto the wooden back porch. He vaulted the railing and leaped up the paving stones set into the grass of the back yard leading down to the river. He expected to hear Willoughby's voice, shouting after him. The idea of skulking and snooping in the kitchen was bad enough; being caught at it would be mortifying. Not that he'd done anything particularly wrong. But he should have made his presence known. He should have walked into the parlor, announced that he'd overheard them, and asked the two men to explain themselves. Even if they'd declined to, he wouldn't have any less information than he had now.

No one shouted at him. They hadn't come out the back. He was stepping along behind the barn when he heard the first shot. Then Dr. Jensen shouted. There was the sound of running feet, another shout, and a second shot. Jack ran toward the end of the barn, rounded the far corner, and saw Willoughby standing in the pasture with his rifle to his shoulder. Jack's loft window stood open above. Dr. Jensen's head thrust through it suddenly. He cried, "No! Damn it!" and then saw Jack standing below him. In the distance, flapping almost tiredly over the tops of the oaks that fringed the edge of the pasture, was a solitary crow, cawing shrilly. In an instant it was gone.

"I'm certain I hit it," said Willoughby, turning toward Jack, thinking for an moment that it was Jensen who stood in the shadows of the barn.

"Why?" asked Jack, puzzled.

Willoughby grinned suddenly, as if he'd been caught doing something he oughtn't to do. "Almonds," he said. "The thing's been eating my almonds. They've stripped half the tree. Greedy things, crows."

Jack nodded. Here was his opportunity to ask a question or two. Dr. Jensen joined them, feigning a look of mild surprise to see Jack there, but unable to hide the concern that tugged at the corners of his mouth and eyes. "Well," he said, running his hand backward through his hair. "I can't hang around here all morning helping you bag crows. There's too many of them anyway to ever get the job done right. Take it from me. You can kill two dozen crows this morning, and the horizon will be black with them by this afternoon. It's a scarecrow you want, Willoughby, or a rubber snake wound into the branches. It puts the fear into them, a snake does. I'm on my way now." He pulled out his watch and scrutinized it, reminding Jack overmuch of MacWilt checking his pocket watch and studying the hills through his telescope.

"The shoe's launched, Jack," continued the doctor. "I hauled it down this morning early. Tide goes in an hour, so I'd better run. I'll see you, I suppose, in a day or two."

"Come back," Jack said.

Dr. Jensen nodded. "I have to. I've got promises to keep. But there's a couple things I'd like to know, a couple things I'd like to see, and I aim to try. I can't wait another twelve years." With that he strode away toward his wagon and left Willoughby and Jack standing on the wet grass.

It hadn't been his father that the two men were talking about. Jack knew that suddenly, and as soon as he did he leaped away toward the barn door, took the stairs to the loft three at a time, and shoved his hand in under his mattress. His book and candle and cup had been knocked off the nightstand and onto the floor. The wind through the open shutter might have blown them off, but Jack didn't think so. His bottle was still there. He pulled the shutter closed, retrieved and lit the candle, and hauled out the bottle, twisting off the lid. The barn was filled at once with the odor of the bay at low tide, mingled with the wildflower smell of a windy spring meadow. Not a drop had been stolen. He looked around with an eye toward a safer hiding place, but there were none. He could hide it in the woods, of course, but there was no telling who or what might be watching him if he went outside. He screwed the lid on tight, slipped the bottle into his pocket, grabbed his coat, and set out for the orphanage.

They watched Dr. Jensen from the cavern in the bluffs. His sailboat shoe rounded the headland, appearing and disappearing beyond rolling seas. He seemed to be making almost no headway, sailing against the current, blown toward shore by the winds. The little boat rose atop a feathery crest, then sank again in the trough; even the tip of the mast dipped out of sight for a time. Then it appeared again, rolling across the next swell before it was gone.

They watched for over an hour, eating bread from the bakery and drinking coffee. The shoe tacked back and forth still, a half mile out. It made almost no headway. By nightfall Dr. Jensen wouldn't have sailed beyond the mouth of the Eel. He'd spend the night hobnobbing with floating skeletons. It occurred to Jack that if you could so easily sail there—to wherever it was that Dr. Jensen was bound—half the village would have been on the ocean days ago. The doctor assumed, quite likely, that it was the particular *sort* of boat you used that made the difference, just like MacWilt and his telescope lens. And there was probably truth to the idea, but apparently not enough truth to overcome the wind and tide.

Jack and Helen and Skeezix wandered up to the Coast Road when the coffee and bread were gone. Dr. Jensen would have to take care of himself. The carnival was alive with villagers. It seemed like half of Rio Dell was there, along with no end of people from Moonvale and Scotia. There was fresh paint on the plywood sides of the fun houses and on the iron framework of the thrill rides, or at least there was a newness and freshness to it that Jack hadn't been able to see when the debris of the carnival had lain yesterday in the wet meadow grass. The wooden arch over the road was papered with posters, a sort of kaleidoscope of carnival images, almost sinister in their profusion.

The bicycle-riding clowns and the top-hatted skeletons grinned out once again from where they were painted. There was the smell of fresh sawdust in the air, of engine oil and burning cedar logs and coal, of greasepaint and barbecued duck. Booths sold beer and skewered meats and hot oranges, and it seemed uncannily like the carnival was enormous, that it stretched away up and down the coast and across the meadows toward the distant smoky village. Here was a paint and plywood structure of two-dimensional domes with the words MOORISH TEMPLE painted over a curtained doorway; there was a covered wagon bearing unspecified CURIOUS FREAKS. Lean-tos and tents dotted the bluffs, and in among the people filing in and out of them, paying ten cents to see a creature half fish and half man or a bird with the head of a pig, were Miss Flees and the Mayor's wife, MacWilt's nephews, the fisherman who'd had ill luck on the pier the previous day, and even old MacWilt himself, his eyes bandaged, tapping his way into the heart of the carnival with a stick.

No end of people shouldered their way through milling crowds, and on the otherwise silent ocean air Jack could hear the flap of canvas and the creak of iron rubbing against iron and the thunder of the fire in the great oven, all of it against the hum and roar of what might have been thousands of laughing and chatting voices.

Calliope music underscored the rest, steamy and wild and seeming to pipe out in time to the turnings and cavortings of the carnival rides, each of which flew and swung and rotated in symphony with all the rest. Skeezix tried his hand at knocking down iron milk bottles with a baseball, but he had no luck. Helen won a rubber pig with a look of surprised grief on its face by pitching three dimes onto a plate. Jack kept his money, but not because he was cheap. He had his eye on the Ferris wheel. He couldn't seem to pay attention to anything else. Lantz, of course, no longer rode it—if it had been Lantz.

It might as easily have been someone else—testing it, perhaps. It certainly ran well enough now. The rust and grime that had coated it the previous day had been scrubbed away. It was painted gaudy colors, and the little swings jerked up and around, their occupants pointing away down the coast, catching a glimpse, perhaps, of church steeples in Moonvale or of the tower of the grange building down the coast in Ferndale.

It seemed to be twilight, as if it were six in the evening rather than an hour before noon. Jack glimpsed stars in the dim purple sky, although they seemed to flicker and vanish and might easily have been the tiny lamps strung overhead from one end of the carnival to the other, which were still lit, despite its being midday. There were a half score of booths occupied by fortunetellers and by people who claimed to speak to the dead, and from one or two came the plaintive, wheedling voices of the dead themselves, demanding attention, asking after unfinished business, complaining about the sorry accommodations of the hereafter.

Peebles strode out from within a tent, staring at his hand and nearly running into Skeezix, who leaped clear as if to avoid touching a poisonous reptile. Neither Jack nor Helen nor Skeezix said anything. The recent events in the alley and in Miss Flees's kitchen seemed to have made small talk impossible. Speaking turned out to be unnecessary, though. Peebles sneered at the three of them, as if he'd sooner talk to bugs, and then he hurried away toward the Moorish Temple, where the alligator child was advertised. Jack saw, as Peebles hurried away, that his severed finger was partly restored, like the arm of a starfish, and that Peebles peered at it two or three times before he disappeared through the door of the temple.

Jack stepped across to the booth that Peebles had hurried out of moments earlier. He pulled back the canvas door and looked in, seeing in the light of an oil lamp a man bent over a makeshift desk, reading a book with his face a half inch above the page, as if he were straining to see it at all. It took a moment for Jack to realize that it was Dr. Brown sitting there, but the lank hair and the bullet scar across his cheek gave him away when he looked up. He grimaced first, then grinned, and asked, "Do you want something?" in a voice that suggested the man's certainty that Jack indeed *wanted* something, whatever it might be.

He seemed to have fleshed out considerably since Jack had seen him on the bluffs the day before. He wasn't half so— what?—transparent, maybe, and not half so shriveled. He was still pale, as if lit with the silver reflected light of the moon rather than with yellow lantern light, and his face was drawn and haggard with lines that expressed unspeakable emotions. He wore his black topcoat and a black cravat, and his hair hung black and oily about his collar and stooped shoulders, and even as he sat placidly smiling, his hunched shadow darkening the canvas behind him, it seemed to Jack as if he might easily be a great feathery crow.

There was a strange litter of debris behind and around him: packing crates heaped with yellowing carnival posters, kegs of iron gears and flywheels and bolts, and toppled stacks of books, all of them old and half ruined, with pages thrust out and covers soiled and torn. A smell of iron filings and gear oil mingled with the musty smell of old damp books and the sawdust that covered the weedy dirt floor to the depth of an inch.

Jack shook his head in answer to the man's question. He was certain, suddenly, that he was confronting Algernon Harbin, the man his father had shot to death twelve years earlier. There couldn't be much doubt, all in all, not when you added up everything Dr. Jensen and Willoughby had said. And the bullet scar. It made Jack almost glad to see it. By what unholy means the man had contrived to return from the sea and become the proprietor of the Solstice carnival, it was impossible to say, and it didn't make much difference anyway. Jack knew at once that he didn't want to kill the man. He didn't want to kill anyone. He just wanted to be rid of him, that and know what it was the man had come back for.

Jack thought suddenly of the bottle in his pocket, but stopped himself from patting it with his hand. The doctor must have read his fear in his eyes, though, for he smiled at Jack and nodded his head, as if to say, I know. I'll take it when I please.

Jack backed out into the sunlight. Skeezix and Helen had gone on. He glanced behind him at the Moorish Temple, from which issued the sound of flutes being played to the accompaniment of wailing, and there was Peebles, watching him from behind the door, darting back into the darkness when Jack caught sight of him.

He found his two friends in the shadow of the Ferris wheel. He told them what it was he'd figured out about the supposed Dr. Brown of World Renown. Helen said it didn't surprise her a bit. The only thing that surprised her was that it had taken Jack so long to see it. Skeezix said he didn't care *who* Dr. Brown or anyone else was, not until they cared about *him*. Jack's problem, said Skeezix, was to think that he was involved in some great plot. Which was all vanity, quite likely. There weren't any plots, as far as Skeezix could see; that would make things too easy, you could guess everything out. "My advice," said Skeezix, nodding shrewdly at Jack, "is to open that bottle of liquor you've been hiding and give each of us a taste."

Jack shook his head. The idea seemed too risky to him, for reasons he couldn't entirely put his finger on. The bottle certainly wouldn't contain poison, after all, else why would he have been given it in the first place? And why would Dr. Brown, or whatever his name was, have been skulking around trying to steal it? And is that entirely why it was that Jack had brought the bottle with him, to prevent its being stolen? He could as easily have hidden it in the woods. It would have been safer there than in his pocket, despite what he'd told himself that morning. He'd brought it because somewhere in his mind was the idea of doing exactly what Skeezix suggested they do.

He looked around, startled all of a sudden to find himself surrounded by milling people. "I don't know . . ." he said to Skeezix, and Helen nodded her head, as if to say that she didn't know either. Skeezix, in reply, hastened across to a man selling cider, bought a cup, and stepped back across, grinning at Jack.

"Nothing ventured . . ." he said, nodding at the cup.

"Don't," Helen said. "There's trouble in this. Dr. Jensen would tell you to pour it down the drain."

"Dr. Jensen would drink the whole bottle and set sail in a shoe," said Skeezix. "We're not asking *you* to be in on this. We'll scout it out first, and if it's safe we'll tell you." Skeezix smiled benignly at her and patted her on the shoulder in a fatherly way. Helen immediately slugged him in the arm and said he was an idiot. She wasn't going, no matter what he said to her. Skeezix insisted that he didn't *want* her to go. She was like a little sister to him, he said, and must be kept from harm. There were some pony rides, he said, that might interest her, and then he gave her a dime and two nickels, winked, and nodded once again at Jack and the cup. Helen dropped the three coins into the cider and insisted that she *was* going. She wasn't going to drink any of Jack's elixir; she was going along sober, to act as a sort of sea anchor when Jack and Skeezix lost their minds.

Jack unstopped the bottle and dribbled a bit into the cider, looking around him guiltily as he did so. There was no sign of Peebles or of Dr. Brown. Skeezix wasn't happy with the small quantity of elixir, though it had stained the brown cider a seaweed green, but Jack wouldn't add another drop. Better too little than too much, it seemed to him. And in truth, he didn't want to waste it. He had no idea what it was or how he was intended to use it, or even if anyone *intended* anything at all. Jack and Skeezix shared the cider between them.

With the rush and whir of the Ferris wheel behind him and the ratchet click of the crank as it rotated the little cars one at a time across the boarding plank, Jack had already begun to feel giddy. He didn't half like heights, and he didn't at all like the feeling of falling. There was something in the carnival air, too, some sort of enchantment, that charged it with the uncanny feeling of something pending, as if Jack and his friends, even while they were standing there in the sawdust handing the cup back and forth, were rushing toward something, or perhaps as if something—a train or a sea wave or a leaf-laden autumn wind—was rushing toward *them*. They waited in line to board the Ferris wheel, neither Jack nor Skeezix feeling anything more than that.

It seemed to Jack that it took about three quarters of an hour for the Ferris wheel to make a single revolution. They jerked upward, stopped, swung there, then jerked upward again. The little car seemed to sway and buck with every gust of sea wind. Skeezix found the swaying and swinging invigorating, somehow, and he set in to make the most of it, leaning back and forth and hooting with laughter until with each swing it seemed to Jack as if he were about to pitch straight out onto the ant people that milled around miles below. A little iron bar had been closed across their knees. The man operating the wheel had tugged on it and nodded, as if *he* was satisfied that all was safe and tidy. The bar didn't amount to anything as far as Jack could see, beyond some sort of vague joke, and so he held on to the structure of the Ferris wheel itself with his right hand, and put his left arm around behind Helen, grinning at her weakly in an effort to make it seem as if he were merely trying to make her comfortable.

Under better circumstances he would have liked almost nothing better—sitting there like that with his arm around Helen. But he knew he looked pale. He *felt* pale, if such a thing were possible. He flipped Skeezix on the ear with his middle finger and then grimaced at him behind Helen's head when Skeezix looked at him accusingly. Skeezix grinned and rocked the car again, giving Jack a heightened eyebrow look, as if he were surprised that Jack wanted even more rocking.

"Hey!" shouted Helen, and she hit Skeezix on the chest,

after which he calmed down, satisfied to make a horrified face every time the car canted forward.

Helen shouted again. When Skeezix began to complain that he hadn't done anything, she told him to shut up and pointed out toward the ocean. They'd risen high enough to see over the oaks and alders that lined the bluffs. The ocean was a deep translucent green, like bottle glass. Spindrift flew from the tumbling peaks of little wind waves, and the ground swell humped along beneath, rolling in to break continually along the cliffs and coves, sounding like the booming rush of an express train.

Out on the sea, tossing on the swell, rode the shoe sailboat of Dr. Jensen. It pitched and yawed unsteadily, waves breaking across the toe and laces and threatening on the moment to swamp the boat entirely and send it to the bottom of the sea. Dr. Jensen bailed furiously, holding onto the sheet, his hair blowing about his head. The wind billowed the sail, jerking the sheet from his hand, and at first it seemed as if he would go after it, but he didn't. He gave up on the sail, which flapped and danced in the wind's eye as if giddy with freedom.

He bailed with both hands now, his craft lying dangerously low in the water. The wind and current pushed him southeast, back toward the cove where Skeezix had found the shoe two nights earlier. The three on the Ferris wheel watched him anxiously. There was nothing any of them could do to help. It was Dr. Jensen's affair entirely. He could swim, at least, and he wasn't any more than three hundred yards offshore, and with the current sweeping around toward the cove there . . . Jack wasn't half as worried about Dr. Jensen's fate as he was worried about his own just then. He knew that to be uncharitable, but the knowledge didn't at all change the way he felt, and it was what he was feeling as the car looped around the summit of the arc that made all the difference.

They plummeted toward the green of the meadow. Jack's stomach leaped in a giddy rush toward his chest. He crushed at the seat back with his left hand and gritted his teeth, certain that at any moment the car would rock too far forward and he'd slide out into the open air. He pressed himself back against the leather of the seat cushion and held his breath as the car swooped round past the grinning operator, started to rise once again, and then jerked to a stop and hung there. The business of unloading and loading cars began again, and they ratcheted up one lurch at a time toward the summit. Jack's grip relaxed. He forced a smile and aimed it at Helen, happy in spite of himself to see that her smile was forced too. Only Skeezix seemed to be enjoying himself, although he had lost, apparently, his inclination toward tilting them all out of the car.

They swung skyward. There was Dr. Jensen again—closer to shore now, still bailing. He was in among the kelp beds; the wind chop had died, and the swell was broad and oily. He'd make it in. Jack was happy about it, but he wasn't so happy that the doctor's journey had been in vain. He had rather hoped that Dr. Jensen would find what he was looking for.

Skeezix reached across Helen and tapped Jack on the chest. He pointed off toward the northeast, toward the Moonvale Hills. The twilight sky seemed watery deep, like the sea, and it shone with pinpoint stars that flickered and winked like eyes in a dark wood. It seemed to Jack that he'd never really gotten a good look at the Moonvale Hills before—never from that height. Willoughby's farm, it's true, was on a rise some ways above the village, which itself was several hundred feet higher than the bluffs. Add to that the height of the barn loft, and it would seem that he *must* have viewed the hills from even greater heights a thousand times. Perhaps it was the curious angle of vision here, or perhaps it was that the sea wind had scoured the sky particularly clean and he was simply seeing things clearly for the first time.

There seemed to be the shadow of a city there again—the same city, it seemed, that MacWilt had been searching for the previous evening. There was the spire of a church steeple, sloped roofs and steep walls, inns and alleyways. It was all merely a darkness against the hilly horizon, like smoke, hovering there in phantom billows. Helen saw it too. It wasn't the elixir. It sharpened and seemed to set, the smoky shadows turning to stone, shingles and leaves etching themselves into the gray curtain.

The Ferris wheel soared over the top, and Jack held on and closed his eyes as it swept downward this time. There was no more stopping to let on passengers. They dropped in a giddy rush into the peanut and sawdust smell of the bluffs. Jack opened his eyes. There was no use looking so obviously frightened. He glanced at Helen, who stared straight ahead of herself as if she were studying some distant spot in the landscape. Skeezix looked past both of them in horror, mouth gaping. Jack swiveled around, following Skeezix's gaze. There was the ride operator with his hand resting on the iron lever. He grinned at them past gumless teeth. His hair hung like seaweed around his shoulders, and the skin of his face was drawn and leathery like the skin of a mummified corpse. He winked. Jack heard Helen mutter *"Really,"* as if she were half insulted by his being familiar, and as they swung skyward she said, "I wish he'd quit giving me that look. I can't stand that sort of thing."

"Neither can I," Jack said truthfully, understanding that this time Helen hadn't seen what he and Skeezix had seen.

There was the city again, sharper now, its streets and alleys defined, windows swung open to let in the thin morning sunlight, the dim shades of what must have been people wending their way through the twisting streets. Jack half recognized the pattern of alleys and roads and streets, the short pier that stretched out into a sea of sky. There seemed to be a cut in the hills now, a valley that opened out into the oak trees of the foothills running down into the sea and into Rio Dell. It became a cobbled road.

"Fancy a road through the woods there," said Skeezix with an air of disbelief.

"What road?" asked Helen.

"There on the meadow, leading into the hills. Are you blind?"

"I don't see any road," said Helen.

"I do," said Jack. "But I don't understand it. Maybe we should follow it while we can still see it. Let's get Dr. Jensen from the beach. He'll come along."

But the Ferris wheel spun them dizzily around again. Dr. Jensen was out of sight beyond the cliffs. The music of a dozen distant noises played in Jack's head. He waited for the city to reappear, and it did. It seemed fearfully distant, as if it didn't really sit on the Moonvale Hills at all, but on some point in space far beyond them, as if Jack saw it through a powerful telescope and that, combined with its enormous size, made it seem close by, as if walking along that cobbled road to its gate was a matter of an afternoon outing.

The noises of the carnival faded until Jack could hear only the muted echo of the calliope and the distant boom of the oven and the *skreek* and catch of iron rubbing against iron. He felt as if he were rushing toward something, or perhaps as if something were rushing toward him—a shadow in a dream, a wolf in the woods. It seemed as if he were both the pursued and the pursuer, and he was struck with the wild notion that he was chasing death, closing in on it, swinging toward it in his Ferris-wheel car as it soared again over the top of the little circle of sea air it circumnavigated. The rushing sensation heightened and he could hear the hiss of releasing steam, the clatter and clank of iron wheels, the airy scream of a train whistle that sounded as if it fled toward him across distant wooded hillsides.

Then there was the whirling meadow again, the thousands of people like splashes of paint on a canvas. Jack watched for the ride operator, hoping he wouldn't see what he saw before but far too curious, too caught up in his journeying, to look the other way. The man was gone. Dr. Brown stood in his place, Skeezix's empty cider cup in his hand. He seemed to be sniffing at it, his eyes half squinted shut. He looked up, nodding at Jack as their car tilted past.

They lurched to a stop, one car back from the platform. The sounds of the morning meadow returned in a rush. Jack shook the muddle out of his head. The Ferris wheel revolved a notch, then stopped again. Dr. Brown was emptying the cars. He paused for a moment and ran his finger around the bottom of the cup, licking the liquid slowly, savoring it, studying it. He pulled on the lever and up they went. Then again.

The city in the hills had begun to dim. The road wasn't a road any longer. It was a stream bed lined with polished stones. The water in it seemed to evaporate, all at once, and the rocks in the stream bed were white in the sun. Then they were dust that faded into the green of winter hillsides. The car teetered at the very top of the wheel. Skeezix didn't seem interested in rocking it, or in foolery of any sort.

There was a shout from below, and in a moment, before any of the three of them could make out what had happened, the masses of people milling about the carnival had shifted and moved toward the bluffs. Those at the front of the crowd broke into a run. People shoved and hollered. Some stood still and shook their heads. Jack heard someone call for a rope, and a half dozen people disappeared over the edge of the cliff, climbing down toward the sea.

Dr. Brown levered them down another notch. Jack could see the top of his oily head and the sloppily tied bandage around his arm. He was watching the cliffs too; that was clear. Passengers clambered off and set out in the wake of the rest of the crowd. The rope was brought. A man tied it to a tree, and a hundred hands helped him fling it over the edge of the cliff. Someone climbed back up. The Ferris wheel dropped. Jack wanted to pull his legs in, as if he were dangling them off the edge of a low pier into a shark-infested lagoon. He imagined withered hands clutching at his feet; he could picture the pale face of Dr. Brown, swinging up onto a level with his own, then towering above him as he sat with his legs pinioned by the bar across his knees.

Dr. Brown had set the cup down. His hand fell from the lever and he took a few steps toward the cliffs as if contemplating something. The people in the car below Jack shouted at him to let them down too, but he seemed not to hear them.

"Look!" cried Helen, pointing away up the coast. There, trudging wearily along toward the carnival, up the dusty Coast Road toward the arched mouth of the carnival, was Dr. Jensen.

Jack hoorayed with joy. Skeezix pounded him one on the arm, easily as happy as Jack for reasons he couldn't entirely explain. Dr. Brown jerked around and looked back at them, as if he were suspicious that they might have disappeared, and then he turned and looked up the Coast Road himself, past the lines of canvas tents and plywood lean-tos. He seemed to slump just a bit and he ground his fist into his hand. Then he limped away toward his tent, leaving four Ferris-wheel cars full of complaining people behind.

The next ten minutes were a confusion of tangled activity. Jack climbed down from the car. Skeezix wouldn't. He'd wait, he said. But the comparatively solid scaffolding of the Ferris wheel attracted Jack, who had had enough by then of dislocated swinging. He waved at Helen from the ground, as if to tell her that everything was all right. He'd let them all down, one at a time. She waved back while Skeezix grimaced at him, screwing up his face and thumbing his nose. Jack hauled on the lever, surprised to see a shower of rust flakes scatter across his shoe. The first cart creaked down and two girls jumped off, immediately racing away toward the cliffs. He pulled on the lever again. It seemed to need oil; it was bent and stiff. The carnival wasn't as fresh and tidy as he'd thought it to be; it was old and tired, and the atmosphere of gaiety and color was a figment—an illusion built of calliope music and paint and milling people.

In a moment his friends stood beside him. Skeezix fell to

his knees and kissed the ground theatrically. Dr. Jensen waved at them, then cut across the meadow toward the crowds lining the cliffs. The mass of people parted. The rope was hauled in like an enormous fishing line. A body was tied to the other end, the rope looped under its arms. It bumped over the edge of the cliffs and across the grass and wildflowers. Dr. Jensen set out at a run. Jack bolted along with Helen, and Skeezix puffed along behind them.

"It's Lantz!" Helen shouted.

Jack knew she was right. The buzz of the crowd diminished. They caught up with Dr. Jensen. The meadow fell silent but for the calliope and the oven, like the sounds of the blood coursing through the veins of the empty carnival. There sounded from overhead the cawing of a crow, and Jack looked up to see the distant black bird above them in the sky, circling once out over the sea and then doubling back, dwindling in the east.

8

"THERE WAS A SLIDE last evening," one man was saying, shaking his head and talking past his pipe. It was Dawson, the vintner. "Lots of the boy's trash down there, caught up among the rocks and scrub. Stuffed birds and such. He was in among 'em. Fell, I guess, along with his shack. Must have washed him right down the hill while he slept. Dirty shame, that's what I say. He didn't have but one oar in the water, but he was all right. Better than some I could name."

With the help of two other men Jack didn't know, Dawson laid Lantz's body beneath an oak. The vintner had been the first to see him there, tangled in the roots and branches of cliffside brush. He pulled his pipe out of his mouth with one hand and dusted his pants with the other, shaking his head. "White as a fish, ain't he?" There were murmurs of assent.

The statement, though, didn't half describe the ghostly pallor of Lantz's skin. It was almost transparent, and it seemed to Jack, who had pushed to the front of the crowd with Dr. Jensen, that he could see the yellow-white outline of Lantz's skeleton through the veil of silvery flesh. Dr. Jensen lifted Lantz's head and parted his hair. He shook his own head. Lantz's shirt was torn, although that didn't suggest much, since Lantz seemed to have preferred torn, lacy-thin shirts and trousers to the newer clothes that Mrs. Jensen left for him. He was scraped and cut from his tumble down the bluffs, but the papery-white skin, although chafed and torn and dirty, was bloodless. Here and there, mostly on his fingers and across his forehead, his skin seemed gray, as if the flesh beneath it were faintly charred.

"It ain't hardly natural, is it?" asked the vintner half under his breath. "Rain washed all the blood off but didn't touch the dirt." Dr. Jensen looked at him and shook his head again minutely. The crowd gaped and craned their necks, trying to assess exactly how awful the tragedy had been so they could tell the story appropriately later. Most of those to the rear, who had tired of leaping and asking futile questions, had gone back to the carnival, and when Dr. Jensen threw his coat over the body and Dawson the vintner jogged off to get his wagon, people drifted away in twos and threes until only a half dozen remained. Peebles was there. Jack hadn't seen him in the crowd, but he'd no doubt been there all along, watching. He continued to peer at the corpse, as if he could see it through the coat, and he rubbed his hands together nervously until he noticed that Skeezix was staring in horror at his newly sprouted finger.

He cast Skeezix a withering look and started to speak.

"Get out of here," Skeezix said.

"I'll—" began Peebles.

Skeezix rushed at him, slamming him in the shoulder with his open palm and grabbing a handful of his jacket. Peebles reeled and then jerked up straight as Skeezix brought his free hand back, fist clenched.

Dr. Jensen leaped in, caught Skeezix around the shoulders, and hauled him away. Peebles followed, his jacket still clutched in Skeezix's fist, his arms flailing, a look of terror in his eyes. He made a mewling sound which sickened Jack—not the sound of honest fright but of something cracked, broken, demented. Jack would gladly have seen Skeezix hit him. There was something in Peebles's regard for Lantz's corpse that oughtn't to have been there. Jack felt like hitting something himself, and Peebles was the closest thing worth hitting. There had been something in Peebles's eyes that had suggested he'd had a hand in Lantz's death. Lantz hadn't slid down any cliff in the night. He'd been pushed, maybe, but he hadn't slid. He'd been in town and at the carnival. Dr. Jensen knew that. Peebles knew that. Jack was sure that Peebles knew a great deal.

Skeezix let loose of Peebles's jacket and stood glaring at him, clenching and unclenching his fists. Dr. Jensen wedged himself between them to fend Skeezix off. Peebles, in a venomous rush, spit first at Dr. Jensen, then, in a single move, bent around him and spit at Skeezix, leaping away down the Coast Road before Skeezix could push past the doctor. Jack turned to follow Skeezix, who bolted after Peebles, but Dr. Jensen caught his arm and held on. "Let them go," he said.

Jack looked round at Helen, who sat on a fallen log by Lantz's body. Then he glanced into Dr. Jensen's face. The doctor gave him a look that suggested there was more in this than met the eye; it was the look of a conspirator. Dawson rattled up in his wagon then, braked it, and climbed down, and the four of them lifted Lantz onto the bed. Skeezix trudged back up the Coast Road toward them, Peebles having outdistanced him. Jack could have caught Peebles, but what was the use? What would they do, beat him up because the look in his eye suggested his guilt? That wouldn't do. They picked up Skeezix on the way back to town, the carnival forgotten for the moment.

Dawson stroked his chin nervously and stood a good two feet back from the table on which lay Lantz's body, half covered by a sheet. It seemed as if he didn't at all like the look of what he saw. He was out of his depth, he told Dr. Jensen. The medical arts were a mystery to him—a closed book. He'd sewed up his arm one time when he'd sliced it open with a fishing knife, but that was the extent of his doctoring. But he was as curious as the next man, and maybe, taken all the way around, he had the right to know.

There wasn't any sign on Lantz's body of a blow that might have killed him. He hadn't been shot or stabbed; he hadn't fractured his skull tumbling down the bluffs. But he was soft all over, like a pudding, Skeezix might have said, if any of them, including Skeezix, were in the mood for such a thing.

"Reminds me of what they call 'the last press' in my business," said Dawson, as if having failed to understand the phenomenon in medical terms he was having a go at it from the vintner's point of view.

"I'm not familiar with wine making," said Dr. Jensen grimly. "What is a 'last press'?"

"It's getting out—what is it?—the *essences*, you might say. The remainders. Pressing out the skins when it seems there ain't nothing left. And when you're done, there ain't, either. This boy looks pressed out to me. But I ain't no doctor, as I said. Something's done away with his blood, though, hasn't it?"

"More than that." Dr. Jensen peered at Lantz's scalp line through a heavy magnifying glass. "It's like his nerves have incandesced. I'd swear he was burnt up from within, if such a thing were possible, which it's not."

Dawson widened his eyes and shrugged, as if to suggest that there were things in the world that ought not to be possible but were possible anyway.

"Lantz rode the Ferris wheel for hours last night," said Jack, feeling half like a fool. Lantz's riding the Ferris wheel couldn't conceivably explain his condition, and yet it seemed to Jack that it must. And this was no time to conceal things, no matter how they made you feel. At least it wasn't the time to conceal much. He'd keep the bottle of elixir hidden, of course. He'd reveal it to Dr. Jensen if he thought the doctor might want to share it, but he was fairly sure that the doctor would suggest pouring it down the sink.

"How do you know?" asked Dr. Jensen, suspecting, perhaps, that Jack himself had spent some time at the carnival last night and not at all liking the idea of it.

"I saw him through the loft window. It might not have been him, but I *think* it was. He went off in that direction after the business with the crow. We told you about that. I watched him with my telescope hours later—early morning, actually."

Dr. Jensen nodded, as if it seemed reasonable, taken all the way around. Then, abruptly, he drew the sheet over Lantz's face and set in to wash his hands in the basin. "I don't know what's going on here," he said, not looking at anyone, "but I'll tell you that what happened to our friend Lantz is the same thing that happened to the man I found in the tide pool yesterday." He turned around now and looked particularly at Jack. "Here we have the Solstice, the carnival, and all the rest of it—you kids know as much about it as I do, maybe more. It can't all be coincidence. That's what I say. Watch out for that carnival. Watch out for Dr. Brown. Watch out for crows, for goodness' sake. The Solstice peaks in two days. If I were you I'd lay low. Spend some time reading. In the library. If you go about the village, go together. Don't get caught out alone. And give up your silly ideas about the Mrs. Langley business. At best you'll just get wet."

He cinched up his trousers with that, the cuffs of which were still soaked with seawater. White smudges of salt spray had dried on them, and his shoes were dark and wet. His hair, combed by the wind, looked as if someone had been at it with a harrow. He must be grievously tired, and rightly so, thought Jack, suddenly sorry for the doctor. He'd set out that morning with a destination, and not the corner market either. It had been a destination unthinkably vast and colorful and mysterious, with unmapped shores and heaven alone knew what sorts of dreams, waiting to come true. And here he was, cold and wet and itchy with dried salt, dead tired and knee deep in the mire of other people's worries.

Still and all, Mrs. Jensen was glad to have him back. She couldn't keep the evidence of it out of her eyes when she'd seen them ride up on the wagon, until the sight of Lantz lying there dead had obliterated it. It could as easily have been the doctor himself lying in the wagon. He'd gone out on the same errand that Lantz had pursued, hadn't he? And wasn't Jack headed straightaway down that same road, a road that lay golden in the sun, across the grassy meadow and into the foothills? He and Skeezix had seen it, and he and Skeezix would walk along it before they were through. Helen too.

Everyone filed out the door to see Dawson off, leaving Jack

alone with Lantz. He reached for the sheet, to have one last look at Lantz's face, regretting all the chances he'd had to make things a bit easier for his friend but had passed by. There had always been tomorrow, hadn't there? He fingered the hem of the sheet but didn't lift it. There was no use. It wasn't Lantz who lay beneath it any more. What had been Lantz had seeped into the air above the bluffs last night, had been breathed by the dwindling carnival. He shook his head. That was nonsense, wasn't it? There was no use *inventing* horrors, the world was full of enough of them as it was.

On the counter, beyond the basin, was no end of empty jars and vials and glass tubes. Jack stepped across and looked at them. He pulled the vial of elixir out of his pocket. There were two inches of the green liquor inside. He could afford to part with half of it. Pulling the stopper out of an empty little bottle from the shelf, he unstopped his own vial and tilted it over the mouth of the empty bottle. A scraping sounded at the door—someone coming in. He corked his vial and shoved it into his pocket, then put the empty back onto the shelf and pretended to look at a sidewise heap of books. Dr. Jensen strode back in and stopped abruptly inside the threshold. He wrinkled up his nose, gave Jack a look, started to speak, thought better of it, and sat down heavily in a chair. The smell of the elixir hung in the air of the room. Jack nodded at Mrs. Jensen, who followed the doctor. Then he slid out and joined his friends, the three of them walking away in silence toward the harbor.

"What's to do?" asked Skeezix, kicking a stone along in front of him as they walked.

"Kill time," said Jack.

"Seems like we're waiting for something, doesn't it? Waiting for something to happen. That's what killing time is all about. Maybe we have to *make* it happen. Chase this thing down."

Helen gave Skeezix a look. Obviously she wasn't keen on "chasing things down," whatever Skeezix meant by it.

"There's probably nothing to chase down. Or if there is, it isn't what you think. You probably won't want to catch it if you see it. MacWilt isn't happy with what he saw. Dr. Jensen said to keep out of it, and he's right."

"Huh!" said Skeezix. "Dr. Jensen sailed out of the harbor in a shoe. Where was *he* going? Fishing? When he takes his own advice I'll listen to him. What does Mrs. Langley say about it?"

"Mrs. Langley talks about her dead dog, mostly, and about a haircut she got at Miss Pinkum's that made her look like a fool. She can't forgive Miss Pinkum."

"I mean in the book," said Skeezix.

"Oh, the *book*. Not much. I haven't read it all, mind you, but it's mostly one of those books that avoids saying anything in particular by being very abstract. Mrs. Langley was full of philosophy and mysticism. Most of it's a mess, I think. She's never actually been there as far as I can tell. There's mention of roads and rivers, but all very allegorical. Not a specific road, like the one you two claim to have seen."

"We don't *claim* anything—" began Skeezix.

"Let's walk out to the hills," Jack interrupted. Somewhere against the back of his mind, like an afterimage on the inside of his eyelids, the road he'd seen from the top of the Ferris wheel still meandered across the meadows.

"What for?" asked Helen.

"The road," said Jack. "There's probably nothing there now, but there might be. Some sign. Something."

"Of course there might be," said Skeezix. "We've *got* to see; And there's nothing better to do, is there?"

Helen shook her head. She had the look of someone who was skeptical of Jack and Skeezix's road.

"Oh, *you* didn't see the road," said Skeezix theatrically. "That's right; you were the sea anchor. Well, Jack and I saw it well enough, leading up toward the Moonvale Hills. Both of us did. If only one of us had seen it, it wouldn't count. But there's something there, all right, even though it faded. We could find it, I bet."

"Of course we could find it," said Jack.

"*You* can find it all you want. *I'm* going back to Miss Flees's. Don't be stupid."

Skeezix shrugged at her, as if to say he didn't care what she did, but as for him, he was the sort who took risks, stupid or otherwise. "All I want is the treasure," he said, after which he turned up the alley that led past Mrs. Oglevy's orchard and then out over the Tumbled Bridge and into the hills. Helen didn't take the bait. She said, "So long," and walked away up the High Street.

"What treasure?" asked Jack. "I didn't see any treasure."

"Neither did I," said Skeezix, laughing. "Helen will worry about it all afternoon, though. I wouldn't be surprised if she got halfway back to Miss Flees's and then turned around and followed us."

Jack trudged along in silence. He hoped Skeezix was right. He'd rather have Helen along. And what with Dr. Brown skulking about the village and Miss Flees necromancing and Peebles hating them all, the three of them ought to stick together. Dr. Jensen had advised that too.

It was a half hour's easy walk to the hills. The sky was blue and white with scattered clouds, and the meadow was patched with moving shadows. The air was silent but for the distant cawing of crows in the almond orchards below the bridge. They could hear their own footsteps and the sound of their own breathing, and the few times that they spoke, the conversation languished at once and fell off again into silence.

Jack didn't like the crows, not at all. There seemed to be some safety in there being dozens of them—it was a single crow they feared—but then Dr. Brown could easily enough hide himself among them—supposing, that is, that Dr. Brown could turn himself into a crow. Willoughby and Dr. Jensen supposed he could; that was certain. They'd shot him— winged him was the word, perhaps. Dr. Brown's arm hadn't been bandaged yesterday, but at the carnival that morning it was.

They watched the ground once they were out onto the

meadow and climbing into the hills. What they were looking for they didn't know: something, anything that signified. The meadow grasses and wildflowers were high and green, though, rising above their waists, blowing back and forth in the wind like sea waves. Jack climbed into the branches of a nearly lifeless oak in order to "spy out the country" as Skeezix termed it. But from his perch he saw nothing that reminded him of roads, or of stream beds either. There was a movement near the Tumbled Bridge: a slash of blue and white that was gone as soon as he saw it—Mrs. Oglevy, quite likely, out beating her almond trees with a rubber mallet.

He could see landmarks, such as they were, that he remembered from the Ferris wheel, although now he was looking at them from the other side and from a different angle. Somehow, from the dizzy height of the Ferris wheel, nothing had seemed quite so distant as it proved to be now. A stand of trees that had appeared to be a couple hundred yards from, say, an outcropping of decomposing granite now was closer to a quarter mile from it. And the bank of stone that traced a little fault line, along which a hill had slid in an earthquake some distant time ago, didn't seem to point straight toward the north at all but toward the southeast now, as if it had shifted around cunningly in the last hour so as to confuse the two of them.

"Give it up," said Jack when he climbed down again. "Helen was right. There's nothing out here anyway, except the wind and the grass."

But Skeezix was already hiking up the hill toward another stand of oaks, and so Jack followed him, knowing that in truth it wasn't results Skeezix wanted so much as the quiet and the empty desolation of the foothills. With the coming of the carnival, the cove wasn't empty enough for him—too many strollers and shell collectors. Skeezix poked at the ground with a stick, overturning stones, ferreting out clues. He found a broken penknife and a bit of cloth and an empty bottle that had turned purple in the sun. He held the bottle to his eye and peered through it, as if through the distorting lens of its heavy concave bottom he might see what it was he was searching for. "Somebody's following us," he said, turning around and continuing his walking.

"Blue shirt, maybe?"

"Yes. He's down along the creek, angling up through the willows so as not to be seen."

"He?"

"I don't know. No, of course not. It's Helen. Didn't she have a blue jacket on a white shirt?"

"I believe she did," said Jack, who couldn't absolutely recall what it was Helen had been wearing. But it sounded right. "Let's wait for her."

"Let her catch up." Skeezix walked farther along, more slowly now, though.

"We can wait at the hilltop," Jack said, anxious, actually, to get a glimpse of the countryside from a more elevated point. Already they could see far enough to make out the edge of the Eel River delta, fanning out toward Ferndale and Sunnybrae. And there was the carnival, down on the bluffs—not so big now at all, just a scattering of tents and sheds and a half dozen creaking rides. Smoke from the oven rose above it and was blown to nothing in the wind. Surely from the top of the hill, thought Jack, they'd see even more clearly the land laid out below them, revealed all at once, nothing hidden from view.

"Look here," said Skeezix suddenly. He bent and poked at the ground with his stick. The grass had thinned and now sprouted in tufts from sandy soil, as if it were growing out of a river bottom long ago gone dry. Round, bleached stones like enormous eggs lay half buried among the grass tufts. The old stream bed was some fifteen feet across and meandered upward toward a cleft in the hills. They followed it, forgetting about Helen, stooping now and then to unearth bits of metal trash: an old railroad spike, bent and rusted; a blunt pickax with a bit of twisted oak limb shoved through it and wedged with a sliver of obsidian; a button cut from abalone shell as broad as Jack's hand. There were fossils in the stones, like sepia-toned paintings, and there were little spiral seashells scattered in the sand as if they'd lain there half a million years.

But it was the button that interested them—Dr. Jensen would want that. It drew them into the hills that closed around them, blocking out the sight of the bluffs and the ocean and then, after they'd rounded behind the first of the hills, of the village too and of the bridge and Mrs. Oglevy's orchards. It was then that Jack remembered Helen. He stopped Skeezix, both of them agreeing to climb out of the stream bed and up the hillside to wait for her. They'd be able to see her from up there, no doubt, and wave their jackets at her or something to attract her attention.

Skeezix was sweating despite the ocean wind, and he huffed and puffed as he talked, stopping every six or eight steps to rest. "Do you know," he said, "I don't think these are river rocks at all. Not most of them."

Jack shrugged and climbed on.

"They're cobblestones is what they are. This is the road we saw. I'd bet on it. This giant button proves it. Let's drink some more of your elixir—just a taste—and see what we see. I bet it'll be a road."

"Let's not," said Jack, thinking suddenly in the lonesome, windy silence that Helen made a very good sea anchor indeed. "Let's wait for Helen before we do anything. Do you see her?"

"No. I don't see anybody. Wait. Yes, I do. Down there among the trees."

Jack looked where Skeezix pointed. There was a long line of oaks, stretched out almost in a single file, then muddling up into a stand of alder that bordered the woods edging the meadows. There was the blue again, moving through the trees. Something about it was strange. It wasn't Helen. He was sure of it. It was someone hiding himself. But from whom? From them, obviously. If it were Helen she'd be in the open by now, probably yelling for them—mad that they hadn't waited. It was impossible to think she'd be skulking through the trees on the edge of the wood, not on a strange and empty afternoon like that.

Skeezix seemed to agree. "Who do you think it is?" He whispered it, as if suspicious that the sea breeze might carry his words down across the waving grasses.

"Not Helen," said Jack. "And not Dr. Jensen. He was done in when we left."

Whoever it was drew closer. They'd lose sight of him in a moment if he kept on along the woods, and he'd come out just on the other side of the hill adjacent to theirs, where they couldn't see him. No doubt he was harmless—someone out strolling, taking advantage of the few hours of sunshine. Jack told himself so. Somehow the whole business of the Solstice was getting to him. He was seeing things when there wasn't anything to see. He was suspicious, suddenly, of everything. Skeezix was too. Jack could see it on his face.

"Let's go," said Jack, standing up. "We're doing nothing out here but spooking ourselves."

Skeezix shook his head and held the button aloft. "We found this. Imagine what else we might find when we get back up into the hills. Maybe it's the curious Dr. Brown." He nodded toward the woods, where, for the moment, nothing at all could be seen except the shadowy trees.

Jack shivered. "Maybe," he said, recalling the look on the carnival owner's face when he'd run his finger around the cider cup and tasted the result. Then he remembered Lantz, white and dead as the stones of the stream bed. "I say we head west. We can hit the Coast Road where it winds inland beyond Table Bluffs Beach. There's always someone on the road. We can catch a ride into town on a wagon."

"I mean to see where this stream comes from," said Skeezix. "I'll go alone if you don't want to. It won't be much farther, one way or another. We could hike across the hills to Moonvale before dark, if we had to, and spend the night there. I've got enough money for dinner."

Jack wasn't fond of the idea. But then he couldn't leave Skeezix out in the hills alone either, especially not with someone abroad in the woods like that. "Let's get at it, then. I won't go as far as Moonvale, though, even if the stream *does* lead us in that direction."

They set out again, scrambling through the scree along the edge of the hill and down onto the stream bed. It wound along through the little valleys separating the hills, now widening, now narrowing, now disappearing beneath the grass only to reappear a hundred feet farther up where the soil was sandy enough to make the grasses sparse. It would have been more to the point for them to climb a hill again and determine the general direction of the stream, and then head there straight-taway, instead of following around every loop and bend.

Skeezix wasn't satisfied with that though. If they'd found the giant button, he said, they'd find something else—maybe something that would lead them to conclusions. The sun fell in the sky, and the twilight on the horizon spread down to-ward them. Jack wondered if in Moonvale it was already eve-ning, perhaps had been all day, or whether the odd twilight shadowed their horizon too, and, if so, how far north and east a person would have to travel to catch up with it. Maybe you couldn't get there merely by traveling, by chasing it.

The afternoon grew almost hot back in among the hills. Flies buzzed around Jack's ears. The silence was complete. A cutaway hill loomed up on their right, angling out over the stream bed as if in the distant past the stream had undercut it, and now a little root-tangled triangle of hillside defied gravity by hovering there, shadowing the white sand and stones.

They heard the scrunch of the stick before they saw it, both of them standing at the edge of the stream bed where it wrapped around the hill. There was the sound of the stick shoving into the sand and gravel. Then the tip of it thrust into view, followed by MacWilt, whose eyes were wrapped in a single strip of black cloth.

Jack's feet seemed to root themselves to the stream bed. Skeezix's face was frozen in disbelief, staring at MacWilt's blue denim jacket, at the billowy white shirt misbuttoned beneath, its tattered tails half tucked in. The tavern keeper paused three feet away from them and sniffed the air. He cocked his head, leaning into the wind. A grin stiffened his face. There was something odious in the grin, malevolent. His head swiveled once back and forth, and his cheeks twitched and shivered.

Skeezix took a step backward, carefully, and drew himself up, ready to bolt. Jack set himself to follow. He could outrun a blind man; that much he knew. But then the idea of it struck him suddenly as ludicrous. Obviously MacWilt was still at it. He'd been struck blind when he'd peered through his telescope, but he'd seen enough to send him out on the same search that Jack and Skeezix were engaged in. MacWilt wasn't following them at all; they were simply bound for the same destination. He'd stuck to the edge of the forest because he could follow it blind. On the open meadow he'd be lost in an instant. Speak to him, Jack told himself. Say something—anything to break the silence. Jack opened his mouth just as Skeezix turned and ran, stumbling first in the soft gravelly sand, then howling away in a wild rush, hollering at Jack to follow. Before Jack could, before he could speak or straighten up, MacWilt's stick swung through the air and struck him on the shoulder.

"Hey!" Jack shouted, leaping back. "I didn't—" A shadow passed over the dry stream bed, and Jack looked up to see a single crow, high overhead, circling. MacWilt tugged at the bandage over his eyes, exposing nothing but white, and he threw his head back and craned his neck, as if there was some little corner of vision that he could find if he contorted himself sufficiently. He cursed, cut the air again with his stick, pulled the bandage back into place, felt the air with his free hand, and took a step in Jack's direction, holding his stick like a saber.

Jack leaped out into the open stream bed and faced

MacWilt. The man, surely, had made a mistake. The crow was a coincidence. A rock whistled past Jack's head and caught the blind man in the shoulder, half spinning him around. He shrieked and whirled back toward Jack, cursing and lunging. "Strike a blind man, will you?" he cried. "Help! Murder! Hit a poor blind man!" And then he stepped in neatly and cracked Jack across his right kneecap, hauling the stick back with both hands to hit him in the head. He bubbled with sudden laughter. The shadow of the crow passed overhead again.

MacWilt wasn't blind. He couldn't be blind. Jack knew that as he rolled away, the stick whistling past his ear. MacWilt cursed again and hobbled after him, holding his head up unnaturally. The cawing of the crow sounded nearby. Jack looked for it. There—in a dead tree along the stream bed. Another rock sailed past, chunking into the hillside. Skeezix appeared, crouched, scooping up a baseball-sized rock. He hefted it once and then threw it straight at MacWilt's head, but the old man shifted and ducked. He'd seen Skeezix throw it. Jack picked up a rock of his own and edged away toward Skeezix. MacWilt mumbled and chirped, talking to himself maybe. He reached under his coat and drew out a shiny blue gun. For one ludicrous second Jack thought it was a toy. Skeezix didn't make the same mistake. He turned wonderfully fast and dove into the bushes behind the hill. Jack threw his stone wildly as MacWilt aimed the pistol.

The blind man dodged to the side, Jack's stone sailing past his head. Jack heard it thunk the weedy gravel of the stream bed as his shoulder hit the sand and he rolled against the side of the hill. There was no place to hide, though. He couldn't burrow into the earth like a gopher. He smashed himself against the cutaway hillside, scrabbling for another rock to throw even as he turned to run. He angled across toward where Skeezix had disappeared, and he shouted as he ran without thinking about it, maybe so that he wouldn't hear the crack of the gun when it fired.

He heard it anyway, over the shouting. The bullet zinged

against the granite ledge beside him, and he dove into waist-high weeds, rolling away down the little valley between two hills. There was a shout and a curse behind him, and Skeezix hollering his name. He stopped and turned, expecting to see MacWilt, head canted, stumbling after him with a smoking pistol.

The tavern keeper reeled like a drunken man, throwing his pistol into the brush, prodding the air with his stick, waving his free hand. "Wait!" he shouted. "Don't leave me here! Hello!" He *was* blind now, disoriented. Skeezix dropped from the edge of the hill above, wrenched the stick from the man's hand, and threw it end over end up the brush-covered hillside. Jack leaped back toward the two of them. Skeezix crawled in the weeds on his hands and knees, looking for something—MacWilt's gun.

"Forget it. Leave it," Jack shouted. "Let's go."

"The crow!" Skeezix shouted. "Kill the crow! I hit it with a rock, but it's not dead! I'll shoot the filthy thing!" But he couldn't find the gun. It had landed out of sight when the old man had thrown it, in his surprise and fright at suddenly losing his vision. The crow had been his eyes, and Skeezix had knocked the crow silly with a rock. Jack should have thought of that. What had he been meddling with MacWilt for? MacWilt was a pawn, used by Dr. Brown because the doctor was lame. Jack plucked up a rock, wondering at once whether he could kill an animal at all. Peebles could, but that was half of the problem with Peebles, wasn't it? Skeezix scrabbled in the brush, complaining under his breath and puffing with exertion.

There was a rustling of weeds beyond the dead oak and a sudden uncanny cawing, sounding half human, half like a crow. "There it is!" shouted Skeezix, meaning, perhaps, both the pistol and the crow. He lunged into the brush, coming up with the gun. He shook sand from it, pointed it at the sky, and pulled the trigger, turning his head away and grimacing.

The crow flapped once or twice on the ground, hopping across weeds and stones. Skeezix stepped toward the crow, pointed the pistol, and shot. The bullet cracked into the tree trunk, a yard wide of where the great crow stood twisting its head, looking about itself with its small black eyes. MacWilt, ten yards down the stream bed, howled and cursed. He tried to run, stumbled, climbed shakily to his feet, and felt his way forward. "Don't shoot!" he cried. "Don't shoot a poor blind man. Scum! You're scum to shoot a blind man!"

Jack had half a mind to hit him in the back with a rock, but he didn't. He yelled at him to shut up and be gone. Skeezix stopped, looked at MacWilt as if contemplating something, turned back to the crow, steadied his hand, and fired again; then again and again, squeezing off rounds one after another and all of them scattering dirt and gravel and weed. The crow hopped onto a fallen limb and flew away cawing, although the cawing sounded to Jack overmuch like cockeyed laughter as it evaporated on the still air overhead. In a moment there was nothing but the sound of the hammer clicking against empty chambers and the diminishing curses of blind MacWilt, who felt his way around the edge of the hillside and disappeared from view.

9

WHEN THE CAT had chased him out through the crack in the barn wall he'd almost gotten lost in the high grass. Thank goodness the barn door had been closed and the cat trapped inside. There were few advantages to being three inches high, and even fewer when you were three inches high and growing at such a rate as to make your mouse costume nearly choke you before you'd had enough time to do what it was you had to do and then slip away unsuspected. He should have borrowed a different costume, that was the truth of it, something cats hated.

He'd found his way to the river, though, out behind Willoughby's farm, and he'd hitched a ride downstream on a log, climbing ashore unseen, thank goodness, and finding rags of clothes in the taxidermist's. They fit him now like the clothes of an ordinary man would fit a midget—which was exactly the case, of course. He'd started to grow in earnest, and if he hung round for another hour they'd fit better, but he wasn't concerned with fashion; he had things to do and he hadn't much time left to do them in.

He'd sneaked down to the wharves and scraped tar from the pilings, and he'd gotten dandelions easily enough from the yard. There were enough dishes and pots and the like in the old taxidermist's shop to brew the stuff up. It wouldn't be any real trouble at all; he knew that—he'd seen himself do it once, hadn't he? He wished there was time to brew more, but there wasn't. He would have to make do. A little batch for himself, a batch for Jensen, a batch for the man who in a few minutes would come in through the door and who would very badly want more.

There he was now. A hand shoved in through the broken

window and pawed at the inside of the door, finding and pulling back the lock. The door swung to. In stepped a giant, nearly eight feet tall, but shrinking, of course, just as he himself was growing. In an hour, if the man were around that long, his clothes might fit too. And he *would* be around that long—an hour and a little more, wearing another man's too-small clothes. Then he'd be on his way into the past, to try and fail to find the four-year-old Jack Portland at Willoughby's boarded-up farm, to visit Viola Langley, to journey forward again and deliver the elixir, finally, and be chased by a cat into the tall grass and slip into the river and end up here, in the abandoned taxidermist's shop, brewing up another batch of elixir, in a hurry now. All these unscheduled stops ate away at the few remaining precious hours of the Solstice; and his most important work still lay ahead.

He paused for a moment in the melting of the lumpy tar, remembering his wife. In a few hours, if everything worked . . .

The giant stood in the doorway, looking at him stupidly. It embarrassed him to see it. "Close the damned door, idiot," he said. "They'll see you."

"Who are *you?*" the second man asked, closing the door.

But he knows, thought the small man, or at least he suspects. We look enough alike, heaven knows. And besides, I've been through this business before, so I *know* he knows, or is figuring it out fast. He resisted the temptation to bait the man, to confound him. He still had a few moments to do it in. He couldn't take time for sport, though. "I'm you," he said, "From the future. Do I have to tell you that?"

"No," came the reply, after a moment.

"Then mash up those dandelions. We haven't got a moment to spare."

"But tell me," said the giant, still staring, even though he understood things well enough suddenly. "Tell me what you know."

"You'll find out. Just mash those dandelions and listen. Up to a point you'll do all right. You'll deliver the elixir, but not without considerable trouble. That's right, quit gaping and grind them up. You know how; you've done it before. We won't have enough elixir; you can see that."

"We've got to get more. You're right, of course. I'll go out after the stuff now."

"No, you won't. You'd stand out like a hippo. And besides, here we are, mashing away, aren't we? You'll get to where you're going, otherwise I wouldn't be here, would I? It's *me* we have to worry about. And Jensen too."

"Of course, Jensen. He's missed out, hasn't he? I regret having gone off with the formula and left poor Jensen to his own devices. They must have failed him."

"Don't I know about your regrets? Do you have to tell me about your regrets? There's hardly anything I do more of than avoid thinking about your regrets."

"I can't see a damned thing without my glasses. We should have anticipated that."

"We should have anticipated a boatload of things, but we didn't, did we? More regrets. We'll undo a few before we're done, though, see if we don't." Together they mixed the dandelions and tar, deglazing the pan with ocean water.

"That's it!" cried the big man as the elixir in the pan turned color and started to steam. The aroma of it filled the air, wafting round on the little bit of ocean breeze that blew in through cracked panes.

"Of *course* that's it. Here I am, aren't I? Ssh! There's a noise through the window."

The small man stepped across, trailing his rolled pant legs, and shoved open the door. A girl stood outside, under the pepper tree, lost in a reverie. She came to herself and looked at him, half surprised, as if she recognized him. He smiled at her—no use setting her off, after all; they still couldn't afford to be found out. "Who are you?" he asked, assuming that there might be some purpose in her spying on them.

"I'm . . . Helen," she said. "Excuse me for staring. You look just like a friend of mine. It's uncanny, really."

"Is that right? What's his name?"

"Jack," she said, then turned to leave.

She was frightened; he could see that. But she knew Jack. He couldn't let her go, but he couldn't chase her either. "Wait!" he shouted. She was running, though, even as he said it. "Tell Jack to try the Flying Toad!" he hollered. "Please!" It wasn't exactly a comment meant to slow her down any, but maybe it would do the trick. He'd meant to leave a note, to do more than whisper into Jack's ear, but the damned cat had spoiled the business. Well, there was no time to make amends. They'd do another batch, cook it all down, bottle it, and be off.

It was over an hour later when a ruckus started up outside again. It was dark out and raining off and on. There was a shout and a scuffle. "That's yours," said the small man.

The big man was asleep on a table, catching forty winks, he'd said, leaving the boiling down to his smaller counterpart. He woke up now with a start. "What?"

"This one's yours." There was another cry and a terrible cursing. The tall man leaped for the door. Someone was in trouble out in the night. It wasn't his business, but he couldn't very well let it go.

The small man knew that as well as the other one did. He sighed, remembering the blow he was about to receive on the side of the head. He reached up and felt the lump it had raised, and as the door swung open he said, "Watch out! You'll meet someone out there you recognize—Harbin. I'm certain of it. Take this with you; you won't see me again, ever." He handed across a jar of elixir with the lid screwed on. There wasn't much in it, but there was enough to get him back onto the train, so to speak, back to the depot. Along with it was a tiny stoppered bottle containing more of the same, a bottle the size that a mouse might carry, if a mouse were inclined to carry a bottle of elixir.

The giant shoved them into his pocket and wrenched the door open, looking back in wonder at his companion and nodding a goodbye. Then he pushed out into the wet night and was gone.

Helen hadn't any desire to wander in the hills with Jack and Skeezix. Not really. She wasn't wildly excited about magical lands. She was perfectly happy being where she was. Well, almost perfectly happy.

Helen wasn't sure about Skeezix, though. He needed someone around to look after him sometimes. He talked very bravely, but Miss Flees was spiteful and jealous, and Skeezix had always been an easy mark. He was as close to being a brother to Helen as anyone would ever get. There'd been rough moments two years back when he'd fallen in love with her, or thought he had, and she'd had to put an end to it. Then he'd fallen in love with Elaine Potts, the baker's daughter. Elaine Potts hadn't put an end to it, even though sometimes she pretended that she didn't care about him.

Helen could see the truth about Elaine Potts when they stopped in at the bakery. And it wasn't surprising either. Skeezix was one of those plain sorts of people who become less and less plain the better you know them. Helen appreciated that sort of thing. One of her favorite authors had written that beautiful women should be saved for men with no imagination. The same could be said for men—really handsome men, that is. Skeezix had one of those interesting faces that, admittedly, would never become handsome, but would become—what was it?—attractive. That was it. He had the sort of face that would paint well, if you could capture what it was that made it so.

Elaine Potts seemed to sense that. She was the same way, although she didn't know it. That's part of what made Skeezix like her—her not knowing it.

Jack wasn't anything much like a brother, and never had been. He was strange, in his way: gazing out of his loft window through his telescope, wandering in the woods, collecting glass bottles and old books. And now his elixir; he'd gotten it from a mouse, he'd said, or else from a tiny man dressed as a mouse. That was just like Jack.

Helen smiled. The High Street was almost empty. Everyone was at the carnival, Helen supposed. Only a single fisherman sat on the pier, whittling idly. The wind blew down the center of the street, whirling a yellowed old sheet of newspaper into the air and picking up leaves. Helen was suddenly lonely. She wished that she *had* gone with Jack and Skeezix, and for a moment she thought of turning round and following them. But there was no telling, really, where they'd be by now. Jack was good company. It was too bad he was so solitary, kept so much to himself, although it was that, partly, that made him as interesting as he was. Interesting, thought Helen. What a rotten word for it.

There was the taxidermist's shop. Jack and Skeezix and she had sneaked in there one night and stolen a stuffed ape that they'd given to Lantz. She'd felt bad about it for a long time, but that was two years ago, and bug-eaten animals still sat in there doing nothing. Riley the taxidermist was dead. He'd made a "visitation" that morning at the carnival, or so she'd overheard some people to say, and he'd talked ceaselessly about the quality of glass eyes, carrying on until they'd pitched cold water in the face of the medium and shut the taxidermist up. There was a light in the shop now, way in the back, only a little light, like maybe someone was burning a candle in there.

It had nothing to do with her, of course. She had better things to do than be curious about candlelight. Jack and Skeezix would investigate, if they were there, and would probably end up being chased up the alley by a tramp. They'd investigate anything. Skeezix would come home gloating this afternoon, boasting about what he'd found, full of theories, clucking his tongue and shaking his head that Helen hadn't been with him. What had she been doing? he'd ask, feigning interest. Then he'd nod broadly at whatever she'd been painting and say something smart about it and then sigh. Then he'd swagger off making furious faces, which, he'd imply, Helen was making at *him*. Helen wouldn't be, of course. She'd ignore him utterly.

She found herself halfway around to the back of the taxidermist's, tiptoeing along. She wouldn't go home empty-handed. She'd have an adventure of her own, is what she'd have, and throw it in Skeezix's face.

The rear windows were dusty and dark and had been covered with newspaper, glued on long ago. Here and there the newspaper had dried out and yellowed and peeled off in patches.

She glanced up and down the river. It was empty. The fisherman on the pier wasn't in sight. She edged along the rear of the shop, wincing at the sound of gravel and trash scrunching underfoot. There was the light. She could see it past a ragged rent in the newsprint covering the window. She peered through, holding her breath, squinting against the dimness of the room within.

A lumber of stuffed animals littered the floor, looming half in shadow. She could just make out the head of a bear, the dorsal fin of a shark, a clutch of moony-eyed squid, mounted in a long line as if they drifted in the current atop an offshore reef. A hand moved. A man in an artist's smock worked at a bench. It wasn't candlelight after all; it was the glow of a little fire that was cooking a pan of something. Helen realized with a start that the heavy smell of ocean and tar on the air wasn't blowing in on the sea wind after all; it hovered in the room beyond, leaking out through the hole in the window.

There were two men in the room, not one. One, in the smock, was far taller than the other. The smock was undersized, now that Helen had a moment to study it. The man worked at a bench, grinding something up. He was the tallest man Helen could remember having seen—easily seven feet tall, maybe taller. He bent over his work so that he looked at it from about an inch away, as if he were fearfully nearsighted but had lost his spectacles. The other man stirred the pan on the fire. He was a midget for sure, not just small in relation to the giant that he labored alongside, but shorter than the top of the bench. He stood on a stool to work, and he wore outsized clothes, his sleeves and trousers rolled. It was too dark in the taxidermist's to make out much detail. The men might easily have been brothers, mismatched twins even.

What should she do? What would Jack or Skeezix do? She could walk away, but what she'd seen wouldn't make much of a story later on. She'd tell it as well as she could, but then she'd get to the end and Skeezix would say, "What did you do then?" She'd say, "Nothing. I came home." That wouldn't do. The smell of tar and ocean was cut suddenly by the sharp odor of dandelion. The beaker bubbled and fizzled. A cloud of greenish vapor tumbled up out of it, dispersing through the room, and the smell of elixir, of Jack's elixir, weighted the air.

Helen reeled back against the trunk of a pepper tree. Her eyes were misted by the elixir, and she was overwhelmed with longing and with regret for all the places she'd wanted to go in her life but hadn't, for all the wonderful places she'd been and had to leave, for all the places she longed to see but wouldn't. Before her eyes was the fleeting vision of rolling springtime countryside glimpsed through the window of a train car, and she anchored herself to a tree limb with one hand, fearing that she'd pitch over into the grass with dizziness. In her ears was the sound of the rush and surge of the ocean and of the clatter of train wheels on a railroad trestle, and for one brief moment she seemed to be standing on the train tracks above the bluffs, waving at a receding train and at a man and woman she didn't know who waved back at her from where they stood on the last car. In an instant they diminished to specks on the far-flung landscape and disappeared.

She realized abruptly that someone was watching her. It was the small man. He'd pushed the rear door ajar and was looking out, smiling at her. She let go the tree limb, shook the mist out of her head, and smiled back, although it was a troubled smile. He had an oddly familiar face. "Who are you?" he asked.

The encounter didn't last a minute. He looked like Jack, and she felt compelled to tell him so, but that's all she'd tell him. This wasn't the sort of thing she was fond of. She didn't need to chat with oddly clothed men outside an abandoned taxidermist's shop.

"Wait!" he shouted as she turned and ran. He didn't follow her, though. He stepped out into the shade of the tree and hollered, "Tell Jack to try the flying toad!" Then she was gone—around the side of the shop, up onto the High Street, pounding along toward Miss Flees's. She went in through the back door, silent as she could and wondering about "the Flying Toad." Maybe Skeezix would know. Or Jack. It was Jack she was supposed to tell, after all. She'd save it for him. Jack would love the mystery of it.

Up the attic stairs she climbed. She pushed into the room, locked the trapdoor behind her, and turned around to see Peebles sitting there in the darkness, sucking on his finger. Mrs. Langley's book lay open on the desk, as if he'd been reading it. The canvas that had rested on the easel had been slashed and torn with a pocketknife and the easel kicked over. Her box of paints lay on the floor, brushes and tubes and hunks of chalk scattered and kicked.

Helen stopped and stood still. She edged back toward the door but didn't dare reach down to open it. Peebles grinned at her stupidly, a look that suggested he'd happily push her downstairs if he had the opportunity. She was overcome with a sudden rage. The filthy little brute, getting into her stuff, knocking it around. On the floor before him was a crockery bowl, a heap of twigs, some sulfur matches, and what must have been chicken entrails. Skeezix and Jack had told her about that.

"I'm tired of you," said Peebles, lighting a match with his thumbnail and watching it burn down toward his thumb.

"Not half as tired as I am of you."

The match burned down to where he held it. He didn't twitch—he let the flame burn him, seeming to like it.

"Very impressive," said Helen, looking again at the slashed canvas. "Why don't you light your shirt on fire and burn yourself up?"

"I might just burn us all up." He lit another match and held it to the edge of the canvas. The fire caught and spread, eating across the half-painted canvas, the paint flaring.

Helen took half a step toward it. The painting was ruined as it was; she didn't care about that. It was the house she cared about. He might very easily burn them all up, exactly like he said. She stopped, though. She wouldn't give Peebles the satisfaction of seeing her stamp out the flames. And besides, he was probably half bluff. He talked too much. He was too showy. His glasses were tilted and his hair was mussed, and if it came to it, she'd beat him senseless. One of the candelabras was in easy reach. She could pluck it up and persuade him with one good blow. Then she'd kick *him* downstairs. The thought of it made her heart race, and she found herself trembling. She hated this sort of thing.

Peebles smirked at her. "Scared?"

Helen said nothing. She stared at him intently, as if she were assessing the nature of his peculiar behavior. It was a look that would drive him mad. She'd used it on him before, implying that she saw very clearly that he was sadly insane and was "scoping him out," as Skeezix would say.

Peebles peered at his new finger, wiggling it uncertainly. It grew out of his hand at a cockeyed angle, like the grownback arm of a starfish. His smile faltered for a moment. He lit a match, then bent down and lit the twigs in the crock, blowing them into flame and dropping on the gizzard, or whatever it was. Then he pulled a silver needle out of his coat and pricked his new finger, holding it up for Helen to see. She stared at him stony-faced. He pricked it again, and then again and again. No blood flowed from it. He grinned, as if proud of himself, and pricked the finger next to it. He pushed on it, holding it over the bowl, but nothing happened. A second prick accomplished nothing either. Then, in a sudden rage, he stabbed away at his fingers at random, but they seemed equally bloodless. A look of awe and fear flickered across his face, turning into sudden loathing and desperation. He jammed the needle into the palm of his hand, squeezing a globule of blood onto the half-burned twigs.

With a hiss and a sizzle smoke poured out of them, congealing in the air above the bowl, whirling and seeming to pulse on the still attic air. Vague shapes formed. Airy pictures danced in front of her: a sheep with a gash in its neck, the face of an insect, a gibbet with a man hanging from it, his hands bound. Peebles grinned through it. Helen was horrified, and her face gave her away. She leaped forward and kicked the smoking herbs into the wall, stamping them out against the floorboards.

Peebles cried out in surprise and then leaped up and rushed at her, shoving his needle into her arm. Helen lurched aside, crying out even though she hadn't felt any pain. The needle had caught in the heavy seam of her coat, and when she jerked away it pulled out of Peebles's hand. He seemed to writhe with anger. He stood with his mouth open and working, as if he were probing his teeth with his tongue. His chest heaved. He pulled out another match, tried and failed to light it with his thumb, and then plucked a matchbox out of his shirt, spitting out a curse and lighting the match with shaking fingers.

Helen wasn't near the trapdoor any more. She was against the street windows now. The candelabra wasn't within reach either. The canvas on the floor had burned itself out. She'd brain him with the chair, that's what she'd do. She'd smash it to flinders over his tiny head. She'd—

But before she had a chance to do anything, even speak, he held the match to the tattered muslin curtains. They went up in a rush of flame. He backed toward the trapdoor, lighting another match as he went and looking around for something else to burn. There was the ragged end of a tablecloth, draped over a table on the edge of the stacked furniture. Peebles held the match to it, until flames crept off across the table, licking up along the legs of a chair that sat atop it. He bent down suddenly, grinning maliciously at Helen, and reached for the latch of the trapdoor. He meant to leave her there. He meant to climb down and brace the door shut and leave her there.

Helen picked up the chair he'd been sitting in, lifted it over her head, and pitched it at him. He dodged it easily—surprisingly easily. It was as if he'd been snatched out of its way. Helen turned and pulled at what was left of the curtains. They tore away in a wash of sparks, and she dropped them to the floor and danced on them, stamping out the flames. She leaped across to tear the tablecloth off the table before it set the whole heap of old furniture alight. But there wasn't any need to. The tablecloth floated hovering in the air, burning out over the floor. It wrung itself out like a washcloth while he stood transfixed, gazing at it, his hair standing on end as if it were yanked up by someone's fist. He stood on tiptoe, jigging like a mechanical ballet dancer, hooting out one clipped-off shriek. The fallen chair floated into the air, righted itself, and sat down hard on all four feet at once. The trapdoor opened with a bang. Peebles teetered on the edge of it. The tablecloth shook itself out like a rug and collapsed in a burnt heap on the floor as Peebles seemed to step involuntarily out over the abyss, shaking his head and looking about him and then falling suddenly with a shout onto the steep stairway below. He managed to cast Helen one last befuddled and venomous glance as he fell, and she heard him bang down the stairs. The trapdoor slammed shut. The latch slid into place, and the attic was deathly silent.

Helen wanted company. No, that wasn't quite right. Someone was in the room with her. She could feel the presence, and she knew straightaway who it was. It was Mrs. Langley. Mrs. Langley hadn't at all wanted to see Peebles burn the house down. The burned tablecloth had infuriated her, and she'd dropped Peebles down the stairwell like a sack of oranges.

Helen suddenly wanted to put things right, to pick up the burned tablecloth and carry the chair back over to the table, to gather up the fallen paints and chalk. But she didn't dare. Perhaps it would be best to let Mrs. Langley cool down a little—let Mrs. Langley make the next move. Nothing happened, though. Helen waited. The afternoon was drawing on and the attic was slipping into shadow. She bent down finally and reached for Peebles's box of matches. They lay on the floor where he'd dropped them when Mrs. Langley yanked him up by the hair. Helen half expected the matches to be snatched away, to fly into the air, to skitter off across the floorboards. They didn't, though. She lit the candles in the candelabra and set it very carefully back onto its table. Her heart no longer careened quite so wildly behind her ribs. She was better off quit of Peebles. She'd been friends, as far as it went, with Mrs. Langley, but she'd never been friends with Peebles, although she'd tried. Peebles hadn't let her, even years ago when such a thing would have been possible.

She picked up the chair and then stepped across with it to the desk, looking around her as she walked and half expecting something to happen—a ghost to appear or a disembodied voice to moan out of a dark corner. She scrabbled around the floor, retrieving bits of chalk and tubes of paint. The box, thank goodness, hadn't been wrecked. He'd snapped one or two of the brushes, though, and she couldn't replace them without sending to San Francisco. A little glue and tape, perhaps . . .

For what capering reason, she wondered, had Peebles decided to take his filthy malice out on her? Why break things up? Just for sport? She shook her head, then gasped in surprise as a gray cat walked out of the shadows of a gable, meowing. It stopped in the afternoon light that still shone weakly though the window and curled up into a ball, falling asleep almost at once. More meowing came from a distant corner, and another cat, a black one now, wandered out, sniffing the air. A third cat appeared suddenly on the table beside the candelabra; one moment there was nothing, the next there was a cat, materializing out of vapor.

Helen didn't know any of the cats and she had the distinct suspicion that no one else in the house did either. A bird chirped. In the dusty brass cage angling out of the stored furniture was a canary, ghostly gray and sitting on a piece of dowel lashed to the cage wire with a bit of string. A fourth cat appeared, out of nothing, out of the air.

Helen's hand shook again. She closed her box and uprighted her easel. Then she smoothed out her jacket and hair. She heard the first faint sounds of someone humming, and for a moment she thought it was Miss Flees, working in the kitchen below, carving cabbages for the soup. But Miss Flees didn't often sing, or hum, for that matter. This was something else. A silver-white light shone near the trapdoor, hovering there above it, seeming to spin, like one of Peebles's enchantments, as if someone had thrown a handful of luminous chalk dust into a miniature wind devil. It was Mrs. Langley, materializing. Helen steeled herself for the confrontation. She hadn't really ever gotten used to the idea of hobnobbing with ghosts. Mrs. Langley hadn't ever meddled in her business before, and she, heaven knew, had left Mrs. Langley well enough alone—only fragments of casual chatting now and then.

The glowing dust whirled upward toward the peak of the roof, then fell suddenly like a heavy mist. Mrs. Langley stood there. At first she was simply a wash of moonlit fog, and then, like the city above the Moonvale Hills, she grew slowly solid until she stood there gray and bent, an old woman in a shawl and outsize bedroom slippers, smiling at Helen. "Have you seen Jimmy?" was the first thing she said.

Helen blinked at her. "No, I haven't. *Should* I have seen Jimmy?"

The old woman squinted at Helen, shaking her head in

rapid little palsied jerks. "He might come across, Jimmy might. He was always one for coming across. I've got to leave a bundle of clothes under the trestle at the cove. I'm late this year. I always try to get it out early."

Helen nodded and grinned. She had no idea at all what Mrs. Langley was talking about. Helen had only heard speaking spirits a couple of times in her life, and they hadn't amounted to much. One ghost had recited its multiplication tables up to eight times eight and then had been very proud of itself and quit. You didn't know what to expect from a ghost.

"Did you drop Peebles down the stairs?" asked Helen.

"Is *that* his name? It sounds like rocks, doesn't it? Very ugly little rocks. I'm certain he deserved to be dropped downstairs. He deserved worse, I dare say. You should have seen him carry on before you arrived. It was shameful. Diseased, is what it was. I had to take the cats into the back, poor things, and I neglected to take Peety with us. Heaven knows what the sight of such things will do to him."

For a moment Helen guessed that Mrs. Langley had mixed up Jimmy and Peety, whoever they were. But Peety, it turned out, was the canary, who'd suffered through Peebles's foul behavior because of having been left behind. Helen was at a loss. She couldn't think of anything to say, but it was impolite to say nothing. She reached down to pet the gray cat, but her hand passed through it. "I'm reading your book," said Helen. "It's really quite nice. The illustrations are lovely."

"Yes, they are," said Mrs. Langley. Then she sat down on a chair and the gray cat jumped into her lap. Helen wondered why she didn't fall through the chair—why, for that matter, she didn't fall through the floor.

"Did you paint them yourself?" Helen asked, and then remembered that she hadn't, that there'd been mention of an illustrator.

"No," said Mrs. Langley, petting the cat, "Jimmy painted them. Before he went off. He'll be coming back, and he'll need these clothes. There's nothing funny about not having a change of clothes when the clothes you're wearing are growing like hops. Be a dear and take Jimmy's clothes to the cove for me. I'm an old lady, you know."

"Not so old as that—" Helen began, thinking to say something nice. But Mrs. Langley gave her a look and interrupted.

"You know precious little about it, young lady. I'm older than you imagine, very much your senior. What I say oughtn't to be questioned, I suppose—not by a girl. *I* have no idea how old I am. I rather lost track of it. An old friend of Jimmy's took the clothes down last Solstice, but he hasn't been around since. He would have been. He and I were fine friends. He was very interested in my writings, but he was a sad case. I fear he's gone across too, for equally sad reasons. He would have been back otherwise, like I said. Very understandable, though, his going across. I helped him, didn't I? I told him what to mix up and what to let alone. You'd know him, perhaps."

Helen shrugged. "Perhaps. What was his name? That was rather longer ago than I can easily remember, though, if it was at the last Solstice."

"Lars Portland. You'd have been a little girl then, wouldn't you? There's a trunk behind the wardrobe."

Helen nodded, startled by the shifting direction of the conversation. Lars Portland! What in the world did *that* signify? Did Jack know that? Did Skeezix, and they hadn't told her? She'd murder both of them. And there *was* a trunk behind the wardrobe. Helen had seen it. It was locked, though, and so she hadn't had a look inside, even though she was eaten up with curiosity about it. She hadn't told Skeezix and Jack, because they'd have wanted to pry it open, and Helen didn't think they had any business prying into Mrs. Langley's trunk. Thank goodness Miss Flees didn't know about it, she'd have been at it years ago with a crowbar. Miss Flees had found a heap of old newspapers once, hidden away beneath the attic stairs, and she'd pulled them apart a page at a time for hours on end, insisting that there might be money between the pages. Old people, she'd said, were clever at that sort of thing—squirreling money away. There'd been only newspaper, though, and she'd flown into a rage and made no supper that night, saying she'd been denied her "windfall" and she couldn't afford feeding ungrateful children.

Mrs. Langley nodded slowly at her and pointed a spindly finger in the general direction of the trunk. "The key is hidden under the handle on the right-hand side, if you're facing the front of it; on the left-hand side if you're facing away. But then you can't see it, can you, if you're facing away?" She waited, as if she expected an answer.

"No, ma'am," Helen said.

"Good. You're a shrewd young lady. Much as I was once. That's why I've let you inhabit this attic. There's a woman downstairs. What is her name?"

"Miss Flees, ma'am."

"How unfortunate."

"Yes, ma'am." Helen waited. Mrs. Langley sat there, gray and thinking, with a hand on her chin. For a moment Helen was afraid she'd run down, like a clockwork engine. The ghosts that talked through mediums at the carnival sometimes did that, as if talking to living people had seemed to be a good idea to them when they set in, but they could see now that nothing would come of it, and so they tired out and went off somewhere, letting their voices trail away into nothing. "The trunk, ma'am."

"Have you seen Jimmy?"

"Not a glimpse of him. I'll keep an eye out, though. I've been seeing some strange things these past few days, to be sure. I wouldn't be half surprised to see Jimmy too. What does he look like?"

"He'll be naked as a fish," said Mrs. Langley, perking up a bit now that the subject had come round again to Jimmy.

Helen didn't much know what to say. There was no denying that he'd be easy to recognize, but all of a sudden keeping an eye out for him didn't seem to be even a half-good idea. "Why will he be naked as a fish?" she forced herself to say.

"Well, he might not be, mightn't he?"

"I hope not, certainly. Is that why you want to take him a change of clothing?"

Mrs. Langley peered at her closely for a moment. "Is there a better reason?" she asked finally.

"Not at all. No. I can't think of one. He *needs* a change of clothes under that sort of circumstance, doesn't he?"

"Of course he does. And you'll take it to him. To the cove, under the railway trestle. There's a heap of rocks along the wall. He'll be coming out of the ocean. At least I think he will. He came up through a gopher hole the first time, but it didn't suit him. Too—what is it?—'subterranean,' I believe he said. Too like a mole. He couldn't tolerate moles. It was his single downfall, if you want the truth. *I'm* as fond of moles as I am of anything. It's the business on the end of a mole's nose, if you ask me, that Jimmy couldn't abide. Also they have mismatched feet. God gave them the feet of some other beast—heaven knows what."

Helen nodded, wondering what to say next. "Who is Jimmy?" she asked—as good a question as any.

"Why he's my husband, child. You've been reading my book. Your young man *borrowed* it from me, didn't he?"

"Yes," began Helen. "That is to say, my friend Jack borrowed it. But I asked him to. He was saving me from having to crawl back in there to get it. He's not my 'young man' exactly. He's . . . just Jack. He lives with Mr. Willoughby."

"*Just* Jack," said Mrs. Langley flatly and nodding her head. "Just Jack." She screwed one of her eyes shut and peered at Helen out of the other. "I had a 'just Jimmy' for years. Then I realized he was a good bit more than that. He painted, like you do. He was better at it, but he was older wasn't he? When he set up as a painter he was a mess—friends from San

Francisco. All of them wore exotic hats and drank far too much champagne and had 'artistic temperaments,' which, of course, means that they were able to behave like fools and infants and get away with it. Ah, poor Jimmy, poor Jimmy. He wasn't as bad as the worst nor yet as good as the best. But then who is?"

Helen thought for a moment, wondering if someone ought to be. It sounded like a mathematical puzzle to her. Mrs. Langley, though, obviously hadn't expected an answer. Her philosophies weren't arguable. Helen remembered suddenly who "Jimmy" was. He was James Langley, no doubt, the man who'd illustrated Mrs. Langley's book. The wonderful paintings of the magical land were his, the cloud drift, the sketchy landscapes, the pastel colors of evening fading into shadow. "Where did he go, exactly, your Jimmy?"

"Why, he went across at the Solstice, child. Years ago. Let me see. Five twelves is—what? I'm worthless at numbers. Sixty. He was back twice. First through the gopher hole, as I said. Cats nearly got him when he came in. He was covered in dirt and twigs and went to sleep in a drawer that first night, tucked into a pile of sweaters like a doll. Somewhere around two he grew too big for it and burst the front right off— spilled out onto the floor and like to have broken his hip. Next morning he was right as rain, though. He walked abroad like a man of stature—not the hint of a midget about him.

"Then twelve years later he went across again, and this time he returned by sea. I missed him, of course. But he was a wanderer—couldn't be tied, he said. The wide world was his canvas, and he intended to paint it all. He was a fearful romantic, Jimmy was. Anyway, it was the most astonishing coincidence, him coming by sea that second time. I was walking along the cove, thinking I'd never see him again, and here he was, out of the seaweed like a god. It was late evening, thank goodness. He was immense. You can hardly imagine. He'd floated in from out to sea somewhere, so he'd had some time to shrink, and his clothes had all fallen off him long before. It was appalling, I can assure you. Bits and pieces of them floated ashore for a week, but we managed to find them all, I think. The weather was foul, so no one frequented the beach much. It wouldn't have done to have the clothes found. I'm not sure why. He was fearful, I seem to remember, that they'd be traced to him, that everyone in the village would be after him for the—secret, I suppose you could say. Men would kill for it, and worse. There's others, like Jimmy, who wouldn't.

"The Jimmies of this world are after something—some little bit of wonderful music they hear playing in the back of their heads—and they're certain that if they listen closely enough they'll be able to capture the tune and remember it and whistle it any time they want. Others, though"—Mrs. Langley shook her head at the idea of these others—"they haven't got any music at all, only noise.

"Your fellow with the herbs and the sulfur matches. He'd . . . well, there's no saying what he'd do. But they get desperate, and the less happy they are with their lot, the more desperate they get. Some people simply go about hating, don't they? I've had an eye on your Miss—what is it again? Bugs?"

"Flees," said Helen.

"Of course. Your Miss Flees. I've been watching her. She talks to herself, you know: gibbers. She hates everything, I think. Everything, and all of it equally. She curses her hair and this house and you children and the weather and the sad broth that she cooks down in the kitchen. And she curses the very idea of cooking something that tastes better. She hates one thing as much as the other, and what makes her very dangerous indeed is that she doesn't know it. Mark my words, child. She hasn't an inkling. Neither does your fellow with the matches. They're certain *you* hate things too, that the world is made out of dirt. But that's what gives you the edge; they can't understand you. Your painting confounds them. The fat child's love of food; that confounds them too. And he laughs a good deal, doesn't he? All of you laugh, for the pleasure of it. That must drive them wild. They're a dangerous lot, and yet there's worse than them, depend on it. They're looking to break out a window in this world and climb into the next. But they'd just break *it* up too. They're stupid. That's what makes them tiresome, isn't it?"

Helen nodded. They *were* tiresome. She wasn't being told anything that she didn't already suspect. It was good to have such things confirmed though—by another party, so to speak. She spent too much time trying to be cheerful to them. She knew that, and had known it. But it would never work for them. There lives were like machines assembled by feeble-minded drunken men. Still, it was as easy to be cheerful, to make the effort, as to declare war openly. At least it used to be. Peebles had rather pushed things this time.

"Excuse me, ma'am," Helen said. Mrs. Langley had drifted into a sort of lethargy. She seemed to hover on the edge of sleep. And she'd become almost transparent, as if she and the cats were slipping away, and with almost nothing solved. "The clothes? Are they in the trunk?"

"Of course they are, dear," said Mrs. Langley.

Helen's heart lurched suddenly. A giant from the sea. Jimmy *had* come home. Of course he had. They'd found his shoe, hadn't they? And his spectacles and cuff link and the crystal out of his pocket watch. Heaven knew what good it would do to tell a dead woman that her live husband had "come across," but she couldn't very well keep the news to herself. Mrs. Langley listened intently, her head cocked, her eyes hopeful. Then she shook her head.

It wasn't Jimmy, she told Helen. Jimmy didn't wear spectacles. And he didn't own a watch. He never had. Time hadn't meant anything to him. He and his artistic friends made a point of that. They *knew* time, they said, and weren't constrained by watches. And cuff links? Mrs. Langley had to laugh. Jimmy's cuffs wouldn't be constrained by cuff links. He and his friends from down south despised cuff links. They probably despised cuffs, for that matter. Helen had found someone else's clothes. It hadn't been Jimmy who had come across.

She peered at Helen for a moment, as if thinking that Helen had made up all this cuff-links business in order to get out of taking Jimmy's clothes down to the cove as she'd promised. But Helen got up then and went after the trunk, asking questions of Mrs. Langley almost continually, fearful that the old woman would drift away without explaining the gopher holes and Jimmy and "coming across" and all the rest. Their conversation hadn't clarified things; it had deepened the mystery. The only thing for certain was that Jack and Skeezix were caught up in the same oddities that had entangled Jimmy.

Helen managed to shove the bits and pieces of furniture around enough to wedge herself back in toward the trunk. There was a bit more room behind the wardrobe than there had been in front of the bookcase, so she didn't have to worm her way underneath things like Jack had. "Her Jack." She grinned with embarrassment and then tried hard to dissolve the grin but couldn't. There was the trunk—an old leather and wood chest with a heavy hinged lid. She thought about rights and lefts for a moment, fiddled with both handles, and found herself holding the right one, which had come away in her hand. Sure enough. The key lay beneath it, slid under a bit of leather.

"I don't understand the part about the gopher hole," she said to Mrs. Langley as she slipped the key into the keyhole.

"What is it about gopher holes that you don't know, child? When I was your age they were commonplace. The garden was a mess with them."

"How could Jimmy have gotten into one?" Helen pushed the lid back. Inside was a sort of wooden box, open on top, filling half the trunk. In it were men's clothes, including a pair of heavy shoes, as Mrs. Langley had promised.

"Why he was coming back across, child, just like I said. He'd gone over into what he called 'the twilight' and he'd found his way into another time. . . . It's all rather complex, for someone ignorant of the entire business. Are you sure there isn't *anything* you know?"

Helen rummaged in the clothes, wondering what to say. "No," she said after a moment.

"Do you mean no, you're not sure or no, there's nothing you know?"

"No, there's nothing I know. Try to explain it to me. I've found his clothes in a bundle. Will he want them all?"

"I dare say he will. He won't have a stitch, will he? He can't wear clothes built for a giant, nor for a Tom Thumb either, if he comes that way. But I very much doubt he will. Every time he thought about running into a mole down there he shuddered. I'm certain it's the growth on their nose."

"Of course it is," said Helen. There seemed to be no mistaking what clothes it was that Mrs. Langley wanted. Below them were what appeared in the dim light to be bits and pieces of costumes. Jimmy wouldn't want those; he'd have troubles enough without finding a rabbit outfit under the rocks.

"Ours is one of many worlds," said Mrs. Langley, quoting from her own book. Helen shut the trunk lid and listened to her. She slid back out into the candlelight. Mrs. Langley sat as before. One of the cats had come around to lie across the old woman's feet, but at the sight of Helen it slipped away.

"How many worlds are there?" asked Helen.

"Only one, actually. I phrased it—how shall I put it?—figuratively there. It's tempting, when you write a book, to color things up. It's time, really, that's meddled with at the Solstice. Jimmy tells me it's like a railroad train, exactly like that, with stops along the line, and each stop a different point in time. All of them falling into line, mind you, at the Solstice."

"That's when Jimmy 'went across'?"

"You really *are* a bright child," said Mrs. Langley. "But art seems to be your forte, doesn't it? The two don't make steady companions, art and science. Some few would argue otherwise, I suppose, but I always found that science made Jimmy's head spin. He wouldn't let it constrain him, he'd say, nor would any of his friends. So it's all very much like a million worlds a-spin—isn't it?—if you can travel from one to the other and find yourself someplace new, or at least in another time. It's—what time is it?"

"Almost four thirty, I should think," said Helen.

"All right. It's four thirty here, and who knows what time at one of those other stops? Midnight, perhaps. Eleven thirty-five. Four thirty and some tiny fraction. Ten years hence, twenty years back. Some of them lurking still in the stone age, I don't doubt. It doesn't matter in the least. The wonderful part is that as you travel forward in time you grow. The universe, you know, is expanding; that's what science tells us. And traveling backward you shrink and can come along forward again, if you're quick, through a gopher hole. Then you'd 'acclimate.' That's what Jimmy called it. You'd find yourself becoming one of them. You might run into yourself there too, living in perfect ignorance. You could knock on your own door and say something clever when you opened it. In the meantime your clothes wouldn't be worth a thing to you. *They* won't oblige you by shrinking or growing, will they? And you'd be mighty thankful that someone had left some few shreds of clothing under some rocks somewhere, wouldn't you? You'd come sailing in on the Solstice tide or creeping up through a gopher hole or popping in through a cave. Or you'd climb up into the foliage of a particularly tall tree and out onto a limb that stretched into another world altogether, and there you'd be, across. Back again. Just like that. Very simple."

"How do you *get* across?" asked Helen. Her head seemed to whirl with it all. She had a thousand questions to ask suddenly. She knew that the answers weren't in Mrs. Langley's book. The book was wonderfully concerned with the whys of the business, but it didn't much explain the hows. "What is it about the carnival?" she asked, without letting Mrs. Langley get started on the first question. The old woman smiled at her and shook her head, as if she found Helen's sudden curiosity a bit like what you'd expect from a child.

She started to speak, seeming to settle to the task of explaining. A knock at the trapdoor nearly pitched Helen out of her chair. Another knock followed. Mrs. Langley's voice dimmed to a whisper. Her shawl turned to mist. For a moment her shoes were all that was left of her. The gray cat hung suspended over the chair, and then shoes, cat, and all were gone.

10

Jack got home in the late afternoon. Skeezix had gone back to Miss Flees's without him, intending to stop at Dr. Jensen's on the way. They were dirty and tired and hungry—mostly hungry—and Skeezix knew that there'd be no hope for food at the orphanage. He could have come along to Willoughby's, but neither Willoughby nor Jack was the sort of hand with food that Mrs. Jensen was. And Skeezix didn't want yesterday's chicken or cheese or bread. He said he was in a mood for pastries. If Elaine Potts were home, he'd pay her a visit—take her a bouquet of wild fuchsia and a sprig of flowering pear leaves. She'd melt at the sight of it, he said, and cover him in doughnuts. But with Elaine Potts out of town, Mrs. Jensen would have to do. Skeezix had seen something on her kitchen counter earlier that looked promising.

They had agreed to meet later that evening in order, as Skeezix put it, to see what was what. It seemed to Jack that Skeezix was being optimistic. The more he saw, the less he knew "what was what." It wasn't tough to figure out, though, what Dr. Brown was after. Jack still had it in his pocket, and there it would stay until . . . until what?

He could pour it down the sink right now, stay in bed for a couple of days, and watch through the loft window as the Solstice passed. Then it would be a twelve-year holiday before things were stirred up again, before the weather shifted and another Solstice tide rose; twelve years during which to ponder a million unanswered questions and in which to wonder what, exactly, would have come to pass if he *had* seen the mystery through. And what would Skeezix do? Something foolish, to be sure. Skeezix wasn't one to hide from this sort of adventure—whatever sort of adventure it was.

Willoughby's wagon was gone. The farmer was probably

in town examining pint glasses. If he was, there'd be no one around the farm but Jack until after midnight, and it would only be the weather that prevented Willoughby's sleeping the night away in the back of his wagon, halfway up the road from town. Jack liked solitude well enough; he welcomed it usually. But now with the sky half twilight and clouding up again and the moon already up over the woods and no sound on the wind but the lonesome barking of a dog somewhere out toward the Tumbled Bridge, he began to wish he gone on to Dr. Jensen's with Skeezix. He hadn't any good reason to be always mooching off the doctor, though, not like Skeezix did. Jack had plenty to eat at home. But still he couldn't see any profit in sticking around the farm now. He'd clean up, shove some food together, and be off. He shouted for the cats; they'd be some company anyway. But even the cats had gone off—after food, probably, like Skeezix.

He unlocked the barn door and went in. The air was heavy with darkness and the smell of cheese. He reached for the lantern, but it wasn't on the hook, so he stood for a moment letting his eyes adjust to the little bit of daylight that shone in through the cracks in the shutters over the high window and cast little streaks of light slantways over the books along the wall. He'd left the shutters open that morning; he did every morning unless it was raining straight in, in order to air the place out. The wind must have blown them closed.

From the dimness of the barn floor the books seemed to be tumbled and heaped and tossed about, but that was probably a trick of the waning light. He climbed the loft stairs two at a time, stopping with surprise when he got to the landing. The candle and book that had been on the table by the bed were on the floor now. So were his clothes, flung around, some of them hanging over the railing. Someone had been at his things, had torn the place up. He picked up his brass kaleidoscope from where it sat half under the foot of the bed. The front lens was cracked and bits of colored glass had leaked out. One of the long mirrors inside slid out into his hand. The bedclothes hadn't been mussed; he was certain of that. The mattress wasn't lying askew. It should be, if someone had been at it. A thief would look under the mattress. An interrupted thief might not have had time to.

The barn door had been locked. He'd just unlocked it himself, hadn't he? He stood very still, listening. His mind raced. He knew at once what had happened—who it had been and why it had been folly to leave the shutters open. Was he still in the barn? Of course he was, unless he'd flown back out the window and away. But then the shutters wouldn't be closed, would they? And why would he leave with the job half done? He wouldn't, of course. He'd wait there in the darkness for Jack, who'd been fool enough to shout for the cats when he was coming up the road. If he hadn't shouted, then he'd have caught the man at it. He'd have run, is what he would have done, and he'd be running still.

Jack pushed the shutters open and looked out over the meadow. He held his breath, hearing nothing but the sound of blood rushing in his veins. There it was—a stirring in the darkness below, in the barn. He was gripped with the urge to pitch the lantern over the railing, to illuminate the barn floor with a puddle of burning oil. He had to look, but he couldn't bear to. Whoever it was had hidden there and let him climb the loft stairs, thinking to corner him.

There was the hissing of a struck match, the glow of it burning, illuminating the hand that held it. The hand touched the match to a lantern wick, and there was Dr. Brown, trimming the lantern, smiling up at Jack, who stood now at the railing. He'd come in through the window—flown back from where Skeezix had stunned him with the rock, from where he had left MacWilt blind and alone on the meadow.

He leaned on a carved stick, and his hair fell black and oily around his shoulders. The lamplight in front of him cast his shadow onto the wall behind and stretched it nearly to the loft railing. His black coat was cuffed at the sleeves and open in front to reveal an old-fashioned frilly shirt of the sort that hadn't been worn in a decade. He nodded, as if out of respect, and said, "Well, Jack, here we are, now, aren't we?"

Jack didn't speak; there could be no profit in it. His voice would simply give away his fear.

"You know what it is I want. And I'll have it too, or I'll have your blood. Do you take my meaning?" He grinned then, his face lit from below.

Jack took his meaning well enough. He'd seen Lantz. Dr. Jensen had told him about the man in the tide pool. Without looking away, Jack hooked his foot into the pile of the rope ladder under the bed. He tried to calculate how long it would take to hook the ladder over the sill and be down it. He'd climbed up and down the ladder hundreds of times; he barely used his feet—just a few quick, sliding clutches and he'd be away, into the woods.

"I believe it to be in your pocket. Shall I look for it myself, or will you bring it to me?"

"No," said Jack. "I mean, it's not in my pocket. I wouldn't carry it—would I?—I don't want to break it. What is it, anyway? I don't know."

"You don't know! That's a fine lie. You know who you are, don't you? You know who your father was. You know who *I* am; that fool of a doctor would have told you. Where did you get the elixir, from the man in the moon? You don't know!"

"I got it from a mouse," said Jack. The ladder was caught on the bed leg somehow, wrapped around it. Jack couldn't afford to look. He had to pretend to be hesitating because he was scared, because he didn't want Dr. Brown near him. "At least I think it was a mouse. It might have been a man in a costume."

There was a silence below as Dr. Brown regarded him from the shadows, obviously thinking about mice and bottles of elixir. "A man in a costume . . . a big mouse, then?"

"Not big, at least not like you mean it. Three inches tall, maybe."

"When?"

"Days ago. I've had it since, but I don't have any idea—"

"Where did this mouse go?"

"Through a crack in the wall. Into the woods, I guess. I don't know. What was it?"

Dr. Brown didn't answer. He stood there thinking, rubbing his chin and leaning on his stick. How lame was he? Jack wondered. How quickly could he rush up the stairs? What if he *didn't* rush up the stairs? What if he saw Jack going out through the window and just walked calmly out the barn door and met him on the meadow?

"Give it to me now, boy. I won't hurt you or your friends. I don't care about you or your friends. I want the elixir. You know that I can't wait past tomorrow."

"Did you kill the old Chinese man?"

The question seemed to take Dr. Brown by surprise—as if he hadn't any real idea of the extent of Jack's knowledge. He took two steps toward the stairs, stopped, and squinted up toward the loft. He shook his head slowly. "No," he said. "But I'd kill him now happily if he weren't already dead. He cheated me into taking the damned carnival and letting him die. You can't imagine how many years he'd owned it—or it had owned him. How do you know about Ling?"

"Dr. Jensen knew him." Jack gripped the headboard with his left hand and pulled steadily up on it. It was heavy, built of oak and iron. The corner of the bed rose with it—a half inch, an inch. He scrabbled at the rope ladder with his foot, hauling out coils, pulling it clear. There it was, in a heap around his feet. There was no telling what sort of tangles it had gotten itself into. He'd toss it from the window and there'd be nothing but a mess of rope hanging there, swaying back and forth fifteen feet from the ground. "Give it up, if you detest it so. Was it the carnival that saved you when my father killed you?"

"You're a smart lad, Jack. You might have been my own son. You know that, don't you? You and I."

He paused and shook his head, regretting, he seemed to

imply, that he and Jack weren't good friends, that he had nothing but Jack's well-being in mind and wasn't a murderer at all. Jack hated him for it.

"My agreement with Ling saved me at the same time that it killed him." Dr. Brown smiled up at him and stroked his chin again. "I'm tired of it, in truth. And I'm bound for greener shores, so to speak. What about you? Doesn't eternal life appeal to you? We could strike a bargain, couldn't we? Haven't you dreamed of owning a carnival? It's right up your alley, I'd say. There's nothing to it. It maintains itself with a little help, and you get used to that soon enough. You'll see lands you haven't suspected exist."

"You'd die, wouldn't you, just like Ling? You're dead now." Jack could see that Dr. Brown was edging toward the loft stairs, out of the circle of radiance thrown by the lantern and into shadow. Jack pushed open the shutters, letting in the feeble early evening light. There Dr. Brown stood, regarding him with a questioning look. Was he stupid enough to think that the idea of "maintaining" such a carnival would appeal to Jack? Probably he was—evil men no doubt suspected everyone of being equally evil. "It would be almost worth it, if we'd get to see you die—turn to dust."

"Of course it would be. Take your friends along. There are inevitable periods of—what shall I say? Self-denial, maybe—when the fat boy would lose a few pounds. But it would do him good in the end, and he could flesh himself out, if you take my meaning, in good time." There was a pause. Jack glanced down at the floor, calculating where the two bent bars were that he'd have to grab in order to hook them over the sill. He couldn't afford to paw through the rope mess to search for them. He'd have to pluck them up and go. He'd have no second chance.

Wham! Dr. Brown's stick cracked against the pine floor. "Give me the bottle, boy. Now. You're fooling away my time. I have an aversion to killing you, but that doesn't extend to your friends, especially to the girl. It doesn't extend past my patience, either, which is running out." He shook his head slowly. "You look a bit like your mother. Maybe that's why I haven't killed you yet—"

He was still speaking when Jack threw the table at him. He picked up the table by his bed, raised it into the air, and flung it with all his strength at the man below him. Then, without waiting an instant, he snatched up the end of the rope ladder and jammed the hooks down onto the sill, dropping the ladder out after it, watching for the second it took to unreel.

The crash and clatter below ended even as he let go of the ropes. He hoisted himself through the window, saw the black hair of Dr. Brown rising into view on the stairs. Jack dropped, feeling with his feet for the rope rungs. He got a quick view of a face twisted with rage, heard a shout, a curse. He slid toward the grass, half expecting to be reeled in like a fish. The ladder heaved suddenly and he dropped, let go, and fell, closing his eyes and gritting his teeth and bumping to the grass almost at once. He'd been only two or three feet up. Dr. Brown hung from the window, his hands on the ladder. He bent back in, thrust out again, and threw his stick at Jack's back as Jack ran for the woods.

The road would do him no good. He'd have to take to the woods. He knew the woods around Willoughby's farm better than anyone else. He could hide out until late, then circle around to Miss Flees's. No, he couldn't. He had to get there now and warn his friends. It would do Dr. Brown no logical good at all to carry out his threats against Skeezix and Helen, but then logic hadn't played much of a hand in this affair so far. He thought suddenly of Lantz lying dead beneath the tree on the meadow. It could as easily be Skeezix next if he didn't hurry. Or Helen. It didn't bear thinking about.

He ran along through the darkness of the forest, leaping over fallen limbs, smashing through the wet, spongy grass. Oaks and alders and occasional clumps of redwood cast the forest floor into darkness. What little sunlight there was wouldn't last out the next ten minutes. He'd get along easier in the woods then Dr. Brown would, if only because he knew them. There were a dozen places he could hide, especially along the river. He slowed down when he thought about the river. He stopped, listening for the sound of Dr. Brown coming along behind. There was nothing—only the chattering of a squirrel and the crying of birds. It wasn't safe, though, to sit and think. He was off again, angling through the trees, back in the general direction of the farmhouse and the river, where it ran along behind, placid and slow and broadening out into a natural pond and then emptying into the harbor a mile and a half down.

A crack of thunder echoed out of the mountains. Rain began to fall—big, cold drops that caught on tree branches and misted down over him. He wished he'd grabbed a sweater to put on under his jacket, but there hadn't exactly been time for that. There was open meadow ahead, high grass and skunk cabbage and the river beyond. He stopped and listened again, out on the meadow. He could see all around him, and there was no one, and not a sound of pursuit. Dr. Brown had given up. He couldn't run in the first place; that's why he'd taken MacWilt with him up into the hills. Jack was safe enough for the moment.

He hunched over and ran for the river, hauling his jacket over his head. The rain thickened, beating down around him. For a moment he thought of going home. There'd be no profit in Dr. Brown's hanging around there. He knew well enough that Jack had the elixir, had seen through Jack's lie. Jack could lock himself into the farmhouse and wait for Willoughby to come home. He could sit in the darkness, letting Dr. Brown think he'd gone on into the village. But then what about Skeezix and Helen? And what about sitting alone in the dark, wondering whether Dr. Brown was skulking around out in the rainy night? It wouldn't do.

He leaped across the last few yards of meadow, down onto the muddy little path that ran up toward the farm. In a moment he was on the dock, such as it was, untying the painter of Willoughby's rowboat. It was half swamped with rainwater. Jack bailed it with a dipper even as he pushed off and settled onto the middle thwart. He unshipped the oars, plunged them into the water, spun the boat half around with the first crazy heave, and then settled to it, pulling out toward the middle of the pond and letting himself drift down as he bailed.

He was safe—wet and cold, but safe. He set his feet on either side of the boat spinning toward town. With the current he'd be there in no time at all—long before Dr. Brown would suppose. There'd be time to think, to plan. They could go to Dr. Jensen, perhaps, and get his advice. Jack looked up into the falling rain. The sky was dark and whirling with clouds torn to bits by wind. The moon was high by now, showing through the clouds themselves, then through the sudden rents between them, then disappearing altogether and leaving the earth dark and cold.

Circling above, illuminated for a moment in moonlight, was a bird—a crow, following the lazy course of the river. When the moon blinked out beyond storm clouds the crow was gone with it, invisible against the night.

Helen pulled the door back and found Skeezix on the stairs, grinning up at her. "Smells like the devil up here," he said, wrinkling up his nose and looking around.

"I've been burning the curtains," Helen said to him.

"Ah. Look what we've found, Jack and I."

Helen looked at the thing in his hand, a disk as big around as a saucer. "What is it? Looks like it's made of seashell."

Skeezix looked around warily, surprised, perhaps, to see that Helen *had* been burning the curtains, or someone had. "I thought I heard voices. Were you talking to someone?"

Helen shrugged and took the disk out of his hand. It was a tremendous button, with two holes drilled into the center of it, made of abalone, probably, and a monstrous abalone at that. "This *is* fascinating, isn't it? You'll give it to Dr. Jensen, I suppose, and he'll put it with his other giant trinkets, and you can go over and look at them on rainy Sunday afternoons and wonder where they came from."

Skeezix gave Helen the dubious eye. "Sorry you stayed behind, are you? You missed it up in the hills. Dr. Brown was there; MacWilt. He nearly killed Jack."

Helen flinched a bit despite the "nearly." "Is Jack hurt?"

"No. I hit him with a rock—Dr. Brown, that is. He's a shape-changer, you know. Half the time he flies round the countryside as a crow. He was in a tree, and I hit him with a rock. Pow! Just like that." Skeezix thumped himself in the chest with his balled-up fist, then reeled back with a look of surprised chagrin on his face, imitating Dr. Brown as a crow.

Helen nodded. "Just like that? He was a crow? How did he *almost* kill Jack, peck him in the forehead?"

"Not the crow—MacWilt. Blind as a cave fish, but seeing through Dr. Brown's eyes. It was spooky, I can tell you. Here he came, around the hill, tapping with his stick. I could see that something was wrong, so I circled back around and hid. Jack stayed to talk. It was just like Jack—very polite to a blind devil with a gun." Skeezix grinned and shook his head, recalling it, glorying in his own good sense. Helen gave him a withering look, though, and he went on, telling her about slamming the crow with the rock and the two of them going for the gun and very nearly getting rid of the crow for good and all, and MacWilt staggering away sightless and shouting while Jack and Skeezix ran down over the hills toward Mrs. Oglevy's orchards, looking to get another crack at the crow.

"You didn't get him."

"No," said Skeezix, sitting down at the table and idly thumbing Mrs. Langley's book. "He was frightened for his life—flew like he was shot from a catapult. I wouldn't be surprised if he packed up his carnival and left. If he was smart, that's what he'd do, and without waiting for an invitation." Skeezix brushed his hair back out of his face and squinted at Helen. It was the look of someone who'd done a dangerous job and done it well.

"You *nitwit*," said Helen, squinting back at him and giving him a smarmy sort of look—a look that made it clear she saw right through him. "Pack up and leave! I told you not to go out there meddling around. So did Dr. Jensen. What did you find? I'll tell you what—nothing, that's what. You nearly got killed, and what for? So you could come back here and carry on. Well, I've had a few adventures of my own. I've met a couple of curious people."

"Like who?"

"Like Mrs. Langley."

Skeezix looked around him all of a sudden. The sarcastic face he was making dissolved.

"She'd gone now. She disappeared when you came fumbling at the trapdoor. She was on the verge of telling me everything. Her husband's been there, and —"

"Been where?"

"Why, to the magical land, idiot. Where do you think, San Francisco? Arcata? Where else would he have been?"

"All right, all right." Skeezix held up his hands in a gesture of resignation. "Relax, will you? Take a few deep breaths; you're all worked up."

"I'll relax you with this button." Helen menaced him with the button, holding it over his head with both hands. "Anyway, her husband's been across, and back again. You can find all sorts of worlds over there, she's been telling me. Worlds full of giants here, bull of tiny little men there. And after a bit you grow or shrink to size—very convenient, except that your clothes don't grow with you. I promised I'd take this change of clothes down to the cove where her husband—Jimmy—is supposed to come in. He won't have a thing to wear, otherwise."

"The filthy—" began Skeezix, but Helen waved him silent.

"He isn't filthy anything. He's a wonderful man and he'll seem like a giant to us, but then he'll shrink out of his clothes. He probably already has and they're scattered down the coast by now."

"The shoe!"

"No, *not* the shoe. That stuff wasn't his. I asked Mrs. Langley."

"Then whose is it?"

"How should *I* know whose it is? I got all this from Mrs. Langley. She's a ghost, for goodness' sake, and lives in this attic. She's no oracle. Her husband's come from *little* worlds, too— crawled up through gopher holes. There's any number of ways you can come across, but she recommends coming by water. It's too dangerous the other way. You're at the mercy of every mole you run into."

Skeezix grimaced. "I dare say. And bugs, too. Imagine running into a potato bug when you're shrunk down to the size of a worm. It's horrifying, isn't it? So what did you find out that we can *use*? This is all very nice—first-rate gossip. But look at the source. A ghost, after all."

"Sshh!" said Helen, widening her eyes. "You should have seen what she did to Peebles. He tried to burn the place down, with me in it, and—"

Skeezix stood up and punched his fist into his open palm. "I'll murder him. Where is he now? He's downstairs, in the kitchen. I saw him there. I'll feed him to the dogs."

Helen pushed him back over into the chair. The look on his face seemed to her to indicate that he'd do what he said. "Wait a moment. I'll help you do it, but there's more to tell you first. Mrs. Langley *threw Peebles downstairs!*"

Skeezix blinked hard, then looked around slowly. "Good for her!" he said with an air of sudden overwhelming approval. "That's just what I've been saying about her, haven't I? Isn't it? I've got nothing but admiration for a woman like that—living up here like a monk, nothing but the finest furniture all heaped around like this. It's a wonder, isn't it? I mean really." He gestured roundabout, then peered into the shadows, grinning weakly as if half expecting Mrs. Langley to materialize there, perhaps intending to pitch him down the stairs too.

"Relax," said Helen. "She likes you. She told me so. She likes Jack, too. Jack isn't hurt, is he?"

Skeezix shook his head. "I got there in time. Jack was lucky."

"I'm sure he was," said Helen. "Anyway, I've got to get these clothes down to the cove, the sooner the better." Then in a whisper she said, "I don't think he's going to come, actually. He's been away years now. But she's such a dear old thing; I want to do it just to satisfy her."

Skeezix nodded. He could see the value in that. "Smells like someone's cooking something awful."

And it did. There was a rotten, fishy sort of odor coming up through the vent—clearly not cabbage soup. The two of them stepped across and peered through. There was Peebles, rolling out dough on the wooden counter. The bucket that had held the strange fish still lay on the table, empty now but for two inches of bloody ocean water. The fish lay beside it, flayed and hacked and boned. A heap of its little fingerlike fins lay alongside the muck cleaned out of the fish, into which had been shoved the creature's severed head, eyes open and staring.

Helen turned away, sickened. There was something in the cut-off fins that reminded her of—what? Peeble's regrown finger. That was it.

"Look at this!" whispered Skeezix.

"I can't. It makes me sick."

"He's making up a pie, a fish pie! Good God! He thinks he's going to feed us Solstice fish!" He walked over to where Helen sat at the table. "Let's go down there right now and make *him* eat it. Raw. Every bit of it, guts and all. What in the world do you suppose would happen to him? I bet he'd become immune to gravity, float right up into the sky until the thin air exploded him. He'd rain down over the village like—"

"Shut up, will you? Enough about guts."

"Of course," said Skeezix. "Let's go down and see what's up. We've got to meet Jack anyway in a couple of hours, and we might as well haul these duds out to the cove first. No telling when this naked Jimmy will reel up out of the weeds." He scooped up the clothes and headed for the trapdoor.

Miss Flees met them in the hallway. She had a distant,

glazed look in her eyes, as if all the conjuring and chasing after magic had tired her out. Her eyes were red-rimmed, and she smelled of wine. She stopped them by putting her arm across in front of them. "Where are *you* going?" she asked.

She's been drinking, thought Skeezix; he grinned at her and widened his eyes. "In to eat."

She stared at them both, as if she were trying to think of something to say—some reason that Skeezix's answer wouldn't do. She stood just so, reeling slightly, then nodded. "Watch yourselves. You two are a *little bit* too high and mighty these days. Coming and going at all hours. Lying. What do you do up in that attic?"

"I talk with Mrs. Langley," said Helen, looking straight into her face. "Mrs. Langley threw Peebles down the stairs today. I asked her to do that."

Miss Flees stiffened. She knew about Peebles and the stairs. She'd have to; Peebles had cried and shouted enough. Helen had heard him carrying on during her conversation with Mrs. Langley.

Helen kept at her. "Peebles tried to burn the house down two hours ago; do you know that?"

Miss Flees jerked herself upright, trying to paint a proud look onto her face, but succeeding only in sort of pinching together her mouth and chin. She licked the palm of her pawlike hand and touched her hair with it. "Young Mr. Peebles is an intellectual," she said. "You two wouldn't know about that. Children like him are often frail. They're . . . prodigies. That's what they are, prodigies, and it's not for the likes of you to judge them. We understand each other, Mr. Peebles and I."

"I'm certain you do," said Helen. "Birds of a feather, I suppose. You were a prodigy too, weren't you? Wasn't that what you were telling us?"

"Well," said Miss Flees, shrugging, "I won't say I wasn't, in my time."

"You must be a very fortunate lady. I was telling Skee—

Bobby here that I envy people of genius like you—the things they might accomplish."

"Envy is a sin, of course. In this case I can understand it, though." Miss Flees seemed to have gone blank, as if someone had reached into her head and switched off the bulb.

Skeezix gritted his teeth at Helen, as if he could hardly stand it and at any moment would say what he meant. Saying what he meant wouldn't hurt anything much, of course. He'd done it before. Miss Flees couldn't pitch him out because she'd lose the little bit of income the village paid her, and besides, Skeezix had too many friends, including Dr. Jensen. So did Helen. That in itself was maddening. But saying what he meant would end in shouting, and shouting would end in Miss Flees ordering them out, and that wouldn't do any good, because what they wanted was to see what it was that Peebles was up to.

"Peebles is cooking something nice, isn't he?" asked Helen, placating Miss Flees, who smiled broadly, showing off her tilted teeth.

"I'm sure he is. There's nothing for you children, though. Perhaps you could eat out. Our Mr. Peebles says there isn't enough to go around. He's making me a pie. He won't let me into the kitchen. 'His little surprise,' he says, and that's just like him, isn't it?" She shook her head, thinking of her dear Peebles.

Skeezix grinned. So that was the way it was. Peebles was going to feed *her* the Solstice fish. And she'd be too addlebrained to know what it was she was eating. Or maybe, heaven help her, she *did* know, was going to eat it on purpose. Things were getting desperate indeed. He'd give anything to watch, but from the look of Peebles, messing around in the kitchen, Miss Flees wouldn't begin to shove it down for another forty-five minutes. Maybe they could get down to the cove and back by then. He nodded at Helen and gestured toward the front room, toward the door. She nodded back, and both of them pushed past Miss Flees and set out.

"What's that bundle of clothing?" the woman asked after them, suspicious suddenly. "You can't steal those clothes!"

"There's a naked man on the beach," said Helen over her shoulder. "These are for him. It's Mrs. Langley's husband, come home from the wars. Save some dinner for him." And with that they were through the door and gone. They could hear Miss Flees sputtering as the door slammed shut. She'd have no idea what to make of talk like that. Having no sense of humor herself, she couldn't recognize it in others. She'd understand everything literally, and it would confound her. Just as well, Helen thought. In the last couple of hours she'd somehow come to the conclusion that such people deserved what they got, although it was a bit much that Miss Flees had gotten Peebles. Almost no one deserved Peebles.

The tide was up, washing very nearly across the entire beach. The strip of sand that lay exposed was littered with kelp and seashells and driftwood and flotsam out of the ocean. Rain had fallen and had wetted things down pretty thoroughly, but it had let up again and now the night was dark and windy beneath a cloud-hung sky. Skeezix carried a lantern that he'd gotten from Miss Flees's shed. He and Helen stood beneath the trestle, looking at shadows and wondering what, exactly, to do with the clothes. Somehow simply leaving them there seemed foolish—as if they were leaving an offering to a sea god that both of them knew didn't exist or, if he did exist, wouldn't show up to claim the gift.

Skeezix set the lantern on a high shelf of cut stone beneath the trestle and began poking around beneath it. Rocks were tumbled and heaped there, the cracks between them jammed with weather- and ocean-worn debris—broken mussel shells and sticks and tangles of dried seaweed. "We can hide them here," Skeezix said. "They're sheltered enough from the rain, so they'll stay dry, except that the fog will get at them. A really high tide will get them too, but there's nowhere else as good, not if Mrs. Langley wanted you to leave them at the cove."

"That's what she said." Helen pulled rocks loose, letting them roll down onto the sand. Little beach bugs scurried away, and a big red crab scuttled back into the shadows, eyeing them warily. "Here, what's this?" Helen reached down into the rocks, half expecting to be pinched or bitten. A bit of blue material lay just visible in the light of the lantern, wedged under two round stones. They both pulled stuff clear, levering one big rock loose with a stick and jumping back as it thumped onto the sand.

Helen got a hand on the cloth and pulled, tearing a chunk away and hauling it out. It fluttered in her hand—a piece of shirt, maybe, with the button still attached. "Darn it," said Helen. "I didn't mean to rip it. Let's get it out of there. I've got this curious suspicion." And the two of them pawed through the rock pile until the cloth was exposed. It was a shirt, just as Helen thought. Beneath it were trousers, neatly folded, and lying across the top of a pair of shoes with socks stuffed inside them. Helen looked into the collar of the shirt, and there, scrawled in ink, was the name *J. Langley.*

"Well, I'll be," said Skeezix, wondering at it. "I wonder when—"

"Twelve years ago."

"She was dead last Solstice, wasn't she?"

"She got someone else to do it, like she did me."

"Who? How do you know?"

Helen gave him a look. Here was a chance to play one of her trump cards. "Lars Portland, Jack's father."

"No. You're making that up."

"So don't believe me. *I don't care.* Believe what you want. Revel in ignorance, prodigy."

Skeezix made his cabbage-broth face at her, then reached into the rocks and yanked out one of the shoes. "Look here," he said, pulling the sock out of it. A rock had been shoved into the shoe along with the sock, to weight it down, perhaps. Under the rock was a bit of paper, folded very neatly. There was writing on it in a shaky hand, the ink lightened and spidery from years of misty air. Skeezix held it to the lantern. *Three*, it said simply. There was nothing else on the paper.

"It beats me," said Skeezix, turning the paper over and back again.

"Not me." Helen took it from him. "These have been here longer than I thought—twenty-four years. I'd bet on it. She said he'd been gone five times and had come back twice. These were left at the third Solstice, after he'd been and gone a couple of times already. He never came back after them, either."

"Look inside the shoes you brought."

Helen did. There were rocks inside. Mrs. Langley had been thorough, leaving nothing to her courier except the burying of the clothes. Under the rock in the right shoe was a folded paper. *Five*, it read.

Skeezix nodded, satisfied with himself. "She's keeping count."

"She wants him to know that she's been faithful, that she hasn't missed a year. It's very romantic, isn't it?"

"It's nuts," said Skeezix. "Where's four, do you think?"

"Someone's taken them. That's obvious. No telling when. That's pretty rotten, unless it was Jimmy. But Mrs. Langley would know if Jimmy'd come back. He would have gone to her. They were that way, very faithful."

Skeezix shook his head. "They were nuts. I bet number one and number two are down there someplace. Do you want to find them?"

"They aren't there. He came back the first time through a gopher hole. Didn't I tell you that? Listen next time, smart aleck. Then the second time he came back by way of the cove, but there weren't any clothes here. Mrs. Langley was here herself, by accident. *She* found him that time, luckily."

Skeezix nodded. "Put the clothes back in. If he *does* come, all of them ought to be there. If she was keeping count for him, we'd better not mess it up. It's touching, really, isn't it? Like something out of a penny romance magazine. Very artful. Makes your heart go, doesn't it?"

"You're a jerk. Let me put the clothes in. *You'll* mess it up."

A gust of spindrift-laden wind blew up the beach as they laid the last of the rocks over the clothes. Helen shoved bits of shell and wood into the cracks and scattered weedy sand over it all; then the two of them backed away, swishing out their footprints with a clutch of kelp so it wouldn't look like anybody'd been messing about there. The wind and tide would no doubt do it for them before the night was up, but somehow it seemed to both of them that, all things considered, they couldn't be too careful with the whole business. More was going on than any of them had suspected earlier that day. They turned their backs on the cove and headed toward the lights of town.

Part Three

DOCTOR JENSEN'S CRAB

11

Jack slumped, deadly tired all of a sudden and almost hope-less. Small as the river was, as it neared the harbor it did nothing but get broader. Trees overhung it on both sides, but even if he rowed in toward shore and stayed there he'd be seen easily enough from the air. And he'd probably just tan-gle himself up in thickets anyway. There was nothing to do but put his back into it and go. In five minutes he'd be in town, come what may. If it came down to it, he'd lay odds on his being able to elude almost anyone in town. There wasn't a street or an alley he didn't know. He'd played hide-and-seek in his time across every inch of it, from the harbor to Dr. Jensen's.

He passed the first riverside house—old Mr. Dingley's tumbledown mansion with its tilted dock and grassy, sloped rear yard. Then two more houses: the White sisters', sitting side by side. On a sudden impulse he brought the rowboat around and in toward shore. The current drove him on down, past another half dozen houses.

The crow was gone, or at least it had disappeared for the moment. That wasn't good. It certainly hadn't flown away. . . . He bumped ashore. The stern swung round in the current as he leaped onto the bank and grabbed the trailing painter, hauling the bow high up on the weedy sand. There was nothing to tie up to save the pepper trees, farther down, but there was no time to tow the boat to them. So he dragged on the bow and then grabbed the rear thwart and lifted the stern entirely up out of the water. The rain had fallen off, but if it started again in earnest, the river could easily rise a foot by morning. It wouldn't do to let Willoughby's rowboat wash into the harbor and drift out to sea with the tide.

In seconds he was hunching along, up the bank toward the rear of the taxidermist's shop. He could hide inside, if it came to that. He knew which windows weren't locked like they ought to be. But what if Dr. Brown cornered him there, among the dusty animals, all of them going to bits, some of them without eyes? That wouldn't do at all. The crow might easily be sitting in one of the pepper trees now, watching him.

The thought of it slowed him down. He mustn't blunder into anything. It occurred to him that he'd been doing too much blundering that day. But the fault wasn't all his. When he and Skeezix had gone up into the hills they'd had no idea what they'd run into. They could hardly have expected what they'd found.

Jack stopped, listening to the silent night. There was a light on in the taxidermist's. He and his friends weren't the only ones, apparently, who knew about unlocked windows. Was it Dr. Brown? Probably not; he wouldn't light a candle to announce his presence, would he? Jack crept forward in a crouch. It could, of course, be a tramp, getting in out of the rain. If Lantz weren't dead . . . but Lantz was dead. Rainwater dripped from the limbs of the pepper trees, and vague disembodied noises filtered down from town, from the inns along the High Street. Someone was singing, low and quiet— from inside the shop. Jack cocked his head and listened, half relieved to hear the singing, as if villains wouldn't be interested in singing.

He edged into the shadows of the three trees. The weeping limbs nearly touched the earth. He couldn't see much; the windows were too dusty and full of pasted-on newspaper. He'd have to take a closer look. He felt like a conspirator, glancing back down the river to see that he wasn't followed. There sat his boat, high and dry. He looked once toward the harbor, saw no one, and stealthily took a step forward.

A hand grabbed his elbow. He shrieked and jerked away, but the fingers closed round his arm. Another hand covered his mouth, a hand smelling of musty bird cages and of leather crumbled with age. The forefinger and thumb clawed at his eyes. He bit the hand, but it was like biting rubber. A knee shoved into the small of his back, and the hand let go of his arm and patted at the pocket of his coat.

Jack slammed his elbow back and flailed around to get a look at his attacker. The hand on his face dragged him over backward, and he stumbled and fell, striking behind him with both fists. He jerked free of the hand over his mouth and looked up into the stony face of Dr. Brown, who clutched him now by the jacket, hauling up on it so as to pull Jack nearly off the ground. Jack hollered and twisted. He felt the tip of Dr. Brown's stick prod him hard in the ribs. He gasped, hollered again, and sluffed off the right sleeve of his jacket, sliding away through the wet grass, clambering onto a knee and one foot.

There was Dr. Brown, his stick raised over his head, a look of loathing twisting his face into something inhuman. Jack lurched halfway to his feet as the stick smashed into his shoulder and rose again for another blow. He hollered, raised his arm to cover his face, and felt someone brush past him even as he heard footsteps rushing up. There was a grunt and a curse as Dr. Brown went over backward, striking now at a white-coated man, weirdly tall, in his stocking feet and sadly undersized clothes. Jack reeled away, grabbing his shoulder. It was a tramp, apparently, come to his aid, and furious, by the look of him.

Dr. Brown retreated toward the river, limping along, stopping to chant something over his shoulder. The tall man cursed at him. He knew him—called him Harbin. Jack stepped toward the corner of the building. Perhaps he *hadn't* been saved by some sort of kind stranger. Perhaps this was a double-crossed conspirator, some old enemy running into Dr. Brown by chance. The two stumbled into the river and rolled out into the current, sweeping away down toward the harbor and into darkness. Jack turned and ran, ducking round and onto the High Street, pounding away toward Miss Flees's and wondering vaguely at the strange smell of tar and wildflowers that seemed to drift along behind him. He was halfway up the block before he realized what the smell was.

Helen and Skeezix pressed themselves against the wall of the house, trusting to unpruned junipers and berry vines to hide them from the street. They'd put away Miss Flees's lantern, then sneaked back around in order to see in through the window. Helen hadn't told Skeezix about the other window she'd looked through that day; there'd be time enough for that revelation when they met Jack.

Miss Flees sat alone in the candlelit parlor, a tablecloth thrown over the old library table that she used to sit at when she had séances. She daintily spooned up cabbage broth, tapping her mouth with a crumpled bit of cloth in between mouthfuls. Skeezix was half fascinated by the idea that Miss Flees not only ate the cabbage broth she served them but seemed to relish it, fishing in it for stray pieces of the flabby bacon she flavored it with. Tonight it was only the first course, though.

He could see through the half-open door that joined the parlor and the kitchen. Miss Flees had her back to it, which was just as well. She wouldn't want to see what it was that Peebles was doing to her pie, Skeezix was fairly sure of that. If there was one thing that was certain to Skeezix, it was that before Peebles spiraled down into whatever loathesome pit he was digging for himself, Skeezix would tweak his nose. He'd throttle him, is what he'd do. What Peebles had needed years ago was a fist in the face. It wasn't enough that Peebles lived in a world of self-built misery and meanness, and in the end would scuttle his own ship. Skeezix would kick a hole in it to move the job along. There was no use taking a chance with Peebles.

Heaven knew what was in the pie he was sawing away at in the kitchen. Solstice fish surely wasn't the only loathesome thing. There were sure to be herbs and meats in it that no human being ought to eat, even Miss Flees, if she qualified as human. Skeezix had become convinced, though, that Miss Flees indeed knew what it was she was eating. Her tiresome efforts with the bloody chicken and the rigamarole on the floor had accomplished nothing more than the loss of Pebbles's finger and the singing of hymns by a dead woman. She had gotten no closer to her goal than MacWilt had when he looked through the telescope. Skeezix wondered if Miss Flees would get off as easily as MacWilt. Were there worse things than being blinded and then set adrift in an open meadow? Well, she was doing it to herself, chasing down her sad destiny like a racehorse jockey.

There was a noise on the street—footsteps, running. Skeezix grabbed Helen's arm and yanked on it, stooping behind a juniper. They parted the foliage and looked out. It was Jack, in a terrible hurry. He slowed down when he drew up to the orphanage, darting in to hide behind an adjacent bush. He had no idea they were there. He peered around him, looking at the sky as if he expected to see something. Skeezix could guess what it was.

Helen picked up a pebble and reached back to throw it, thinking, clearly, to hit Jack with it and silently alert him to their presence. Skeezix stepped out from behind his bush, got in the way of the flying pebble, and poked Jack in the small of the back. Jack gasped and pitched forward, sprawling across his bush. He seemed to be strangling. Helen rushed up and hit Skeezix in the shoulder, then thwacked him on the earlobe with her middle finger.

"Ow!" cried Skeezix in a hoarse sort of a shouted whisper. He covered his mouth and lurched away, laughing. Jack had recovered and stood up, staring in shocked surprise, first at Helen and then at Skeezix, who quit his lurching, swallowed hard, and hunched his shoulders. "I couldn't help myself. It was too easy. I can't resist temptations when it's that easy to give in. You should know. You've seen me at Potts's bakery."

"You look like hell," said Helen, grimacing at Jack. He smoothed out his hair and tugged his coat straight, wincing as pain shot across his shoulder. Helen put a hand on his arm. "You're hurt."

"It's nothing," said Jack. "I'm okay. Just a . . . bruise, let's say. Nothing at all." He winced again, as if the pain had decided to return, but the wince actually had more to do with the sudden thought of his flopping atop the bush like a fool with Helen watching. He'd fix Skeezix for that—feed him a bologna sandwich with the meat cut out of a piece of purple rubber.

"Hsst!" Skeezix whispered at them, back at the window. He windmilled his right arm a couple of times, and Jack and Helen crept over toward him, all three of them taking up the old position again.

Peebles had brought in the pie. Miss Flees seemed to be delighted with it, and yet at the same time she looked at it skeptically. She squinted at Peebles and asked him something, but the three outside caught almost none of it, except the name "Dr. Brown," uttered twice. Peebles nodded, a wide theatrical nod intended to convince Miss Flees utterly. She sat half up and drew a thin dark book out from where she'd been sitting on it. Then she waved Peebles back into the kitchen, as if she were suspicious that he'd try to get a glimpse of the book, and she read it carefully, pressing her nose almost against the book and swiveling her head back and forth to follow the lines of print.

She looked up at the window—straight at them. Skeezix, Jack, and Helen slid out of sight, then crouched there silently, waiting for Miss Flees to start shouting. There was nothing. With all the candles lit around her, she hadn't seen them. When they peered through the window again the book was gone, and she'd forked up a piece of the pie and was diligently scraping off the crust. She blew on it to cool it.

Peebles watched from behind the kitchen door, a look of malevolent wonder on his face, as if he was certain something curious was going to happen to Miss Flees but didn't at all know what it was. She touched her tongue to the pie, barely tasting it. Her face screwed itself into a heap, and she seemed to gag, slouching back into her chair and resting there, thinking. Then she lifted the fork again, and, with the same face she occasionally used to try to stare down Skeezix and Helen, she stared at the bit of cooked flesh dangling from the end of the fork. They could see the muscles in her face tighten. She jammed her eyes shut, held her nose, opened her mouth, and shoved the morsel in, chomping away at it with a forced will. Her eyes sprang open as she swallowed it, and she lurched for her water glass, knocking it over onto the cloth. She stood up, clutching the table, and went after the rest of her soup, picking up the bowl and draining it at a gulp, then staggering back and kicking over her chair.

"Mr. Peebles!" she croaked, turning around. But Peebles was gone. He'd left her alone. She stumbled toward the kitchen, calling him, her voice whistling weirdly, like the voice of a bird. "Mr. Peebles! You!" she whistled, then clutched at the swung-open door to steady herself. She seemed to recover a bit. She straightened and shook her head. Then she straightened some more until she stood like a post, her neck stretched unnaturally long.

"She's got a fishbone in her throat," whispered Skeezix. Neither of his friends responded. They watched her reel around toward the table then, striding away toward it like a woman hypnotized. Her mouth opened and shut like the mouth of an eel, and she emitted little flurries of canary song in lip-quivering rushes. She lurched forward, falling over her downed chair. The book she'd been reading tumbled from her bodice, straight into the fish pie. She stood up, reeling, seemed to reach for the book, but plucked out a handful of pie instead and shoved it into her mouth, swallowing it almost without chewing. Then she spun away around the parlor like a dervish, warbling and shrieking and utterly mad.

There was Peebles again, in the living room now, hidden behind a stuffed chair. He watched Miss Flees spin and sucked methodically on his unnatural finger. When the book tumbled into the pie he half stood up, as if he would grab for it, but he settled again when it was clear that Miss Flees hadn't any interest in it any more. She clearly hadn't any interest in anything on earth.

A sudden crack of thunder seemed to rattle the house. Rain washed across the night sky in a sheet. The candles around the parlor dimmed and flared, as if blown by winds, and a vast shadow fell obliquely across street and lawn, as if it were cast by a swiftly opening door. Fireflies, thousands of them, rose in a cloud from the suddenly shadowed bushes and rushed skyward like a swarm of backward-shooting stars.

Jack, Helen, and Skeezix fled from the window toward the back yard. Something cold in the shadow pushed them like a vast, compelling hand, and they tumbled together against the shingled wall of the carriage shed, pressing against it, watching through the distant half-lit window. Miss Flees stood like a swamp bird, skinny and still, unmoving, waiting. She shimmered like ocean water stirred by wind and then was gone along with the candle flames, all of them blinking out in an instant. Jack fancied that he saw the angular shadow clipped off, as if the door that had opened had suddenly closed. He huddled under the eaves of the carriage house, the water running off the roof in a line that soaked his shoes. He expected that Miss Flees was still standing in the dark room, that it had only been the candles going out that had made her seem to disappear.

A light winked on. Someone had lit a match and, one by one, was relighting the candles. It was Peebles. Miss Flees was gone, vanished. Peebles's hand shook so he could barely keep the match lit. He pulled one of the candles out of its holder and lit the rest with it, clustering them around the center of the table, over the broken pie and the book still thrusting out like a sail. He plucked the book out and wiped it off carefully on the corner of the tablecloth. Then he put his fingers to his mouth, to lick off the fragments of pie smeared across them, but thought better of it, apparently, and turned to the tablecloth once again.

Abruptly he stepped to the window and looked out into the night. He cupped his hands round his eyes and stood there, then crouched and looked skyward. Helen, Jack, and Skeezix stood still, trusting that they were concealed by shadow and rain. They watched Peebles tuck the book under his arm and pick up the pie. He walked into the kitchen, idly sucking on his finger as he disappeared from view, leaving the candles to burn themselves out on the parlor table.

When he crawled out of the ocean onto the rock ledge, grappling at kelp strands and heaving for breath, he still clutched his stick. He'd held on to it even as the tide had swept him out of the harbor and into the ocean. He hadn't gotten a clear look at the man's face, but what look he'd gotten had convinced him it was Lars Portland. He'd come back across; there was no doubting it. Too many signs pointed to it, and now this—a giant in the taxidermist's, mixing up the elixir. It had to be Portland. And he would have killed him too. The years seemed to have put an edge on his hatred. If he'd had a revolver, he'd have killed Portland twice there under the pepper trees—once for the sake of his miserable wife, and once for the sake of his son, who'd have given up his precious bottle gratefully enough if things had gone uninterrupted for another minute.

Well, they'd pay; both of them would pay before he was done. He'd be across this time around or be damned, even if he had to float there on the blood of the whole lot of them. He crouched on the rocks, catching his breath. He was weak, frightfully weak, and not just from the chase. And he could feel himself being drawn north, up the coast, to where the carnival, his carnival, labored on without him. There'd be people aplenty on the bluffs, lingering too near the shadows, curious about the darkened interiors of freak shows. He could walk among them in half an hour if he chose. But time grew thin. The passing moments shaved away at the lingering Solstice. He could almost feel the night rumbling with it, like a railway station full of the shriek and steam of a departing train. He had business to finish—old insults to avenge, people to see.

He walked across the headland toward the village, slogging along in wet shoes. He didn't feel the cold; he felt almost nothing at all but a powerful weariness, as if he were wasting away bit by bit with the passing seconds, evaporating into the night air. He'd have to hurry.

He angled up the alley that led to the rear of Dr. Jensen's surgery, stepping past ash cans and rusted buggy springs and tin cans, past chicken coops and vacant lots thick with berry vines and jimson weed. He'd come this way before, several times, watching Jensen. He'd have his way with Jensen too, before he was done—the meddling pig of a surgeon. He'd see him dead and drained, just for sport, as a parting gesture before he went across.

There was the house, the surgery lit by·gas lamps glowing from wall sconces. Jensen bent over the slab, over the body of the boy he'd gathered up that morning on the bluffs, the fool. He must be mystified, wondering what sort of outrage this was, what sort of monster lurked in the night, yet knowing the answer at the same time. The hypocrite. He'd been as anxious to have his way with Jane Henderson as any of them. He'd pretended cheerful defeat when she'd wed Lars Portland, but Harbin had seen through him; he's seen through them all—their lies, their sham happiness, their nothing little lives played out as if they weren't doomed, weren't living in the shadows of impending ruin on a wet and decaying corner of an indifferent world. Harbin spat into the dirt of the alley and narrowed his eyes.

He wiped wet hair from across his forehead and shaded his eyes from rain he hardly felt. It was another irritation in a world filled with irritations, one of a number demanding his attention, begging for it. There was a second man in the room, a short man dressed in the clothes of a clown, in floppy pants and a shirt that hung on him like a sack. He was loathesome, fit to be crippled and shown in a freak show. The two were talking, gesturing at the dead boy on the slab, shaking their heads. They stopped and looked at each other.

The small man handed something to Jensen—two things, one of them a jar, it seemed, full of liquid. They spoke. Their heads nodded, shook, regarded each other seriously, as if what they did there meant something.

Harbin braced himself against the pickets of the waist-high fence along the alley and sagged with impatience, with the effort of waiting. He saw Jensen hold up his hand near a gas lamp. He'd slipped a ring onto his finger, apparently, and he regarded it narrowly, then nodded his head again and slipped it off, laying it on the counter next to the jar. They walked away together. Harbin hurried across toward the gate, leaning on his stick and hopping almost like a crow. He stopped and craned his neck, but he couldn't see them. He was through the gate, stumping toward the window through the rain. He heard the front door slam and knew the small man had gone out. He could follow him easily enough, track him through the evening streets and throttle him at his leisure. But a ruckus in the streets might cause trouble, and trouble might waste time, might alert Jensen unnecessarily. And Jensen, after all, would make prettier carrion than the small man would. Jensen would have some flavor to him.

The back door was unlatched. The man was a fool. Did he think he was immune? He'd come into a sudden bit of knowledge tonight—more of it, perhaps, than he'd appreciate—but it would do him a nation of good, being dead would. He'd have time to spin philosophies. They could summon him back at the next Solstice carnival and ask him about life beyond the pale. He could recite the ingredients in the cure for poison oak or discuss the mysteries of the periodic tables, maybe read them off backward. He'd provide no end of amusement for a thousand sorry little people.

Harbin slipped in through the door, careful of his stick, and stood dripping on the asphalt tiles of the floor. He crept forward silently in the semidarkness, listening, smiling, imagining what the next ten minutes would bring him. His hearing seemed suddenly to be honed on a strop. The music of the

calliope, the rush and roar of the oven, the creak and groan
of the carnival rides spun in his head as if they were alive in
there, propelling him forward.

He stood in the doorway, looking across the hall into the
surgery. His vision narrowed, as if he stood at the far end of
a dark tunnel and watched Dr. Jensen working alone in the
gaslight of the room beyond. The back of the doctor's head
bobbed as he nodded over the little jar of liquid. There was
a something in the air—dandelions, tar, ocean. Harbin's nos-
trils flared. He was suddenly giddy with the smell of it. He
lurched forward, raising his stick, propelling himself into the
surgery. He seemed to be moving far too slowly, as if through
dense air. Jensen turned and shook his head. He twisted the
cap onto the jar on the counter, tried to push it back, to hide
it somehow. He opened his mouth to shout. His spectacles
flew half off, dangling there from his left ear as he made to
duck away, to ward off the descending stick. Flailing his
arms, he fell over backward, cracking his head against the
sharp edge of the counter, then smashing over sideways into
shelves full of chemical glass.

The clatter made Harbin lurch. He shook his head, trying
to rid it of the noise that whirled there, that tugged at the
hand that held the stick and tried to compel it to strike again.
He swept his free hand across the countertop, sliding dishes
and beakers and dried tide-pool animals off onto the floor. He
clutched at the jar—picked it up and swirled it in the lamplight like a man might swirl a glass of wine. He twisted open
the lid and breathed the vapors, his eyes widening with anticipation.

The reek of it drove the noise from his head, and for a moment it seemed to him that he drove a buggy along the Coast
Road, down from the freshwater lagoons to the north. Jane
Henderson sat beside him, dressed in lace, and in the back,
wrapped in wet grasses, were a half dozen trout, caught on
flies he'd tied that morning. For a moment he remembered
feelings that he couldn't quite fathom, as if he'd heard a
sound—a few notes of music, the drone of bees on a warm

day in summer—that recalled something from his youth, something he could no longer define. He twisted the lid onto the jar. This was a dangerous business. It demanded care, or he'd make a fool of himself yet. The memory faded, winked out like a dream and was gone. He bent over the fallen doctor and pressed the tip of his stick into the doctor's neck, leaning on it gently at first.

Jack, Helen, and Skeezix heard the gunshot when they were fifty yards from Dr. Jensen's front door. There was nothing to indicate that it had come from the doctor's house, but they began to run anyway, without a word. The idea of flying bullets slowed them some when they got to the gate, but a deadly quiet within the lighted house prodded them on, and Helen, with the two boys on either side, beat on the door with her fist.

"Come in!" shouted Mrs. Jensen's voice, half crying it. They pushed the door open and found her in the surgery. Dr. Jensen lay on the floor, rolled over onto his side. He clutched his neck and coughed.

"Shot!" cried Jack, looking at the revolver that lay on the slab, tumbled atop Lantz's shrouded body.

"No, he's all right," said Mrs. Jensen evenly. "The man's gone out the back, a thief, I suppose." She bent over her husband, rubbing at his neck with cotton wool soaked in alcohol, loosening his shirt.

Skeezix was out the back door in an instant, with Jack and Helen at his heels. They stopped at the fence, peering down the dark alley, wondering who had fired the gun. Dr. Jensen hadn't been bleeding; *he* hadn't been shot. Somehow they know who it was they searched for. They cocked their heads and listened, the night having trimmed their sudden bravery a bit. There it was—they could hear it—the hurried *tap, tap, tap* of a stick on pavement. He'd gotten out of the alley onto the road.

"Let's go," said Skeezix, and started out at a trot. Jack kept pace, not nearly so anxious.

"Why?" asked Helen, slowing down as Skeezix huffed along. Jack wondered the same thing. He trotted along mostly because it was expected of him, but he hadn't any desire to run headlong into Dr. Brown when he'd just gotten away from him an hour before.

"We missed earlier; we'll get him this time," said Skeezix.

Helen stopped and crossed her arms. "No, we won't. He'll take to the air. You know that, unless all the stuff you were telling me was just nonsense. We're wasting our time. At worst he'll get *you* this time, or all of us."

Skeezix stopped too and turned around to argue with her. It was clear there'd be no budging her, though. And it was true. What would they accomplish? They hadn't any stones or any gun. Also, speaking of guns, it must have been Mrs. Jensen who shot at Dr. Brown. Why else would the revolver lie in the surgery? What had he been after? Had he come round just to murder poor Jensen?

"We gave up," said Skeezix as the three of them trooped back in. Dr. Jensen had sat up. He didn't seem to be badly hurt, but he didn't look particularly comfortable either. When Mrs. Jensen laid a compress on the back of his head, he winced at the touch of it. The surgery was a ruin of broken glass and crockery. There was the faintest aroma of something on the air—something oddly compelling. Jack knew what it was. He felt in his pocket, panicked that he'd somehow broken his bottle. But there it lay, stoppered and dry. He cast a glance around the room, but there was no sign of elixir. That's what Dr. Brown had been after.

Dr. Jensen stood up and retrieved the revolver from where it sat, cold and menacing. "Thanks," he said to his wife, and he grimaced just a little when he said it, but waved her away when she reached for the compress. "I'm all right. A little hoarse, maybe, but all right. He would have done for me, though."

"Why?" asked Mrs. Jensen. "For goodness' sake, couldn't you have given the man what he asked for? Nothing's worth being murdered over."

"My mistake," said the doctor. "I've learned a bit tonight."

"He got away with it, though, didn't he," said Jack. He looked at the clock on the wall—nearly ten. The night was passing; the Solstice was passing. It would peak in a matter of hours, or so Mrs. Langley had said in her book. The night was uncommonly dark outside, except for the ribbon of twilight and stars along the Moonvale Hills, and even as they talked Jack could hear the sound of hailstones clacking against the roof. The wind in the alley had been heavy and wet, and it had an exotic smell to it, as if it were saturated with the essences of a thousand foreign lands and with countless memories and anticipations and regrets, all of it distilled into atmospheric perfume.

Dr. Jensen regarded Jack for a moment. "Yes, he did. I didn't have a chance to save it. He wanted me dead too."

"Who did?" Mrs. Jensen looked at him with surprise.

"Algernon Harbin."

"He's been dead these twelve years!"

"I believe he has," said the doctor, "in a sense. It's a complicated business. Jack has most of it by now. Harbin struck a deal with Wo Ling twelve years ago. Lars Portland swore he'd kill Harbin, and Harbin took him seriously. Lars Portland always meant what he said. Harbin tried to get in before him; he meant to kill Lars himself and steal the elixir and get across, but he didn't. There was the business on the bluffs—you know about that—but Harbin didn't wash downshore in the current like everyone thought he had, like *I* thought he had. Wo Ling had traded him the carnival, is what I think, when Harbin anticipated being killed. He could have avoided the whole mess by fleeing. Lars wouldn't have gone after him; he was bound for other destinations. But there was too much at stake for Harbin. His greed wouldn't let him go. He wanted the elixir that he knew Lars possessed. He tried to steal it, but failed, and Lars and Kettering and I followed him out to the bluffs, where Lars shot him before he and Kettering went across themselves. Well, Harbin succeeded tonight, twelve years later. I won't follow him this time, though. I'm through with it."

"Traded him for what?" asked Jack, referring to Harbin's deal with the old man.

"Death. He was tired of being held in thrall, of being the carnival's unwilling engineer. Lord knows how he'd come into it—some horrifying business, I don't doubt. Harbin grasped at it as a means of staying alive, such as it was, until he had another chance of getting across. And here he has it, twelve years later."

Mrs. Jensen looked as if she were anything but satisfied with her husband's ramblings. The doctor had been happy enough to forget the doings on the bluff for the past twelve years, but they'd come round to haunt him again finally. Jack wasn't at all mystified any more, and although Dr. Jensen had claimed to be done with it, Jack wasn't.

"Where did the elixir come from—this stolen batch?" Jack half suspected the answer when he asked it.

"From your father," said Jensen.

Helen jumped with surprise. "The man in the taxidermist's shop!"

Jack looked at her. "How did you know about that?"

"About what?"

"About the man in the taxidermist's?"

"How did you? *I* ran into him this afternoon, mostly by chance." She turned to Dr. Jensen. "That was Jack's father, wasn't it? The big man. He was dressed in James Langley's painter's smock. The spectacles were his, the shoe was his. All that giant stuff was his. He'd come back, hadn't he?"

"Yes," said the doctor. He'd come back. The small man was him too, although the explanation of that is tough."

"The midget," whispered Helen.

"My father wasn't a midget," said Jack. "Nor a giant either."

Helen waved him silent. "Mrs. Langley told me about it this afternoon, about how these other worlds, if you like, are moving along in their own time, not ours, and you might get over into one that's ten years behind us, and then into another that's five years behind it, and be in both worlds at once, and then both of you could slip into a third world and be there at the same time, one of you a midget and the other a giant, and both of you shrinking and growing. There might be another of you there, too, just living normally—although there wasn't in this case because Jack's father had already left it. And all of *us* are there too, will be, or have been, going about our business." She stopped to catch her breath.

Skeezix stared at her with his eyes wide open like the eyes of a fish. He waited for a moment and then asked, "Are you certain?" in a plonking sort of voice. He screwed up his face theatrically, as if he were thinking hard about what she'd said and wasn't at all doing it to ridicule her.

"She's right," said Dr. Jensen.

Helen smirked at Skeezix. "Of course I'm right. Mrs. Langley told me. It was Jack's father who got the last batch of clothes from under the trestle. She'd asked him to put them there for Jimmy before the business with Harbin, and he found them again when he washed ashore. He couldn't just be running around town, could he? Not as a giant. He must have lived in the woods until he was small enough to wear the clothes. Then he set up at the taxidermist's shop. I've got to tell Mrs. Langley. She'll be happy to hear it. All that hiding of clothes hasn't been in vain."

Jack sat silently, half listening. He knew now why the stranger in the taxidermist's had accosted Harbin with such fury. Did he know who Jack was, or was it the old grievance that set him off? Harbin had escaped, clearly. He'd come back around to the doctor's. And Jack had run away. That was the dismal part. He'd run away when he might have seen his father, spoken to him. Now where was he? "I've got to go back to the taxidermist's."

Dr. Jensen shook his head. "It won't do any good. He's gone—they're gone, I should say. Your father came across to pass the elixir on to you. He hadn't wanted to stay. He'd wanted to slip in and have a look at you while you slept, then slip back through. It was him dressed as a mouse; you know that by now. And he came around the other direction too, across the water like James Langley did the second time—like Helen said—and was surprised to find himself here, on the same mission. They brewed up another batch of the elixir so they could get back across—or he did, I should say—and he gave a jar of it to me. He was rushed. I wish I'd had a day— a week—to talk to him, but the Solstice was passing and there wasn't any time. There's a sort of twilight, he said, in between it all, in the shadow of all the passing worlds. He said it would be full of people going across, like a railway depot. And you see things there, apparently, glimmers of the past and of the future. He wanted me to tell you that you'd meet someday; you weren't to worry. There simply wasn't time now."

"Then I'm to follow him across," said Jack. "It's inevitable. He wouldn't have said that otherwise; he wouldn't have brought me the bottle of elixir."

Dr. Jensen shrugged. "Perhaps. I won't recommend it, but then I won't tell you not to either. You'll make the choice for yourself."

"I'm going." Jack looked at the clock. It was time. The night was drawing on. He had hours yet, it was true, but if he missed it, there would be twelve wearisome years before he had another chance at it, and the thought of those twelve years made the few hours left to him seem more like minutes ticking past. It must have seemed the same to his father.

"Did he find my mother?"

"He said he knew where she was, now, and what to do about it," said Dr. Jensen. "That's why he couldn't wait; he couldn't risk losing her again."

"I'm going with you," said Skeezix. "It was my idea in the first place, you know. Helen was the one with the doubts."

"*I* didn't have any doubts. I knew it was foolery from the start, and I believe it even more now. But you still need a sea anchor. You're not trustworthy enough, either of you. I'm going with you this time."

Jack looked at her doubtfully. He ought to protest: Helen, after all. It couldn't be risked. He glanced at Dr. Jensen, half expecting the doctor to do the job for him, to refuse to let Helen go. Skeezix and he were looking for something, after all—heaven knew, maybe, what it was. But Helen; what was she after? What propelled her? Dr. Jensen said nothing, only nodded. Helen moved toward the door, buttoning up her jacket.

"I don't half understand this," Mrs. Jensen said. "But wherever you're going, good luck. Come back, won't you?"

"Either tomorrow or twelve years from tomorrow; sometime," said Jack. "We don't altogether understand this either, but we'll be back."

"Not through a gopher hole," said Helen, as they pushed out into the weather. "Don't look for us in a gopher hole."

"I'm sure I won't," shouted Mrs. Jensen. Silhouetted against the glow of the open door, she waved a handkerchief at them as they hurried out into the windy alley, bound for the bluffs.

12

"ARE YOU SURE he said the Flying Toad?"

"Of course I'm sure. My memory is longer than that."
Helen brushed her hair back and pulled her jacket around her.
The night seemed to have darkened; it lay now out on the
meadows in stark, opaque contrast to the lights of the carnival. The three of them stood in the shadows of the fun house
and looked across toward where little buggylike carts careened along a track, spouting steam like wheeled teakettles,
disappearing into the interior darkness of a plywood building
scabbed together like a house of cards. "Besides, this can't be
coincidence. There's the Flying Toad itself. That's the one,
just like your father said."

They stood in silence for a moment, cold with ocean wind
and with anticipation. Jack shivered. They'd looked for Dr.
Brown but hadn't found him. Jack expected as much. The
doctor wouldn't have clubbed Jensen and stolen the elixir and
then sat around and pondered it. He'd have gone across himself by now.

An oddly jerky and debilitated lot of men operated the rides
and pitched split logs into the beehive oven. What Jack had
seen in the face of the man at the Ferris wheel, that hadn't
been hallucination; he was certain of that now. He'd seen
things clearly in that moment, because of the elixir. He
couldn't be certain that the carnival workers were the recent
inhabitants of the ripped-open graves or of the washed-out
crypts along the Eel River, but he'd bet the quarter he had in
his pocket on it. They were doing the bidding of another
master now; that is to say, if Dr. Brown had been the master. Perhaps the carnival was the master. It was an eerie
thought—one that disinclined him toward riding on the so-

called Flying Toad. There wasn't anything toadlike about it.

A big cleated door sprang open every thirty seconds or so to admit another car, accompanied by a drawn-out mechanical shriek, no doubt triggered by the door's opening. Low laughter sounded from within, clipped off when the door banged shut, then starting up again when a door on the opposite end opened and a car shot out—propelled, it seemed, by an ocean of windy steam—its occupants screaming with fear and wonder at whatever terrible mysteries they'd glimpsed within.

Skeezix shoved both Helen and Jack farther back into the shadows. He pointed down the line of tents. A light had been burning in Dr. Brown's tent, but the shadow of the man slumped over the desk within hadn't been the shadow of the doctor. Now the flag jiggled and flew back. The hunched figure of MacWilt the tavern keeper came out. He wore a robe tied with a rope, like a medieval monk, and he appeared to be shriveled and bent, as if burdened by the weight of his own evil and the trials of the past days.

He'd given up his stick. He walked with his head twisted back so that he had to swivel his eyes around and down in order to see—but he could see; that much was clear. He looked up and down the avenue before him. The few late-night revelers gawked and circled warily around him when they walked past, as if he were a dervish about to run mad. He shuffled toward the three in the shadows, coming their way, it seemed, by chance. Jack could feel Skeezix tense up beside him, ready, probably, to pummel MacWilt into senselessness if he was threatened.

He passed them by, walking toward the oven and cursing at the men who gathered round it. Jack could see his eyes, glowing in the lamplight. They were gray, like the belly of a catfish too long out of water. It was impossible that he wasn't blind. It was impossible that Peebles's finger had sprouted too. It had been Dr. Brown's doing, is what it had been, and now Dr. Brown was gone. MacWilt was in charge. The carnival had a new operator, a worthy successor to Wo Ling and Algernon Harbin.

When MacWilt disappeared around the corner of the fun house, Jack stepped out into the light. Skeezix and Helen weren't slow in following. Jack couldn't imagine they were eager, but they knew, as he did, that standing and shivering wouldn't work any magic. Sliding in through a hinged waist-high gate, they climbed aboard a buggy and waited there. Out of the corner of his eye, Jack watched the rain drizzle down through the light. It was taking an eternity. MacWilt would return and there'd be trouble. They would only have one chance that night.

They lurched. The wheels creaked into motion, and the buggy shot forward suddenly along its track, rushing toward the still-closed door. It flew open in their faces when it seemed they'd slam against it for sure, and then it swung shut and left them in darkness.

A light flared beneath an enormous grinning skull, and the body of a man swung out on a boom, into the light, whumping into the fender of the buggy. Helen shrieked. The man's head flew off, tumbling goggle-eyed across in front of them and whacking with the sound of a split melon into a basket of heads beside the track. The headless corpse swung back into darkness as laughter chattered out, echoing off the plywood ceiling. A suddenly burning candelabra revealed a laughing skeleton, draped with what might have been seaweed or might have been dried flesh. It sat on a high stool, nodding forward as if to pitch bodily into the buggy, and then it was gone too, back into darkness and silence. They clattered on along a black tunnel, into a cold wind, like air blowing out of a musty cellar.

A light glowed ahead of them. Something was coming up. The ride must be immense, or else cleverly looped around like a maze. There was the facade, suddenly, of a building, standing along the edge of the sea. It was a painted prop, tilted against wooden supports, wound around with the long-dead branches of wild berry vines. Along with it was the smell of fish and tar and sea foam, of steel shavings and dry old leather upholstery and rain-soaked shingles. There were a thousand smells together, and Jack felt compelled to sort them out, to savor each one, except that they were rocketing in through the open door, sliding across wooden floorboards in a rush of oil-tainted steam. A train whistle moaned, sounding rusty and strained and distant through the steam, and then, as if a curtain had been snatched aside, it loomed suddenly in front of them, rushing out of the darkness, its lantern throwing glints of light into the evaporating steam.

Jack threw himself in front of Helen, shielding his face with his arm, hearing Helen shout into his ear. The car spun dizzily, caroming off the rushing train, past car after car of travelers bound for unguessed destinations. Then they swerved off into the darkness, slamming through a wall built of paper and cobwebs and what seemed to be a billion amber wings of swarming termites. They stopped, ratcheted around once, and shot away again, the train whistle evaporating, giving way to an insect hum and once again the bubbling of nearby laughter.

At the sound of the laughter, Helen gripped Jack's arm as if she were going to rip it off. The pressure reminded Jack of why they'd climbed onto the ride in the first place, and he was struck with the strange certainty that if he didn't do something to change their course—to finish what they'd started—they'd whiz and lurch forever through the dark corridors.

With his left hand he plucked the bottle of elixir out of his jacket pocket. There was no time left for indecision. He unstoppered it with the same hand that held it, tilted it to his lips, and drank—just a tiny sip. He handed it to Skeezix. It would have been more gentlemanly, perhaps, to give it to Helen first, except that he was half afraid of it—more than half.

At once there was a patch of illuminated meadow grass,

littered with a basket and crumpled cloth—the remains of a picnic. Jack felt the creakings of vague memories, something suggested by the dilapidated basket, by the yellow checks of the cloth. But they were gone and a light glowed ahead, steamy with rising fog. There was Willoughby's farm—a miniature of it, or else the farm itself, very distant, with oak leaves piling up across the front porch and an autumn wind slamming the screen door shut over and over again. And then there was a pond, fed by a clear stream, with leaf-stained water and grass growing down its banks. He could see trout swimming slowly in the rocky depths, and for a moment, just before they plunged again into darkness, he could see his own face painted in the weedy pebbles of the pond floor.

Glowing windows seemed suddenly to be flashing past them at a prodigious rate, as if they careered along once again beside a train. Darkness slammed down and a howling arose. A clown leered into view, seeming to float in the air, wearing a pointed cap and ruff collar and smeared with whiteface. He turned toward them, as if surprised to see them hurtling at him. Out of the air, out of the darkness, he contrived a bleating lamb and prepared to slit its throat with a billhook, grinning all the while and whistling with the sound of wind blowing under a door. Jack looked away.

There was the shriek of a train whistle once more, of escaping steam. Skeezix handed the bottle back, and Jack turned with it, thinking to give it to Helen and thinking too that Helen mightn't have any stomach for it any more. But Helen was gone. He sat alone with Skeezix. They were aboard a train—inexplicably, instantly—chuffing into the arched mouth of an enormous stone depot.

Jack smashed his eyes shut and then opened them again. He felt for Helen beside him, sure that this was a trick of carnival enchantment. There was nothing beside him but the wood and leather and brass of a train car.

"Am I imagining this?" asked Skeezix.

"No. Helen's gone. She didn't get a chance at the elixir."

Skeezix was silent, waiting. Jack watched out the window, thinking of Helen on that endless carnival ride. It was his fault, wasn't it, taking his time with the elixir? But what could he do about it now?

The mouth of the depot drew toward them slowly, although it appeared that the train they were in was rushing along. Through the window he could see stars in the twilight sky, although somehow it seemed as if that sky weren't very deep, as if it were the cleverly painted ceiling of a vast rotunda. There was fog outside, or steam. Nothing moved and nothing broke the dim monotony of the landscape, if landscape it was. Jack would have expected a town, perhaps, along the tracks—a city, judging from the size of the depot. But there was nothing, not a solitary light, not a shadow. It wasn't a landscape, certainly, that one could walk through; there wasn't even a horizon, just a general darkness that paled gradually into the twilight of the sky.

He felt like a fool. What in the world had he meant by meddling with the elixir? He had thought it was something like fate, like destiny, only he didn't believe in any such thing. It had been his father, luring him along, and Mrs. Langley with her book, and Dr. Jensen with his sailboat shoe, and MacWilt with his telescope built out of the spectacles of a giant.

Two hours earlier he had felt as if he understood the whole business clearly. Here was a village full of people capering with excitement at the idea of going across, but none of them actually getting there. It half appeared as if they hadn't really wanted to cross at all but were consumed with the idea, like a child seeing just how close he could creep to the edge of a precipice without actually tumbling off. Jack had the elixir; he had Mrs. Langley's book; he had a father who'd been across and come back again; he knew where the giant's clothes had come from; he knew who Algernon Harbin was; he knew about the warehouse in San Francisco. He had a suitcase full of information—plenty, he had figured, for a brief visit to

Mrs. Langley's "land of dreams." But now that he was there, he hadn't any idea on earth of what to do, and his wonder and fear of the misty night outside the train windows was over-shadowed only by his desire to be home again, reading by candlelight in the loft and knowing that Helen was safe.

Skeezix punched him in the shoulder and grinned. We made it, his grin seemed to say. Jack grinned back weakly. He upended the bottle that had contained the elixir, letting one last green drop slip out onto his pant leg. Skeezix's grin slumped momentarily. "I hope we don't need more of that to get home," he said.

Jack shrugged, as if to say the die was cast and there wasn't a frightful lot they could do about it.

Skeezix grinned again. "Who cares?" he said "What do we have to lose?"

Jack immediately thought of a half dozen things he had to lose. They quite likely wouldn't have seemed so valuable to him yesterday, but now . . . "I could draw you up a list."

There were other people in the train car, lots of them. Jack didn't recognize anyone. Most of them appeared calm enough, some of them anxious, some of them vaguely frightened, as though, like Jack, they wished suddenly that they weren't there. One man three seats up twirled his hair. A woman across from him talked incessantly, explaining to an old gentleman how it was she'd come across—something to do with a basket of eel eggs and a salt shaker full of dust that had blown in on the Solstice wind that she'd strained out of the air with a sieve made of fishbones and the hair of dead men. The old man looked straight in front of him, nodding now and then. When she left off finally he nodded at his smoldering pipe and winked at her. Jack saw her tilt her head forward, look into the pipe bowl, and recoil with horror. She stood up and lurched toward a different seat, casting a look of revulsion at the man, who shrugged, pulled his hat down over his eyes, and fell asleep.

The depot loomed ahead. It had to be miles away, given

the rate of speed at which they were rushing upon it. But perspective, somehow, was muddled. It seemed to Jack to be a painted prop again, not a real depot at all, suspended in front of the moving train, racing along at a parallel speed like a tin rabbit in front of a greyhound. And then they were there, suddenly and without warning. They steamed into the cavernous mouth of the building and were swallowed up, instantly seeming to be deep inside, with the arched darkness of the entry portal a half mile behind them.

There were no end of trains, pulling in and out, running along beside them, now braking to a stop as they rushed past, now abruptly angling off onto side tracks. Dim violet lamps burned in the steamy distances. Whistles blew. Clouds of vapor whirled up from beneath them, dissipating in the darkness overhead. People walked along beside the tracks, between trains, and up and down companionways leading to upper and lower levels that Jack could only guess at. Some of the people walked with a purpose, hurrying toward a destination. Others looked around them, puzzled, getting in the way, leaping with startled surprise at a rush of steam or the shriek of a train whistle. Vendors hawked hot potatoes and coffee and souvenir hats from wheeled carts. "Last chance!" one man shouted, waving a little pennant over his head. "Time's wearing on!"

"I could use a roll and coffee," said Skeezix as the train lurched to a stop, rolled forward twenty feet, and stopped again.

Jack watched the people milling outside. "I could use a map," he said.

A porter in a blue cap and striped jacket stepped up and opened the door of the train car, peering in at them and grinning. The woman who'd sieved the Solstice wind stood up and rushed toward the open door, gesturing back toward the old pipe-smoking gentleman, goggling in the face of the porter. "That man should be arrested," she announced. Then she gave the old man a last withering look and stepped out onto the platform. People rose and began to file out, Jack and Skeezix following along behind.

Another train eased up alongside theirs and stopped. Jack stopped to regard the passengers—the same mixture of troubled, anxious faces and calm, experienced travelers. One woman wept and another patted her shoulder. A hurried-looking man in an overcoat held his hat and stood in the aisle, as if he were late for an appointment. A merry-looking couple sat side by side, chatting amiably, the man gesturing roundabout and out the window as if he were a seasoned traveler, had been through it any number of times, and was explaining their condition to the woman—who hadn't been, but who trusted her companion entirely.

Jack was struck suddenly with the familiar look of the man. His clothes were ill-fitting, as though they were borrowed and he'd done his best to make them work. There was something in the high cheekbones and sandy hair and in the depth of the man's smile—what was it? Jack had seen him before, and recently. He glanced at the woman. "No!" Jack said, half under his breath, in surprise rather than denial. He slid between the seats, pressing up against the window, fumbling with the latch. The woman wore a black and red velvet dress. Her thick black hair fell about her shoulders, half hiding a gold necklace from which hung a rectangular green stone, a cut emerald. She was his mother, and the man was his father. Jack had seen him for an instant on the riverbank behind the taxidermist's shop when he'd been saved from Dr. Brown.

Jack yanked the window down and shouted, but his voice was lost in whirling steam. He leaned out through the window, holding the frame with his left hand so as not to pitch out onto the tracks. He hefted the elixir bottle with his right hand, cocked his arm, and threw the bottle at their window. Thunk! His father leaped, startled. He turned to look, pressing his hands against the window on either side of his face. He squinted at Jack, obviously seeing him there, wondering at it. Then his eyes flew open in surprise. He said something over his shoulder and immediately Jack's mother was at the window too, waving. She stood up, as if to rush away down the aisle. She started, took two steps, turned, and lunged back to grab the man's arm.

A whistle screeched and Jack's train lurched forward, throwing him into the edge of the window. He pulled himself back inside the car, and found it was empty. Skeezix was gone. The train jerked to a stop and then rolled forward again, smoothly now, gathering steam. "Wait!" he shouted through the open window, and then leaped away down the aisle toward the now-closed door. He thought he could hear his father hollering something about all of them going home, about how it was all right now, but his words were lost in the noise and there was no time to think about them anyway.

Jack wrenched at the handle, yanking the door open, watching the platform slip past him in a gathering rush. There was Skeezix, fifty feet back, waving his arms. Jack leaped for it and hit the platform at a run, catapulting into a crowd of people gathered around a sign that was covered with place names.

He reeled back, apologizing, nearly stumbling off the platform and into the accelerating train. He turned, waving away their curses and complaints, and leaped straight up into the air, looking through the flying windows at the train beyond. It was moving too. It's just an illusion, he told himself, caused by looking through one moving train at another. But it wasn't. The train that held his father and mother chuffed slowly away, alongside his own but in the opposite direction. He ran toward Skeezix, waving and shouting, snatching at his friend's arm, knocking his newly bought roll out of his hands.

There had to be a way to get across. He ran up a stairway, pushing through the crowds until he looked down on both trains, at what seemed to be a hundred trains, coming and going, starting and stopping and starting again as though orchestrated. There was a passage beneath the tracks. He could see the dark mouth of it where it exited on the next platform over. He pushed past Skeezix again, hollering at his friend to follow, and jumped back down the stairs two and three at a time, bouncing off a man in a top hat, shouting an apology over his shoulder.

There was the tunnel. He was in it and running through the half-light, hearing Skeezix puffing along behind and hollering for him to hold up. Another tunnel branched off to the right, choked with people—should he take it? Yet another sloped downward to the left. He hesitated, feeling a warm spring wind heavy with wildflowers and sunshine blowing along up the tunnel toward him, then went on, more slowly now, confused. He seemed suddenly to be groping through a warren of tunnels that angled up, down, and sideways, winding away into darkness. Skeezix came wheezing up, bent over, demanding to know what Jack was up to. He fell silent and followed along when Jack explained.

The depot must have been honeycombed with tunnels. Arrows pointed this way and that, announcing destinations. Train whistles echoed down from above. One moment they were alone; the next moment a sudden crowd of people materialized, clutching coats and handbags and hurrying along. Jack and Skeezix followed their tunnel up toward a platform, hurrying again, and in moments stood in the open once more. A train rolled slowly past, full of passengers. It was impossible to say which train it was, whether it was coming or going. Jack and Skeezix ran along beside it. They sidled past people, leaping now and again to see in through the window, but the train picked up speed, chuffing along into the darkness. They fell away behind. It mightn't be his parents' train at all, of course. Maybe the train just behind it was, or the train beyond that. . . . It was hopeless.

Jack sat down on a wooden bench and stared into his hands. It seemed suddenly that seeing his parents there—his disappeared father and his long-dead mother—had been an illusion. It had to have been. What had Mrs. Langley called it? "The land of dreams." He'd been chasing after figments, hadn't he? But then again, he himself wasn't a figment, and neither was Skeezix. Nobody looked less like a figment than Skeezix did. So why, necessarily, would the rest of the people in the depot be figments?

"We should keep looking," said Skeezix.

Jack shrugged. "I probably imagined it, my parents being there. How could they be? Let's just go. Let's follow these people out—see where we end up."

Skeezix scratched his cheek and looked around. Then he stopped, blinked, and pointed. A dimly lit cafeteria stretched along the wall of the depot, the front of it broken by magazine kiosks and shoeshine benches and pushcarts tended by hot potato vendors and coffee sellers. People filed in and out through revolving doors, disappearing into the hazy interior. The random noise of voices and clinking dishes washed out along with the odor of food—nothing definable, but everything mixed together and boiled up into a stew of smells that was vaguely sickening: boiled peas and carrots and fried fish. Miss Flees might have been cooking. Even Skeezix didn't seem to be tempted by it.

Just as Jack thought about it—about Miss Flees boiling up cabbage for broth—there, standing outside the door of the cafeteria beside a boy hawking old yellowed newspapers, stood Miss Flees herself. She had the unmistakable stamp of lunacy on her face: eyes too wide and staring, a smile empty of meaning, hair like a trodden-on tumbleweed. She'd gotten hold of a sack, somehow, a burlap bag that might one time have held eighty pounds of potatoes, and she spoke to people brushing past her. One man stopped and dropped a coin into the sack. Another shook his head, shrugged, and fumbled in his pockets, pulling out a wrinkled handkerchief and tossing that in. She thanked him obsequiously, but then without warning, in the middle of a broad bow, she began cursing at the man, who ducked in through the revolving doors and was gone, disappearing into the faceless mass of people in the cafeteria.

A wind blew down through the station, stirring up dust, smelling of engine oil and steam. A sheet of newspaper cartwheeled past, and Miss Flees snatched it up, folding it and smoothing it out, trying to read it sideways. She seemed satisfied with it, and she folded it over and over again until it was the size of a playing card before she dropped it into the sack.

"Maybe this is the place where you get what you deserve," whispered Skeezix.

The idea gave Jack a chill. It didn't seem to appeal to Skeezix either, who was clearly troubled by the sight of Miss Flees, come to such a bad end. He seemed half inclined to approach her, to give her something. "She'd go even more nuts if she saw me," he said, shaking his head. "It would do her more harm than good."

Jack nodded. Quite likely it was true. Still . . .

"We can't just go away, though, can we?"

"No," said Jack. "Maybe she won't recognize us." He found a quarter in one pocket and three pennies in another. Skeezix was richer; he counted up a total of eighty-seven cents. They walked toward her, pretending to be passersby, and dropped the change into her open sack. She thanked them by name, and as they walked off, nodding and smiling at her and telling her to take care of herself, she advised Skeezix not to eat so much. Then, as if a switch had been thrown in her head, she began to lecture them about the advantages of roughage in the diet, advising bran muffins, flaxseed, wheat germ, ground fish bones, and sawdust, whining along in a voice shrill with the suspicion that no one was taking her seriously. It was clear, though, that she was talking mostly to an imagined audience, for her eyes drifted away from the two boys and she spoke with a general, detached vagueness at the sides of the heads of people drifting past, the subject of her lecture shifting away and losing itself like the landscape of a dream.

Jack shivered at the sight. Skeezix was silent for a moment; then he said, "I wish we'd had more."

"We didn't," said Jack.

"Maybe we could come back. Isn't that how all of this is supposed to work—you can come and go at the Solstice, popping in at different times? Didn't Helen say there were two of your father at the taxidermist's? That must have been weird."

"I bet it was."

"Sorry," said Skeezix. They found themselves climbing a flight of very long stairs, trudging along without tiring, bound for nowhere at all. They hesitated at the top. Skeezix looked at Jack and shook his head. "I think we screwed up," he said.

"Wrong stairs?"

"No. Coming here and all. I'm hungry enough to eat my arm, but all I want is one of Potts's doughnuts."

"I know what you mean. I wonder if Helen—"

"Will you look at that!" Skeezix interrupted, pointing ahead of them, way off in the distance. There was the train depot, stretching out before them, steamy and loud. There was the cafeteria and the vendors again, appearing to be about a half mile off, although the vendors' voices were clear and close. Skeezix and Jack approached them once more, both of them struck with the horror of tramping round and round through the same circuitous dreamlike depot, finding nothing at all substantial enough to make the place seem real.

Miss Flees still stood with her bag open, accosting the milling crowds. In front of her stood a fat man, who seemed to be dumping odds and ends into the bag. There was something oddly familiar about him: in the way he wore his clothes, in his posture. It was more than just a passing notion. "He's wearing my jacket," said Skeezix. "I wish I had that one now. It's warmer than this one by a mile."

"And your hat," said Jack. "Isn't that your lucky Pierre hat? It's you, isn't it? You've come back."

"By golly, it is." Skeezix hurried forward but stopped after having taken a half dozen steps, struck, perhaps, with the weird notion of coming up behind himself and tapping himself on the shoulder and watching himself turn in surprise, or perhaps in mirth. That would be it: he'd know—wouldn't he?—that he was about to be tapped and would have brought along some sort of gag, a squirting flower or a rubber snake in order to have a bit of fun. Skeezix watched as he—the fat man—emptied his pockets into Miss Flees's bags and then, tipping his hat to her, stepped hurriedly away down a yawning corridor and was gone.

"What would you have to say to yourself that you wouldn't already know?" asked Jack.

"Nothing. I'm glad I came back, though. You know what this means? We get through all right. We must."

"You do, anyway. Let's go."

With that the two of them set out down an adjacent stairway, down and down and down until the dim, flickering light of the depot was replaced by sunlight, flowing up from below. There was a thin edge of blue sky and the green of trees, which grew as they descended the stairs, forming itself into the half circle of a tunnel mouth. They stepped out onto the leafy silence of an oak woods. Brown grass and green fern rose to their shoulders, and mushrooms and fungi on the forest floor sat solid and alien like peculiar rubber statuary. The distant echoes of train whistles had diminished, and one last, long, ghostly blast was consumed by the hooting of an owl that peered at them from the limb of an enormous tree, an oak that towered away impossibly overhead.

The stairs from the train depot was gone. They'd vanished in the shadows. Looming behind Jack and Skeezix was the dark arch of the Tumbled Bridge, near Mrs. Oglevy's orchards. The glow of sunlight shone beyond, and beyond that was the rise of the meadow and the hills where—what was it, yesterday?—they'd fought with blind MacWilt and pitched rocks at Dr. Brown. All of it, the meadow and the hills and the bridge itself, were immeasurably vast, as if they were in a land of giants. Jack stood and stared, feeling as if he would choke. His shirt was too small, and his toes seemed to have jammed up against the ends of his shoes. One of his cuff buttons popped loose and dropped into the weeds.

The air was suddenly full of the rush of wings. "Run!" cried Skeezix, turning and sprinting back toward the dark mouth of the bridge. Jack didn't need the advice. An owl big as a cow swooped down out of the tree toward them. They were mice to it—supper, and a meager supper at that.

They darted into the safety of the shadows, scurrying behind a heap of broken rock, watching the owl fly through and out the other side, beating the air with enormous wings. "What a monster," said Skeezix, hauling off his jacket.

"It's us," said Jack. "We're tiny. That's the way it works, remember?"

"Why didn't you warn me? How long will it take to grow up?"

"I don't know," said Jack. "Not long, I hope. A few hours before it really gets started. These clothes are done for already. We'll suffocate if we don't get out of them. What'll we do?"

"Where are we? Home?"

Jack studied it for a moment, both of them listening for the flapping of owl wings on the air. "In a way."

"Is this a dream, do you think? Some sort of vision? I don't trust any of it."

Jack shrugged and then was struck with an idea. "Let's find Dr. Jensen. He'll know."

"Well," said Skeezix. "He'll be sympathetic anyway."

The stream was low and sluggish. It was still autumn, but the autumn of a dry year. They weren't altogether home, then—which made finding Dr. Jensen a questionable sort of thing. The two of them peeked out from under the bridge, creeping along in the shadows, clambering around rocks that yesterday might have fit into their pockets. The sound of voices reached them on the wind, and they peered over the top of a driftwood log at two gigantic children, playing on a sandy little beach where the stream had receded. A boy meddled with a tin bucket, ladling sand into it with his cupped hand, then upending it to build turrets along either side of a moored wooden boat. A girl, his sister perhaps, arranged dolls on a stump.

"Monsters," breathed Skeezix. "Behemoths. Who are they? They don't live in Rio Dell. Not our Rio Dell."

Jack shook his head. "This isn't our Rio Dell, I guess." His heart sank when he said it. He'd hoped he was home, despite signs to the contrary, but he wasn't.

"Horrifying, aren't they?—children that big. Makes your flesh crawl. Imagine watching them eat."

A voice hollered from away up the river, toward Mrs. Oglevy's orchard, or at least toward what they remembered as Mrs. Oglevy's orchard. The children disappeared up the path, skipping along, leaving their toys behind. "Probably going in for lunch," said Skeezix, stepping out of hiding. "Let's go."

It took them all of ten minutes to tug the clothes off the enormous dolls. To keep things fair, they left their own clothes in a little heap at the base of the stump. Then they cut the painter from the toy boat and cut it again in half with their pocketknives. They left the knives, their good-luck charms, and their caps atop the clothes, pretty sure the children would be well enough satisfied with the trade. Their father, or someone, could build them another boat. This one wasn't worth much anyway. It looked clever enough, with its movable tiller and cloth sail, but the sail didn't much work, and steering the toy vessel was like trying to steer a house. They fought to keep it near shore. If worst came to worst they could swim ashore; there wouldn't be any problem there—if they weren't eaten by a catfish on the way in. It would take them forever to get into town, though, if they had to go overland.

They slid along beneath the trees, dressed idiotically in the doll clothes, not knowing whether to be thankful for them or not. At least they were big—big to the point of falling off. They'd tied the cut pieces of painter around their waists before setting out, and then pulled the hem of the dresses back up and tucked them under the ropes. "You must not feel half as much a fool as I do," said Skeezix, as they rounded a bend in the stream and sailed along past a stand of rushes.

"Why do you say so?" asked Jack, leaning on the tiller.

"I thought you said you were Scottish, somehow—your mother or something."

"That's right. So what?"

"Your ancestors dressed like this, then. Skirts and like that. They ate guts, too, didn't they? I'm getting to the point where I could eat guts. Cheerfully."

"Look there," said Jack, pointing. "It's the farm. There's Willoughby." And sure enough, there was the farmer messing around behind the house, hoeing in his garden.

The sight of him cheered Jack immediately; they were in their own Rio Dell, or something very much like it. But it wasn't the Willoughby who'd given him the carnival circular; it was a changed Willoughby, an older Willoughby. "His hair's gone gray," said Jack, feeling suddenly lonely.

Skeezix nodded. "I wonder if you're in the loft."

"I hadn't thought of that," said Jack. "I guess I might be. Wonder what I'm doing. What if we went to look and I wasn't there? What if my books were gone and there was nothing but hay up there and cats. What would it mean?"

"Nothing. You'd gone somewhere else, that's all. This boat's getting tight, isn't it?"

Jack agreed that it was. But the town wasn't ten minutes off. The boat would hold up until then, if they sat still. Willoughby's farm disappeared behind them and once again they were skimming along through the woods on a journey that had become weirdly reminiscent of the one Jack had taken a few long hours ago. Thinking about it made him wonder suddenly about Dr. Brown. He was struck with the troubling thought that Dr. Brown could quite easily be lurking round about, waiting again behind the taxidermist's shop, perhaps, intent on finishing his score with them.

They put ashore at the first of the White sisters' houses,

hiked up their draped skirts, and ran along under the clothesline and around the side of the house. Crossing the High
Street might pose a problem, except that it seemed to be
midafternoon, and unless life in the village had undergone
some sort of mysterious change, the street should be pretty
much deserted. Beyond the High Street they'd keep to the
alley all the way up to Jensen's. It would be simple, barring
cats and dogs and rats and birds.

They crouched amid overhanging fuchsia and looked out
at the street. There was MacWilt's tavern; only it wasn't
MacWilt's any more. It was called Hoover's now and there
was a wooden sign hanging in front of it depicting a soup pot
and an ale glass. Across the street at the inn three boys were
playing on the balcony, dropping paper helicopters onto the
heads of fishermen below. Even as Jack and Skeezix watched,
the innkeeper poked his head out an open window beside the
nailed-shut door and ordered the boys off the balcony before
he "threw them off."

Jack grinned at Skeezix and retied his belt. Some things
hadn't changed, although heaven knew who the boys were.
When the three had clambered down the drainpipe and disappeared under the dock, Skeezix and Jack scurried across the
road and into the weedy flower bed of Potts's bakery. The
smell of sugared doughnuts staggered Skeezix. He clutched
at his heart and groaned, then blinked in genuine surprise at
the sign over the door. SKEEZIX'S BAKERY, it said. BAKED
GOODS—ALL KINDS.

"This is cruel," said Skeezix. "Land of dreams! I'll—"

"Ssh, look," said Jack. "Isn't that Elaine Potts inside, rolling dough?"

Skeezix smiled a moony sort of smile and nodded his head.
"She's a vision, isn't she? Big, though, under the circumstances. I want one of those doughnuts. Good old Elaine.
She'll see to it that I get one. She always has before, hasn't
she? I think she's in love with me."

"She's not in love with a Skeezix who isn't as tall as her ankle, moron. She'd scream if she saw us, depend on it. And you'd just get sick, eating a doughnut like that. Remember when she smuggled you out a dozen glazed and you ate them all? Wait!"

"For what? I'm going in there after a doughnut, after Elaine, too, I'll—"

"Shut up!" Jack poked Skeezix in the ribs and pointed. There, creeping along in the shadow of a fence two houses down and leaning heavily on his stick, was a rat-sized Dr. Brown—Algernon Harbin—dressed in rags and looking like a storybook goblin. Jack and Skeezix sprinted after him, peering around the corner of the house in time to see him slip through the hinged panel of a cat door, cut in the bottom three clapboards of the side wall, just above the rear stoop.

13

JACK PEERED UNDER the door, squinting into the dim interior of a vast kitchen. Harbin wasn't in sight, although he might easily have slipped in behind the icebox or into the pantry or even be crouching behind one of the flared legs of the stove. They should have followed him in straightaway, instead of waiting. Skeezix pushed Jack a bit and frowned, caught up in the spirit of adventure. Both boys were inside in an instant, running across a wooden floor that seemed to them like a playing field and listening sharp for the arrival of the creature that the cat door was intended for. As he ran, Jack couldn't help but wonder what, exactly, they were doing. What was *Harbin* doing, for that matter, skulking in through a cat door like that? Something connected to their own time, no doubt, to their own Rio Dell. Jack realized that he was following that connection more than anything else, as if it were a road that linked the two worlds, the two times. Who knew where it might lead them?

Half hidden behind a kitchen stool, Jack decided immediately that he liked whoever they were who owned the house. They seemed to have the right sort of inclinations. There were elements that he would change, if it were his, but all in all he felt a sort of affinity to it, as if he was welcome there. The kitchen walls, angling away overhead, were painted cheerfully white, with a stenciled border in red milk paint along the ceiling, the stencils having been cut in the shapes of comical cats that were easily as big as Jack and Skeezix stacked atop one another.

The cats made Jack think of Helen, who would have approved of such things, and who had once sketched a cat on a flour sack and given it to Jack to carry his stuff in. The sack was filled with marbles and bottle glass and Chinese jacks and

227

sat right now beneath his bed in the barn loft. Or at least he hoped it did. He wasn't entirely sure, when he thought about it, *where* the barn loft had gotten to. But thinking about it— the loft and the flour sack and Helen—only made him feel sorry for himself. So he forced himself to think about where he was and what he was doing instead, which wasn't as easy as it should have been, since he had no idea about either.

A pot big enough for them to swim in bubbled away on the stove top, smelling good enough to give Skeezix trouble. Voices sounded in an adjacent room—laughter and the clink of glasses, the abrupt sound of someone quoting poetry that dissolved into more laughter.

On beyond the kitchen, vastly distant, stretched another room, shadowed and dim. Jack could see only that it was lined with books that shared shelves with alchemical debris and clutched bundles of dried herbs. A fierce-looking bust peered down out of the room, half lit by the sun through the kitchen window, bearded and grimacing and with a crack running down its forehead as if slammed with a hatchet. Part of the bearded jaw seemed to have been broken away. The room reminded him of Dr. Jensen's surgery and was just the sort of place he'd like to snoop around in, if he weren't thumb-sized.

Just next to the stool they hid behind stood a wooden pantry, its door barely ajar. Jack and Skeezix reached up together and leaned into it, pushing it open farther, ready to confront Algernon Harbin if the villain were hiding within. He couldn't be up to any good in a cheerful house like this. He was out of his element. The pantry was empty; no one was hidden behind the half dozen enormous Mason jars and the stack of baskets, big as beds. On the floor of the pantry was a flat, open tin of biscuits. Skeezix grappled one out and held it with both hands, working up courage to take a bite. But it smelled awfully of fish and was coarse and grainy and obviously meant for the cat, so he dropped it back into the tin and shrugged.

They left the pantry cabinet open just in case and stepped across to a swinging door that led out toward the talking and laughter. Hiding behind it and peering through the crack between the door and the jamb, they saw four people: three men and a woman. A bearded man stood near the door and partly hidden by it, pulling out one and then another of what must have been a thousand books in a bookcase that covered the wall. He wore a ring on his right hand, a curious band of interlacing gold like ocean waves breaking over and under each other in a line.

"Imagine getting hold of a ring like that," whispered Skeezix, "and bringing it back home and selling it. Either one of us could wear it as a crown."

Jack nodded, only half listening.

"And look at that over there!" Skeezix nodded toward the distant top of the kitchen counter, where a loaf of bread sat atop a cutting board pulled from its recess beneath the countertop. The top of the bread had been torn off, and the fluffy white interior lay exposed, peaked and white like snow-covered ragged hills. "A man could live in a loaf of bread that size. He could chew through it and build rooms, and when it went stale and hard he'd have a house."

Jack still squinted out past the door. He hadn't any interest, at the moment, in houses made of stale bread. Across the room sat a gray-haired, pleasant-looking man in glasses, his face half hidden behind a book—poetry, no doubt. He obviously had one eye on the activities of another man, roughly the same age—or so the back of his head seemed to suggest— who sat opposite him, studying the pieces of a chessboard and smoking a pipe.

In a chair by the window sat a comparatively young woman with raven-dark hair. She might have been Helen's mother, had Helen's mother been more beautiful even than Helen herself. She sat in profile, looking out through the sunlit window into a backyard planted in roses, and gestured to another woman—the wife, perhaps, of one of the chess players—who was clipping off roses and holding them up for inspection.

For a moment Jack considered stepping out into the open and announcing his presence, like Tom Thumb, with a bow and a flourish of his hat. Only he had no hat and he looked like a fool in his doll costume. And almost as soon as he thought about it he heard the swish of the cat door and turned to see an enormous gray tom stride through, sniffing the air and twitching his tail like a predatory saurian. There was no place to run except out among the giants, but if he and Skeezix broke for it, the cat would pounce on them long before anyone understood the meaning of the melee and could put an end to it. Likely enough the giants would think they were mice anyway and let the cat have them.

The beast stopped, cocked its head, and leaped into the open pantry, intent on the fish biscuits. Skeezix was quicker than Jack. He dashed across, headlong into the half-open pantry door, trying to push it shut and trap the beast inside. The door wouldn't budge; it was too heavy for him. Jack threw himself against it too; it was no time to be timid. The cat, thank goodness, didn't seem to care. As the door clicked shut there was the sound of crunching biscuits from within, as if he'd settled in to take advantage of the open tin while he had a chance.

Skeezix immediately set out to climb up onto the first of a series of copper pulls that ran along the fronts of a half dozen kitchen drawers beneath the countertop. Three or four of the drawers were open slightly, which made it an easy enough thing to scramble up, though the top drawer stood open some two giant inches, like an overhanging shelf on a cliff face.

Jack was struck suddenly with the notion that a handful of bread wouldn't be a bad idea at all, and he clambered along after Skeezix, boosting him up around the top drawer so that Skeezix could get his foot and arm into the long cut in the counter face where the breadboard would go. From there Skeezix pulled himself onto the sidewalk-wide edge of the open drawer and from there onto the counter, leaning over to give Jack a hand up after him.

Jack looked back, down toward the floor, and nearly toppled over at the sight of it. He edged away across the marble countertop, which was pale gold and veined with swirls of green that were creviced with fissures into which had fallen years worth of crumbs and gunk. It was an appalling sight, all in all, although a giant wouldn't have noticed. And a giant, probably, wouldn't have seen the gray-white powder that dusted the marble, either. It smelled musty and sharp— faintly like rat poison. A really clean kitchen would require a mouse-sized inspector.

Skeezix had made his way over to the bread and had torn out two handfuls of the coarse white fluff. He stuffed a morsel into his mouth and shrugged at Jack, as if to say it wasn't at all bad, taken all the way around. Steam rose beyond him, from the pot on the low stove. The cat, suddenly, yowled and scratched against the door. Surely the giants would hear it, and they'd come to let it out. Giant cats, Jack reminded himself, could easily leap up onto giant counters.

He looked around him. There wouldn't be time to climb down the drawers again if the cat got out and took a fancy to them. Maybe they could hide in the sink drain. The double-hung kitchen window stood opened and unscreened above him, beyond towering canisters. Jack left Skeezix to the bread for the moment and climbed up onto the sill, brushing shoulders with a half dozen pairs of salt and pepper shakers—comical dogs and pigs and egg-headed men—that stood clustered on either side of the window on the flat sill. He held onto the weighted rope that ran along inside the window frame and looked out. There was a ledge beyond, and a window box planted with begonias, the prickly leaves broad as bed sheets. It wouldn't be an impossible thing, if it came to it, for them to go out through the window, onto the ledge, and down into the shrubs beyond.

In the meantime, he'd eat bread. He was suddenly famished. Heaven knew how long it had been since he'd eaten at Dr. Jensen's—or how long it had been since he'd slept. Journeying through magical lands was adventuresome, surely, but he needed a destination of some sort, a purpose; otherwise he might as well be bumming around his own world. At least there he wouldn't have to flee in terror from kitty-cats.

He stared for a moment from his perch among the saltshakers. Beyond Skeezix and the loaf of bread, where the edge of the counter loomed above the stove, half obscured by steam, lay an upended box. He'd seen such a box before, in Willoughby's kitchen; it was a common enough sight—rat poison, sitting on its side and with a fork shoved under the end of it, as if someone had used the fork to lever the bottom up. It was curious, surely. Someone had dumped it into the soup pot or stew pot or whatever it was, still bubbling merrily while the giants chatted and laughed in the other room. Someone had poisoned the soup.

Jack knew who it was. He had no idea on earth why, unless it was simply out of general villainy, nor had he any notion why Harbin had left the upended box in plain sight. It must have been rough, heavy as the box would have been to a mouse-sized man, to push it out of a cupboard and onto the counter and then drag it to the edge and over the soup pot. Certainly hiding the emptied box and the fork he'd used as a lever would have been an infinitely easier task.

Jack looked around him suspiciously. Then, in alarm, he leaped down and rushed toward Skeezix, slapping the bread out of his friend's hands. "Poison!" he whispered.

"What?"

Jack hauled him around the bread loaf, where they both stood staring at the box. They walked to the edge of the counter, shading their faces from the swirling steam, and peered over. Right below was the bubbling pot, the grainy poison dissolved in the soup. A brief scrape and clink sounded above. Jack looked up, cursing himself for his stupidity, and threw himself into Skeezix as a crockery saucer slid out of a newly opened cupboard and sailed down at their heads. The saucer fell sideways, whumping into the bread loaf, sliding down with a whirling clatter onto the countertop, knocking both of them over and settling across Skeezix's legs. Jack prayed that the noise of it would attract the giants, who were laughing aloud again over their chess game.

Algernon Harbin peered down at them from above, grinning maliciously. He'd started to grow. He'd been back longer than they, perhaps by hours, and he was twice their height— rat-sized now, big enough to tackle the boxful of poison, to climb up into the cupboard and hide himself there. They'd interrupted his meddling with the soup when they'd come in through the cat door. He would have hidden the box, and the unsuspecting giants would have eaten the soup.

Harbin held his stick out in front of him and leaped, his rag clothes ballooning out around him, straight into the center of the bread. He climbed off, advised them sarcastically to wait a moment, and hurriedly limped down to the open drawer, lowering himself into it.

Jack wasn't in a mood to wait. He helped Skeezix from under the saucer and sprinted toward the open window. If the giants wanted to sing comic songs while their soup was poisoned, that was their lookout. He and Skeezix weren't part of it. They could shove a message under the front door—later, after they'd gotten away.

Harbin loomed up out of the drawer with a poultry skewer in his hand, a skewer that would have knitted shut a turkey big as an elephant. He climbed onto the countertop and in three steps cut them off from the open window, jabbing the skewer at Skeezix's head with a viciousness that appalled Jack. Both boys swerved back toward the canisters, leaping along, grateful for Harbin's limp. Jack reached them first, sliding in behind the fat glass jars. Skeezix followed. Either Harbin would squeeze in after them—and he was almost too big for that now—or he'd go round to the other side and cut off their escape. They wouldn't be able to see him easily beyond the flour-fogged glass and the mounded sugar; but then, he wouldn't be able to see them either.

They waited, halfway between the flour and the oatmeal, breathing heavily, wondering which way to run. Harbin was nowhere to be seen. Jack took a tentative step back out, and suddenly Harbin was there, leaning around the sugar canister and stabbing at him with the skewer, held in both hands. Jack dropped, scuttling back into the shadows of the canisters like a crab. The sugar jar thunked abruptly against the wall, trapping them there. Harbin appeared beyond the last, almost empty rice canister, casting a little trifling wave at them as he shoved that one against the wall too, so that Jack and Skeezix stood in little prison, bounded on all sides by the canisters and by the wall. They could see Harbin through the glass now, limping along toward the stove.

He whacked the sides of the box of rat poison, shaking out every fragment, then got round behind it and shoved it along the marble, back past the canisters, tilting it off the edge and into the open drawer. He clambered in after it and was gone for a moment, no doubt sliding it into the recesses. Then he was out again, strolling toward them across the countertop as if he had all the time in the world. Still the giants laughed and joked and sang, as if they'd been at it for hours and were only half done. The cat, trapped in the pantry, kept up a sort of yowling accompaniment.

"Hey," said Skeezix. "Look!" He'd gotten his knee in behind the rice canister and inched the heavy glass jar away from the wall. Jack pushed in beside him and shoved. The canister slid away, and Skeezix was past it, running. Jack followed, straight toward the fork. Jack heard Harbin curse. Something struck him on the shoulder—the skewer, thrown like a spear but flying up endwise and glancing off, then sliding away across the slick marble and onto the floor behind the stove.

Skeezix and Jack picked up the fork together. It was heavy but secure as a battering ram with one of them on either end. They rushed back at Harbin, who fled toward his drawer, faster than they were despite his limp. He tumbled headfirst into it, ducking back out of sight. They stood on the edge, waiting for him to show himself, but there was nothing they could do with the fork if he did appear except drop it on him. They couldn't thrust it downward and both still hold onto it. It was time, perhaps, to leave, while they could still hold the villain at bay.

They backed off toward the window, a step at a time. Jack stepped into a crevice in the marble, fell over backward, and let go of his end of the fork, which clanked down onto the countertop and bounced. Skeezix was dragged over with it, shouting and kicking, and Harbin was up and out of the drawer, hauling a tin tea strainer behind him on a chain. He stood up, glaring at Skeezix, and whirled the strainer around his head as if it were a bull-roarer. Skeezix seemed to pause, halfway to his feet, as if wondering whether there was anything in a whirling tea strainer that would give him real trouble. The grimace on Harbin's face seemed to decide him, and he was up, running for the windowsill, where Jack stood ready to help him up.

Skeezix pulled himself across the sill, resting his chest on it, trying to swing his legs up. He failed and slid down to the counter, huffing for breath and looking back at the capering Harbin, who stepped forward with his tea strainer, grinning but wary. Skeezix smashed against the wall beneath the sill, ducking a swing that would have wrapped the chain around his neck, and reeled back, shouting out loud and leaping nimbly toward the canisters again.

Jack put his shoulder against a saltshaker, a ceramic devil-ridden pig. He tilted it off the sill, and it smashed against the countertop a world away from where Harbin still whirled his device, trying for Skeezix one last time and looking over his shoulder at the open drawer, as if he were wondering what to haul out next—a corncob handle or a potato peeler or a honey dipper. Jack toppled another saltshaker off and then another, making noise. He shouted and screamed and leaned out over the flower box to grab up a pebble that filled his hand.

Harbin turned in a rage and threw the tea strainer at Jack's legs. The chain wrapped around him, and the strainer whipped past, pulling him off his feet, dragging him over sideways toward the ledge. Jack rolled and sat up, still holding his rock, pitching it into the face of the maniacal Harbin.

Skeezix slid out from behind the canister and ran square into the villain's back, knocking him onto his face, then leaping onto his back and vaulting up onto the windowsill. He teetered on the edge, nearly falling. Jack clutched at Skeezix's doll garments, hauling him back across the sill, toward the window and the flower box and the open expanse of the grassy back yard. He shook off the chain, kicking the tea strainer down onto Harbin's head, and then pushed another saltshaker down after it.

There was a shuffling in the other room, a shout, the sound of a book hitting the floor. Jack and Skeezix froze, perched on the windowsill. A man's voice shouted, "That's it! It's me!" And a woman's voice followed: "Hurry!"

"Let out the damned cat!" shouted someone else—one of the old chess players, maybe, who'd finally heard the cat's yowling and somehow understood its plight.

The bearded giant stepped in through the open door, towering above the counter, horrible to look at. The hairs in his beard, neatly trimmed, perhaps, in the eyes of a giant, covered his face like forest undergrowth. His nose was immense, his teeth ridged and broad like weathered slab doors painted ivory. Clamped between them was a pipe with a bowl big around as a tub and glowing like a furnace, the swirling reek of tobacco clouding out of it like fog off a tule marsh.

The giant reached out and plucked up Algernon Harbin, who shrieked and cursed in terror. Then he set the struggling villain onto the wooden floor, jerking his hand back and shaking it, obviously bitten. He reached across and yanked open the pantry door, then stepped back as the cat leaped out, almost onto Harbin's back. The cat hissed and batted with its paw, as if it knew the thing on the floor ought to be knocked down, that it was something worse than a rat. Then, with a screech and a snarl and a gristly snapping that made Jack and

Skeezix look away, the cat picked its prey up in its teeth and ducked out through the cat door, the last of Harbin's shrieks diminishing toward the distant bushes.

The giant turned toward the stove, his face grim. Skeezix nudged Jack and cast him a broad, savage wink, standing very still and with a cockeyed grin on his face. Jack did the same, ready in an instant to bolt for the flower box.

"We eat at Hoover's tonight!" shouted the giant. "Just like I said." The boom of his voice nearly knocked Jack and Skeezix over backward. He pulled his pipe from his mouth suddenly and tapped the ashes out into the soup. Then he twisted off the gas and started back out of the kitchen. He stopped, pulled the open drawer even farther open, and hauled out the empty rat poison box, shaking his head and setting it onto the counter. "Soup's done for," he said. He stepped into the doorway, turned, and looked straight toward the window. Jack nearly leaped out. The giant twisted the ring off his finger, grinned in their general direction, and flipped it end over end in the air, catching it, chuckling, and slipping it back on. He turned and strode out.

Jack and Skeezix had climbed down the bushes, sprinted across the cropped lawn, and ducked under the fence before either one of them felt like speaking. They found themselves on the High Street again, looking across at the harbor. Suddenly the giant world seemed filled with a million perils. A stinkbug big as a dog eyed them from the gutter. A sparrow hawk swooped down to have a look and then swooped up again. They could hear the rustling, padding footsteps of what must have been another cat, stalking beyond the wooden fence they'd just slid under—a fence that rose above them like the wall of a canyon. A cat could scale it in an instant.

"Come on," said Skeezix, and he darted out into the road, angling toward the side of the inn.

"Why?" shouted Jack, following, across the street and into the shadows.

"Why not? Let's hide until we can figure this out. Until we start to grow. Dr. Jensen can wait till it's safer. He's not in any rush." They rounded the inn, hopping down stone stairs toward the bay, scuttling in behind a heap of wooden crates, breathing hard. Skeezix grinned, obviously proud of himself. "He thought we were saltshakers."

"What?" asked Jack. "*Who* did?"

"That monster did, after he set the cat on Harbin. Not that Harbin didn't deserve it. It was our standing there like that that did it, that saved us. I was salt, being the fat one, and you were pepper."

Jack rolled his eyes. "Sure," he said. "What was that gag with the ring?"

Skeezix shook his head. "Damned if I know. And what was Harbin doing there, poisoning innocent people? The giant must have known who he was. Did you see how he just emptied his pipe into the soup like it was nothing, like he was putting in herbs? We're out of our depth here, is what I think. We stumbled into something that was none of our business. Good thing we did, though; it was all the noise and the fight that brought the giant around. They'd have sucked down the soup otherwise and been dead in their beds."

"How long do you suppose Harbin's been here?"

"I don't know," Skeezix answered, shrugging and peering out through the slats of the crate. "A couple of hours anyway. We ought to start growing fairly soon, as I see it. And when we do, we'd better have some clothes to put on or we'll find ourselves in trouble. I'm not going anywhere near Elaine Potts under circumstances like that."

Jack nodded. "We ought to get back down to the river. We could hook some clothes off the clothesline at the White sisters' houses. We wouldn't have to be any bigger than Harbin was to yank a couple of pairs of pants out of their clothespins. Then we could drag them into the bushes and wait."

"Let's go. We've got nothing to do here but crack our heads on the top of these crates."

They crept out, straight into the face of a rat sniffing along the crates. It was immense—fat and with short bristly fur and a tail a foot long. Its upper lip flickered up to expose a row of teeth that might have gnawed off Jack's arm without a terrible lot of trouble. Jack and Skeezix backed away slowly. The rat sniffed after them, curious.

"Back down the ramp," whispered Jack. "He won't go near the guy fishing down there."

Skeezix nodded, mostly because their back was to the broad wagon ramp that ran down to where the dories put in, and there was no place else to go. It was a sound idea anyway, or at least seemed so until it became clear that the rat didn't care who was fishing at the end of the ramp; it followed the two down, its tail twitching, ready to leap.

"He's pig drunk," said Skeezix.

"The rat?" Jack was astonished at the pronouncement.

"The guy fishing. He won't help. Look at him; he's about to lose his shoe, dangling it like that from his toe. He's stinking. The rat knows it; the guy's probably a permanent fixture around here. They can't arrest him for vagrancy as long as he carries a fishing pole."

Jack looked around him for a weapon: a stick, a shard of glass, anything. The whole place seemed swept, as if they'd sent a man around earlier to make sure that there was no debris in the streets that might tempt a mouse-sized man into violence. But there was something—a fish hook, rusted and old and with the eye snapped off. Jack lunged for it, plucking it up and waving it over his head to menace the rat, who stared straight at them through impossibly brown eyes, eyes that didn't notice the hook or didn't care. It was a useless weapon anyway.

Jack bumped solidly into something soft. It was the back of the sleeping fisherman. Skeezix hit the man with both fists, effecting nothing. The rat crept forward. Jack spun around, closed his eyes, and shoved the hook through the man's shirt and into the roll of flesh that sagged over his belt. The fisherman leaped awake, shouting, dropping his shoe into the harbor, waving his fishing pole in a mad, hopping dance.

The rat was gone. One moment he was there; the next he'd leaped away, disappearing into the crates. The fisherman spied Jack and Skeezix and immediately tried to stomp on them. "Rats!" he cried—an observation that would have been true ten seconds earlier—and he reeled back and forth, shrieking with anger when he stepped on a pebble with his shoeless foot, kicking at Skeezix as he ran toward the water.

"Jump!" shouted Jack, and he leaped as he shouted, off the little stone curb that ran along the edge of the ramp and angled down into the water. He landed in the floating shoe, and Skeezix landed on top of him. The shoe listed crazily for a moment, riding up and over a little swell, and then eddied out toward the rowboats moored in the harbor.

The fisherman raged on the shore, hopping on one foot. He reached for the escaping shoe with the tip of his pole, slapping the side, trying to turn it about. But the tide had caught it, and his prodding served only to spin it out farther. He cast his hook at it then, thinking to snag it and reel it in. The heavy hook whirled past, chasing Skeezix and Jack back in toward the toe. It snaked in again and again, finally biting into one of the laces. The shoe jerked about, skidding across the top of the water. Jack dashed out and snatched at it, wiggling the hook out, wishing he hadn't lost his pocketknife. Halfway back to shore he pitched the hook into the water, and the tide picked them up again. The fisherman beat the water with his pole, furious, incapable in his fury of casting into the shoe again. In moments it was lost to him and he knew it. He stood with his hands on his hips and watched it float out toward the open ocean.

A man in a battered stovepipe hat strode down the ramp toward the fisherman, asking about the shouting, and the fisherman told him, gesturing wildly, about the two tiny men who had stabbed him while he slept and stole his shoe and were sailing it out of the harbor. The hatted man shook his head slowly and walked back up the ramp, stopping at the top to say something but failing, perhaps, to find the words. He walked away up the High Street, leaving the fisherman scratching his head in wonder.

The tide ran out quickly, swirling around and out the mouth of the harbor, past the headland, skidding up into a southwest swell and disappearing into the broad Pacific. The sun crept down toward the horizon, and a fog was blowing up, stretching along in a vast gray wall a half mile or so out to sea. Jack and Skeezix sat shivering, watching the land slip past, happy for the calm sea. There was the cove and the bluffs, and way down the shore, shimmering in the late afternoon sun, was the placid expanse of the Eel River. A land wind blew, surprisingly warm but cooling quickly as it traveled across the ocean. When night fell, the lacy doll clothes wouldn't be worth much. They could climb into the shoe to escape the wind, but they'd still have to sit on the ocean-soaked leather of the shoe sole. If the wind freshened, of course, their travels would be at an end. The shoe wouldn't stand a chop.

"There's no carnival," said Skeezix suddenly, standing up and pointing toward the bluffs.

"You're right. And it's still Solstice time too, otherwise we wouldn't have gotten here." He stared at the bluffs for a moment, wondering at their immeasurable height and realizing it was the first time he'd seen them from out at sea like that. "This is just like Dr. Jensen's voyage, isn't it?"

"I *wish* it was," said Skeezix. "Dr. Jensen got pushed in to shore, at least. We're just drifting farther out, into the fog. You know what's going to happen, don't you? Any time now."

It had already begun to happen. Jack untied his belt and then retied it a bit looser. They were growing. A shoe made a fine sort of longboat for mice, and a tolerable rowboat for rats, but it wouldn't amount to as much as a washtub for, say, a possum. "Long damned way to swim, isn't it? Even if we were full size."

"I'm too beat to swim anywhere." said Skeezix. "And imagine swimming in the ocean during the Solstice. A sardine's as big as a shark."

"Don't mention sharks," said Jack. "I don't want to think about sharks."

The shoe bobbed lazily on the swell as the sun set. They drifted into the first of the swirling fog and into darkness at the same time. The wind turned, feeling cold and damp, slanting out of the south, up the coast. The two of them crawled back into the toe, lying down with their heads toward the heel so that when it came time they could pull themselves out. Certainly they'd wake up before they were squeezed senseless by the shoe. Knowing that there was nothing they could do about what would surely come, and too tired to worry about things they couldn't avoid, they untied their belts and lay in silence, listening to the ocean lap at the sides of their craft and watching the misty evening drift into misty night until they fell asleep shivering.

14

WITH A SUDDENNESS that made her gasp, Helen found herself alone in the little cart, whirring along through the weird darkness. For a slip of a moment she thought that Jack and Skeezix had flown out, or were snatched out, or had never been there in the first place and she was dreaming and would wake up.

Then she knew, in a rush. They'd gone across without her. They hadn't been quick enough with the bottle of elixir. Part of her was relieved, but only for an instant. If she'd been someplace else—back in the attic, say, or at Dr. Jensen's—and not hurtling along through this black carnival ride, the relief would amount to more.

She slid to the middle of the cart, where Jack had sat, but slid back again almost at once. There was something safe about being on the edge of the seat. She'd always felt like that, preferring the edge of the sidewalk to the middle of it, the edge of a sofa to the center. Maybe it was because she felt she could get out quicker that way, or maybe it was because it was lonely being all alone at the center of something.

The wheels clacked. Little musty breezes stirred her hair. Cobwebs brushed her face. When Jack and Skeezix had vanished, she'd thought she had heard the sound of a distant train, and she'd smelled salt air and tar and the odor of mussels and barnacles clinging to pier pilings. Now there was nothing but silence and darkness and musty air, like in a cellar, and a light, dim and distant but rushing up at her along the corridor.

She gripped the iron bar across her knees and bit her lip. The cart slammed into the circle of light, and there, sitting on a kitchen stool, stroking the fur of what appeared to Helen to be a dead cat, sat Peebles, grinning at her. She shut her eyes and was past him, into the pleasant darkness again. Laughter hooted somewhere ahead, and there was the sound of a blade thunking against a chopping block and then a cry that gurgled into nothing. Double-time music burbled out and then abruptly shut off. A door slammed. "Helen!" whispered a voice, away off in the recesses of the darkness.

She careened around an S-shaped bit of track, lurching from side to side. A light blinked on and she found herself hurtling toward a wall, painted with a likeness of the carnival itself, centered around the smoking oven. Jerking skeletons fed bleached bones into the smoking, open mouth of the thing, and just before she ducked her head and curled up in anticipation of smashing into it, steam hissed out in a rush, pouring over her, smelling horribly of hot ground bone.

Then she was outside, still moving, aware that the carnival was empty and half dark. She felt suddenly sleepy and exhausted. She could easily lie across the seat and close her eyes. She was drained, was the truth of it, from the excitement of the Solstice, from the too-long day, from the shock of finding herself alone and Jack gone. There was the entrance again, the slab door opening, slowly—a black tunnel into which she was falling, as if down a well toward the soft and steamy center of the earth.

Peebles rattled along in his cart, directly behind Helen. He gnawed at his finger, liking the feel of the rubbery flesh. The numbness in it was spreading along his arm, just as Dr. Brown had promised it would. Shortly, though, when the carnival had finished with Helen, the numbness would be gone. He smiled to think about it. He liked the idea of living at the expense of people like Helen. He hadn't had a taste, so to speak, of Lantz. Helen was his first.

He'd dealt handily enough with Miss Flees, who'd been tiresome. She was beneath him, whining away all the time, looking like a mess, mothering him. The Solstice pie had done the trick. She'd been stark, staring mad before she'd gone across. It was a pity he hadn't any chance to deal with Jack and Skeezix too, but he'd get at them through Helen. And he'd be back, of course. Then they'd see—all of them. The only real regret was that he shared the carnival with Mac-Wilt, but he'd work on that too. He didn't need partners.

He had never been tempted, really, to go across. One world was the same as the next, all of them equally odious. It was power he wanted, that and the eradication of the people who hadn't let him have it, who had scoffed at him and ignored him and tried to save him from himself. He had that power now—over life and death. The only master he served was the carnival itself, and it was a master that couldn't speak, that needed what he needed, that sought, day to day, the same ends that he sought.

He rather enjoyed the darkness of the ride. He could feel something in the air, a sort of electricity, like before a hot wind. It hovered around him, probing, watching him. But he was part of it, in a way, and could ignore it. Helen couldn't, or at least she shouldn't. But then she hadn't any real choice in the matter. She was theirs.

Painted skeletons and headless men appeared and receded. Steam roiled up around him. For a moment he felt the uncanny certainty that it was fog, not steam, and that he occupied a vast, open, and crumbling building somewhere, a building that decayed around him, the floors ankle deep in termite dust, sea wind whistling through gaps in clapboard siding. It felt right, somehow; like home. Then he was back in the cart, angling along the dark corridor. He heard Helen scream from the car ahead. He laughed, imagining her terror and half regretting that it wouldn't last.

Before they left for the south, he promised himself, after he'd seen to Helen, he'd burn down Miss Flees's house. Fire might not kill the old woman who haunted the attic, but it would wipe out every trace of the things she possessed, of her reason for haunting anything at all. He smiled as he rumbled along, imagining the house burning. He'd burn Jensen's house too. He'd have a busy night of it, and tomorrow he'd be gone, beyond where anyone would think to look for him.

Jack and Skeezix found themselves on a beach. Jack woke up first, wondering how long he'd slept. The moon was rising beyond the coastal hills, and only a pale yellow bit of light leaked across the night landscape, so that just the outlines of things were visible. It felt like midnight, or thereabouts. They were in the cove—they must have blown back in, as Dr. Jensen had done. The wet doll clothes hung on him loosely, as they had when he'd first put them on. The foggy weather must have stretched them. It was too much to hope for any other explanation.

There was no sign of fog now, not even offshore, although it might have been hidden by the night. The tide was out, exposing rock reefs and tide pools, shadowy and dark, the still water of the pools barely visible in the pale radiance cast by the hidden moon.

Something moved down the cove, out in the water toward the headland—something big, that clacked and splashed. A ragged arm waved out of the water, the moonlit claw on the end clutching something, a fish maybe, as long as Jack's leg. They'd returned to a world of monsters. This was proof—a hermit crab as big as a house. He could see the mountainous whorl of the turban snail shell on its back. Nowhere was safe. It was curious that they hadn't grown. Harbin had. If he'd lived he'd be big enough by now to walk the streets. He'd have no fear of cats, or crabs, or rats as big as oxen. It wasn't safe on the beach. A crab might as easily take a fancy to them as to a fish.

Skeezix still slept. Jack didn't want to wake him, even though he knew he had to. Despite Skeezix's brave, adventurous talk, he'd be downhearted to find that he was back again, that he still occupied a world in which there was quite possibly another Skeezix, one that had quite conceivably already wooed Elaine Potts, a world in which a passing hermit crab could eat them both before going to bed.

He prodded Skeezix with his foot and peered at the soggy shoe, wondering at it. Something was wrong. They'd gone to sleep thinking that during the night they'd outgrown it, that their increasing weight would swamp it, and that they'd find themselves swimming in the open, foggy ocean. Now it seemed to him that it was even larger than when they'd first leaped into it. Certainly the wet hadn't stretched the shoe and his doll clothes both.

A wave broke behind them, washing across the heel of the shoe, spinning it sideways and beaching it entirely. A sea gull landed on the toe just as the moon cleared the hills, bathing the coast in silver light. Jack stared at the bird for a moment, then blinked in surprise. It wasn't a monster, like the hermit crab or the owl in the oak woods. It was a standard sea gull. It would have had to stand on his forearm to look him in the face. He turned around to look up the beach again. Perhaps the crab was a figment, an illusion, a shadow, a trick of moonlight and darkness. But it wasn't. It was still there, clacking and clambering over rocks, toward them. They seemed to have drifted into some giddy version of the world that was half monster, half normal. But there wasn't any time to be puzzled about it.

"Hey!" Jack shouted, shoving Skeezix again with his foot. He boosted himself over the side of the shoe and onto the beach. The sea gull flew into the air, circling overhead, then landed on the beach farther down. Skeezix awakened, looking about him groggily. Jack waved his hand in Skeezix's face. "Hurry! A giant crab!"

Skeezix blinked wonderingly at him for a moment, forgetting, perhaps, that such a thing as a giant crab was entirely possible. Then he remembered. He twisted round and looked down the beach toward where the crab scuttled along through the shallows. It hadn't seen them yet, but it would. Skeezix tumbled over the side of the shoe and ran, he and Jack both, up the hill and into the cavern overlooking the beach. Jack scraped his head on the sandstone ceiling. The truth struck them both at once. It was Dr. Jensen's crab, coming up at last out of the sea—the last of the Solstice migration. The sea gull, the cove, the cavern they shivered in—all of them were as they should be. They were home at long last.

"Helen," he said. "What about Helen?"

Skeezix shook his head. "We know *where* we are, but we don't know when. Let's get out of here before we freeze."

"We need clothes."

Skeezix grinned, nodded, and bent out of the cavern, sliding away down the slope and watching the great crab dawdle in the waves. Skeezix jogged to the rocks beneath the trestle. They were high and dry; the last tide hadn't risen far enough to soak them.

"What're you doing?" asked Jack, catching up.

"This is where we hid Langley's clothes. You can have number five if you want it. I'll take three. Helen ripped the shirt, but it beats these doll clothes. It'll be a tight fit, though; James Langley was dangerously thin, to my way of thinking."

Jack pulled the rocks out of the shoes, examining the slip of paper. "Where's four?" he asked, pulling on the shirt.

"Your father got hold of four when he came through. If Langley arrives he'll be out of luck. He'll have to knit himself kelp pants. Let's go."

They were off, running up the beach road, angling across the meadow toward the bluffs, hearing for the first time the tootling of the calliope over the rush of the ocean. A low, booming noise seemed to fill the air, to stretch it, as if it vibrated through the earth and rock of the meadow. They stopped for a moment to look back, toward where the crab followed along behind them in the moonlight. It seemed to have seen at last but was wary of climbing up off the beach to pursue them and so was coming on slowly.

The carnival was a wonder of lights, although the rides were silent and empty—all of them except the Toad. Jack and Skeezix could hear the rattling of the carts, the shouted laughter, the intermittent shrieks and ghostly hooting as they pounded along, Jack in front now, Skeezix falling behind but running as fast as he'd ever run and with a look of intensity on his face that seemed to say that he was ready, finally, to confront whoever it was that needed confronting.

Jack could see the beehive oven, its door open, the fire banked and roaring and looking like the arched mouth of the descent into hell. Two men, weed-haired black shadows against the soaring flames, fed fuel in through the open door, one of them pitching in split logs, the other shoveling coal, both of them bending and lurching and casting the fuel like clockwork toys, at such a pace that the oven must have been impossibly full. A banging and hissing filled the night air, rhythmic and slow like a steaming heart—the *boom, boom, boom* they'd heard coming up from the beach—and growing louder with each stroke as if the oven would explode along with the engine it propelled. The calliope sighed and moaned from the center of the dark, still carousel.

One of the men leaned into an iron lever angling out of the side of the oven, aglow in the light of the flame, and at once a rush of steam poured out of the top of the mechanical contrivance attached to the domed bricks in a rising shriek. The beating of the massive heart died to a throbbing pulse. The glow of the lamplit carnival diminished, as if the lamps weren't burning oil but, like the carnival rides, were driven by steam.

Jack slowed to a careful walk as he approached the plywood arch that spanned the dirt road across the bluffs. Skeezix puffed up behind him. It seemed wild and foolish to stride in at the door like that, through the arch, as if they'd come round for pleasure. But there was nothing else to do; there was no hiding on the open meadow. The plywood wall stretching away on either side seemed almost to shimmer, but the shimmering seemed to have nothing to do with the carnival lamps and the burning torches thrust randomly in the meadow grasses.

The colors of the gaudy clowns and demons and apes that decorated the posters covering the walls seemed to shift and deepen. Faces slowly began to appear where there'd been none moments before—staring out from beyond cycling midgets, half obscured by odd, smoky lettering—not the faces of acrobats and strong men and fat ladies but of peering, hollow-eyed strangers, lost in the layers of countless posters glued onto the walls over countless years.

The ghostly faces grew more clear with the slowly brightening paint. Lines of sorrow and fear in their lonely countenances deepened until the shifting and the shimmering became the restless movements of what appeared to be a thousand captured souls, straggling in a procession from impossibly deep within the arched, painted facade. The plywood and the posters had become almost transparent, so that beyond it, through it, could be seen the slowly turning Ferris wheel, the flames of the open oven, the dark swinging door of the Flying Toad.

Jack and Skeezix stood staring at the faces until they realized, at one and the same time, that Lantz was among the spirits they stared at, his face hovering at the forefront of the procession, drawn and tired. And something seemed to be materializing beside him—a pale hovering spirit, looking like dust shaken out of a rug. Jack and Skeezix leaped through the arch, past the wall and running, both of them sure whose face it was that drifted toward clarity.

They could hear the clacking of the crab again as they ducked around behind the row of tents, and Jack looked back, one last time, to see it coming through the arch, the worn pastel colors of its barnacle-crusted shell shining in the glow of the lamps. Immense and startling as it was, there seemed to be nothing incongruous about it, as if an enormous hermit crab was a common carnival fixture. They boys slipped along in the shadows. It wouldn't do to be seen, not just now. And yet if they dawdled—

A hand clutched Jack's shoulder. He shouted in surprise and twisted away, sitting down hard and certain that it was Dr. Brown, escaped from the cat. But it was MacWilt, grinning, licking his lips slowly. His right eyelid twitched as he bent forward and closed his thin and bony hand around Jack's ankle. In his other hand was a knife, its slender blade flecked with rust.

Skeezix hit MacWilt head first in the side, wrinkling him up like a wet scarecrow and tumbling over him into the wall of a tent. Jack leaped to his feet and stamped on MacWilt's wrist, thinking to loosen his grip on the knife. The tavern keeper sat up and spun around fast, his head tilted back and eyes pried open, grabbing Jack's leg and swinging the knife in a wild arc at his stomach just as Skeezix clambered up and fell on MacWilt from behind, knocking him forward. The knife caught itself in Jack's sweater—in James Langley's sweater—and jerked out of MacWilt's hand. A scream sounded—Helen's scream—and Jack was running again, between the tents, the knife bouncing along, entangled in the sweater. He wrenched it out and threw it, hating the feel of it in his hand. In the same instant he heard MacWilt curse, but the curse cut off midway through, folding into the wheeze of a man who's had the wind knocked out of him.

Jack looked over his shoulder to see Skeezix appear from the other side of the tent, running. There was the Flying Toad straight ahead. Steam poured out from under the tilt-up sides of the thing, swirling away in the lamplit night like writhing demons. The air was hot with it, and with the glow from the oven, still stoked by the two men, or whatever they were. One of them, half turned toward them, appeared to be nothing more than a skeleton dressed in rags.

Another jerking ghoul appeared, making toward the Ferris wheel, with Dr. Jensen's crab close behind it and nipping at its neck with an enormous claw. The crab swept through a string of lanterns, knocking them down across the top of the nearest tent. A fire sprang up in a rush, the burning oil pooled up atop the damp canvas and dripping down the sides, brightening the night with running, leaping flame.

"I'm going to shut it down!" hollered Skeezix, climbing over the railing that fronted the Toad.

Jack nodded, shouted "Yeah!" and ran shoulder first into the door, which swung open on its hinge, dumping him into the dark interior. Helen was inside somewhere. He was sure of it. At first he couldn't see, but he could find his way well enough if he stuck to the tracks. He tripped over a pair of pipes that ran in under the wall, but he staggered ahead, hurrying. A light blazed forty feet farther on, almost hidden around the curve of track. It would be the headless man, pitching his head into a basket. Jack started to jog. He could see well enough now. It occurred to him that he might never catch up with Helen. The ride had been unnaturally long, as if it were as much a product of magic as mechanics. Eventually Helen would catch up with him. But he didn't want to wait for that.

The air was heavy with steam that weighed on his shoulders like sacks of sand. It seemed to him suddenly that he hadn't gotten enough sleep in the shoe—he was dead tired. And he realized that he hadn't been warm, not really, in—how long? It seemed like days. It was blood-warm in the ride, though.

He slowed up. There wasn't any hurry. Helen *would* catch up to him. That would have to do. He couldn't chase after her forever, round and round the tracks. He stopped, wavering, feeling as if he were falling forward, down a well shaft—not in a rush but in a slow, lazy, somnolent drift, on a bed of feathers. He slumped against the wall and tried to shake the sleep out of his head. But it was more than sleep, and it wouldn't shake out. Laughter sounded from ahead. There was the whir and clatter of wheels along the track.

That was what he wanted—wasn't it?—to hear a cart coming along. He couldn't remember entirely why. It appeared from behind him, in the dark distance, coming along fearfully slowly, seeming almost to float along through the whirling steam. At first it seemed empty, but it wasn't. Someone lay asleep on the seat. Helen. Even in the darkness he knew it. Jack reeled toward her, toward the moving cart, down the center of the tracks. The cart rolled forward, the wheels barely turning, and with one last *whoosh* of released steam it stopped.

In the sudden silence the air was alive with the sound of pounding, with the throbbing of the oven. The steam dissipated, hovering up toward the ceiling and vanishing, and the weighty, deadening atmosphere of the place lifted with it. Jack heard someone shouting. It was Skeezix. He'd shut the ride down, just like he'd said. Jack blinked the sleep out of his eyes and leaped along the last few feet of track to where Helen lay. He wrenched the bar forward so as to reach in behind it. Helen shifted uneasily. Her face was gray in the dim light, her eyes half open and blank. Jack would have to carry her out—into the ocean air. It was easier thought of than done, though. Small as she was, she was heavier than he would have guessed, and curled up in the cart, and him leaning in and doing all the work with his back—

He was shoved, suddenly, from behind. He heard a little whining grunt of effort, and then he pitched forward, dropping Helen to the seat again, stumbling off balance. He grabbed the edge of the cart and turned around to see Peebles leering at him, sucking on his bent finger. Peebles held something in his hand—a doll, it seemed to be, with an inflated origami paper head, built of feathers and clay and hair, an obscene thing with a chicken's beak on its face and chicken claws for feet and bits of the cut-up Solstice fish stitched on with colored thread.

"Part of this is you," said Peebles, smiling. And with that he plunged a straight pin into it, his eyes shooting open in surprised pleasure at the sudden sight of Jack's face, twisted in pain. He wrenched out the pin and winked. Jack braced himself, remembering suddenly the way he'd thrust the hook into the poor fisherman on the dock and then borrowed his shoe without so much as a thank-you. Well, he hadn't had any choice about that. He'd have to kick Peebles to bits and quickly, too. "Oh, no," said Peebles. "You shouldn't move. It won't be good for you. I can do things to you now that you wouldn't understand."

Jack stood still. He'd let Peebles talk. The hot pain that still throbbed at his side, beneath his belt, made Peebles's threats convincing.

Peebles shouted, over the loudening throb of the oven. His eyes shifted uneasily. "Our fat friend seems to have turned off the machinery. I saw him wrenching at it when I drove past, but Mr. MacWilt is dealing with the problem. In a moment—"

Peebles was interrupted by a distant shriek of steam. The throbbing lessened momentarily. Jack started forward, but Peebles straightened up, jabbing the pin up into the shoulder of the doll and sending Jack reeling. Peebles turned, watching him, ready to thrust it in again. "I could kill you with this, you know. But that would be a waste. I like to hurt you, though. I've got one of these with the fat boy's hair glued on, too. And I've got a Helen doll. I snipped bits of their hair off while they slept. Yours I snipped off one night a month ago when you stayed overnight at Miss Flees's—just the tiniest bit, just enough."

Helen, with a suddenness that made Jack shout, twisted off the cart and launched a kick at the doll in Peebles's hand. Jack slammed back into the wall, as if it had been *him* kicked by a giant foot. The doll sailed into the darkness. Helen stood reeling, looking faint, about to collapse. Peebles sprang at her with a curse. As he swung his fist at her, the lights brightened and steam chuffed up from under the track and out of the cracks at the corners of the ceiling and floor, as if the entire building were an engine, coming to life. The empty cart leaped forward, pushing Helen into Jack, clipping Peebles in the side as he tried to leap clear but couldn't because of the momentum of his swing. The cart rattled away, empty.

Jack grabbed Helen's hand and dragged her back toward the door, down the dark corridor. Helen sagged, and Jack yanked her out of the way of the second cart—Peebles's cart—which hurtled past, materializing out of the darkness and running straight on into Peebles's back as he scrabbled on the tracks after the fallen doll. As Jack bent down to pick Helen up, he heard Peebles scream. With fear coursing through him like an elixir, Jack found the strength to lurch away, carrying Helen against his chest. He held his breath, knowing he wouldn't make it ten steps through the steamy heat of the enlivened darkness if he gave in. Skeezix must have failed; MacWilt must have stopped him. Peebles screamed at his back and staggered along behind, his deformed hand dangling unnaturally, partly severed or broken by the cart. It was bloodless, like the hand of a waxwork dummy. But Peebles was still grinning, clearly feeling nothing, having cried out in surprise when the cart hit him, not in pain.

Jack could hear Skeezix shouting above the din of escaping steam and the throbbing of the oven, which reverberated through the plywood walls. Again, abruptly, the steam died, the lights dimmed, and Jack was running. He felt as if he'd just yanked his feet free of heavy mud. Helen, now that she was balanced and secure in his arms, wasn't so heavy after all.

He saw the door in front of him, wedged open with a stopped cart half through. Ocean air blew in through the door, swirling across them. Outside, the night was aflame. The line of tents and plywood shacks burned in a long orange wall. Six steps from the door a thrill of pain shot through his chest. He staggered against the wall, breathing hard, letting Helen roll out onto the ground, where she half stood up, shaking the fog out of her head.

Peebles waited behind them, twenty paces or so. He held the doll in the crook of his ruined arm, the pin raised. "Wait there!" he shouted. Jack waited. Helen stood up, hands on her knees. The night shook with the pounding of the oven and with the thundering of the calliope—completely wild now, a cacophony of toots and hoots. There was the shriek of steam again, like the sound of a train whistle now, but the pounding didn't dim at all. The bluffs shook with it. Smoke suddenly swirled in under the edge of the building. The walls were afire. Peebles wavered, looking round him, perplexed. "Out!" he commanded, striding toward them, menacing them with the upraised straight pin.

Jack backed toward the door. He had nothing against cooperating. Helen stumbled out before him, coughing in the suddenly heavy smoke. Skeezix shouted Jack's name. He pounded the ride's wooden and iron operating machinery with a three-foot length of railing. A chunk of the machinery broke off, twisting away and hanging there with the audible groan of bending metal.

Beside Skeezix lay the scattered bones of a skeleton that had been whacked to bits. MacWilt lay farther off, folded up across the little broken fence. Beyond, in the leaping glow of the fire, Dr. Jensen's crab jerked and snapped, entangled in the struts and cables of the tilting Ferris wheel. Guy lines ripped out around it. The wheel revolved wildly, carts rocking and hopping as the whole thing smashed over onto the burning tents, sending a *whoosh* of flaming canvas showering across them all. Skeezix threw down his piece of railing and leaped to where Jack supported Helen, then abandoned them at once to chase Peebles, who dashed away, running in a sort of one-legged stoop toward the pulsing oven and engine. Skeezix slowed, guarding his face with his bent right arm, letting Peebles race away into the searing heat.

The oven seemed double its size—immense now, its cavernous door an almost solid white-pink. The metal pipes and canisters and tanks attached to it glowed red. Two skeletons stood before the oven, their clothes and hair burnt off, the fire glowing through their ribs. One of them still shoveled in spadefuls of coal; the other pitched in logs, weirdly, jerkily animated in time to the booming, whooshing steam. The second skeleton paused to lean into the lever, but the iron bar had bent over like a hot tallow candle and nothing at all happened when the thing pushed it. Peebles shrieked at them, waving his arms.

Jack and Skeezix and Helen fled, away from the fire, away from the oven, back out toward the gate and the open meadow and the sea. They heard the roof of the Toad collapse in a rumbling heap, and Jack looked back, watching the crab scuttling down between the flames, stopping to pick up the feebly struggling MacWilt, whose robes smoldered and sparked.

The night was nothing by now but flames and pouring steam and the *boom*, *boom*, *boom* of the beehive oven. The coal-shoveling skeleton bent, oblivious to Peebles's cries, and scooped up a mountain of coal, turned, pitched it in, and stood wavering as if in surprise when its arm flew off and followed along behind the shovel and the spraying coal, straight into the mouth of the oven, dangling there as if held up for the moment by the intense heat, then exploding into fragments. Both skeletons shivered into bits like domino houses brought down by an earthquake. Peebles threw his good arm across his face and loosed one last drawn-out howl that neither Jack nor Skeezix nor Helen could hear, its existence betrayed only by his open mouth and by the wide-eyed fear on his face in the last luminous moment before the oven exploded.

15

JACK WOKE UP in Dr. Jensen's surgery. His head throbbed, and when he pushed himself up onto his elbows, a pain like the sharp edge of a chipped stone stabbed across behind his forehead. He winced but stayed propped up. There was a mist in his head too, and he blinked his eyes to chase it away. He'd been asleep, it seemed, for a very long time. It was late morning, maybe noon. Helen and Skeezix and Dr. Jensen were there. And there was Mrs. Jensen, too, standing in the doorway and whispering to someone in the kitchen.

Jack tried to shift his legs in order to sit up, but he couldn't. His left leg was splinted and stiff. There was a bloody rag tied around Skeezix's forehead. When he saw that Jack was awake and staring at the rag, Skeezix grimaced and shook his head slowly, seeming to say that he'd been through the wringer, that they'd won through, but not without a fearsome price.

"You're cut," said Jack thickly.

"Yes," said Skeezix. He shook his head some more. "It was hellish—the explosion, flying bricks, fire raining down. It was the Cities of the Plain. And that horrible crab—"

Helen reached across and snatched the bandage off Skeezix's head, throwing it onto the counter in disgust. "He scratched himself on a cypress tree pulling you out of the way of the crab. He hasn't cut his head at all."

"I *might* have cut my head. I came close. And you should have seen the crab, Jack. It snatched up MacWilt right before the oven blew up, and then it ran like crazy for the cove—straight at us, and you lying there senseless, hit by a brick and with your leg sprained. The explosion toppled it—blew its small claw right off. Look." Skeezix pointed to the counter where sat an enormous curved claw, some three feet across and faintly blue in the lamplight. "And that's the *small one*! I hauled you in behind a cypress—well, *Helen* and I did— and the crab got up and went right on, carrying MacWilt, right into the ocean and was gone. Anyway, I scraped my arm, but it isn't much of a scrape. The bandage on my head was a sort of joke."

Jack grinned at him, then smiled wider. Then He noticed, next to the great crab claw, a bouquet of cut wildflowers— pink ladies and dandelions and yellow alder leaves. "Gee," he said, not knowing what more to say about friends like that.

"Those aren't for you," said Skeezix. "They're for Elaine Potts. She's coming in today on the afternoon coach. Helen made me pick them. She's says it's time I quit messing around." Jack kept smiling. That was even better—Skeezix giving Elaine Potts flowers.

"Actually," said Helen, casting Skeezix a look and then smiling at Jack, "*I* went out after flowers for you, in the lot next door, and I told Skeezix that he ought to gather a few for Elaine—something he couldn't fathom. Of course *I* had to do it for him, didn't I? He kept picking weeds and talking about making the bouquet look Oriental. In the end he took my flowers and threw his out, which was good, because he would have ruined it with Elaine, giving her weeds. Then Dr. Jensen hollered that you were waking up, so we came in without any flowers at all for you. Sorry."

"That's fine," said Jack. "I—"

Helen interrupted. "Maybe you and I can go out after some later. Together." Then, obviously remembering his injured leg, she added, "After we find you a cane."

Dr. Jensen, who'd been letting Helen and Skeezix catch Jack up, broke in and said, "No canes. Not today. It's not much of a sprain, but with the crack on the head and all, you'll take it easy today. And, Jack, before you three went off last night, before I'd been knocked out by Harbin, I'd wanted to give you something. Your father had given it to me earlier in the evening."

The mention of his father recalled to Jack his efforts to find his parents in the depot. He could picture his mother's face through the train window, behind his shouting father. He had recognized it from the photo—there was no mistaking it, really. But now that he'd actually seen her, he remembered something more than a photo, and the memory was at the same time painful and wonderful. It meant that somehow, in some distant time, his mother hadn't died, that she was alive somewhere with his father. And it meant also—the memory did—that he'd have nothing *but* that brief glimpse of her face as a souvenir.

Dr. Jensen handed him a ring. "Your father said he mightn't be coming back. He didn't know. He was in a terrible hurry, and he might not be quick enough to finish the night's work and get back across. So he let me have this with instructions to give it to you, a memento, I guess."

Jack stared at the ring. He'd seen it before. It was made of gold—a ring of waves toppling over onto themselves. It was the ring that had been on the hand of the giant, the ring the giant had flipped into the air with his thumb. Jack could picture it turning over and over and landing in the giant's enormous hand and then the giant winking at him, inexplicably, before turning away. Jack slipped the ring onto his finger, realizing suddenly who the giant was. And he knew, too, who the woman was who looked so much like Helen, only older. It *was* Helen, and older too. And the giant was him.

"It *was* your bakery," said Jack suddenly, looking up at Skeezix. "The doughnuts were yours."

Skeezix nodded. "I've been thinking so. That means I marry Elaine, of course. I told Helen that. These flowers are nice and all, but not entirely necessary. My weeds would have done the trick."

"You're a jerk," said Helen.

"And you and I—" said Jack to Helen, but caught himself and stopped, blushing. He couldn't be sure, after all, that he had been *married* to Helen in that house near the harbor. They might still be mere friends. Well, he'd see about that. He didn't like the look of himself in a beard. He'd write himself a letter to remind himself. From the perspective of a mouse, a beard was a terrible thing.

"Something's cooking," said Jack, smelling suddenly the odor of baking bread.

"There's fresh bread," said Skeezix, rolling his eyes happily. "And a stew and pie. Don't empty your pipe into the stew pot this time. We can't go to—what was it?—Hoover's. Hoover hasn't shown up yet. Everybody else has, though."

"What?" asked Helen, looking puzzled. "Your pipe?"

"Nothing," said Jack. "I don't smoke a pipe, do I? I guess I'll take it up, to be ready when the time comes."

"There's a little surprise," said Helen, obviously anxious about something.

Jack hadn't time even to ask what the surprise was when through the door stepped a man and a woman—his father and mother. Jack nearly pitched off onto the floor and might have, too, if his mother hadn't grabbed him and hugged him and generally carried on as if she hadn't seen him in twelve years, which, of course, she hadn't.

His father stood beaming, over the top of his spectacles, then very soberly shook Jack's hand. "We've all made it, then," he said. "Even old Jim Langley. He rode in on the train with us; he was aboard when we saw you there, in the depot. He's moved back in."

"And we'll stay on there," said Helen excitedly. "As long as we want, he says."

"I'll cook," said Skeezix. "'Not a cabbage passes the threshold'; that's my motto. Nothing but culinary delights."

Jack's mother had left off her hugging, finally, and stood back to look at Jack, and he at her. She was young—surprisingly so. Years younger than his father—something that ran counter to his recollections but was probably explained by all the popping in and out through time that had been going on. "We've taken a house by the harbor," she said, "behind the tavern."

"I know which one," said Jack. Helen *had* painted the cats. Jack looked at his father, puzzled. "How—" he began.

"Easy," came the reply, "if you're quick enough. It was poison that Harbin had given your mother. I knew that, but I didn't know what kind. She was dying and I couldn't do a thing. Kettering knew, and went across thinking that I knew too, but I didn't. I followed him but couldn't find him in the depot—you know how *that* is. When I finally ran him down the Solstice was passed, and it took twelve years to come back around.

"I planned for every moment of those twelve years—honed it down just right, I thought. Then the run-in with the cat and Willoughby's having taken you north for a year put a crimp in all my planning, and I had to rush around trying to catch up. When I returned for your mother, knowing now how to save her, we talked, she and I, about finding you and taking you with us, picking up where we'd left off, not losing all those years of watching you grow up. But we didn't. We decided that you'd turned out well enough to suit us, from the little bit I'd seen and from what Jensen had told me. And you had your friends and your memories, and we couldn't take those away.

"So we slipped across and came along to catch up to you, thinking we wouldn't make it, thinking that the Solstice would pass us by and we'd lose you again. I had given you the elixir, though. That was our only wild card. Maybe you would have come across too, and if worst came to worst, we'd make a life for ourselves somewhere in time. When we lost you in the station, though . . . Well, never mind about that. It was a bad moment for all of us, but here we are now, aren't we? Skeezix tells us that Harbin is dead. The carnival is gone, destroyed. Jensen didn't get a glimpse of the crab, but he's got the claw, hasn't he?"

He had indeed. Jack couldn't take his eyes off his mother. It would be weird to have one. Would she let him read by candlelight at night, or go in and out the window on a rope ladder? When he thought about it, there was no second story to the house by the harbor anyway. He wouldn't need a rope ladder. He could swing the window open and climb out into his own back yard.

Mrs. Langley's land of dreams hadn't come to half as much as he'd anticipated; though, come to think of it, nobody had ever promised him it would. It was mostly the romantic notion of a ghost in an attic, the pursuit of phantoms. He and Helen and Skeezix had gone round and round on Ferris wheels and trains and through haunted fun houses, and they'd set sail in impossible boats. Now here they were home again, where they'd always wanted to be, in the land of doughnuts and rainy weather, of books and tide pools, of sand-castle dreams waiting for the rising tide. In the spring there would be picnics in the cove. Autumn would be a smoky memory among countless others, blowing across the bleached shreds of an old carnival poster on a sunset beach, piling up sand in a cast-off shoe, covering the brass loops of a pair of lost spectacles crusted with sea salt.